Modern Django Web Development

With Channels, DRF, GraphQL, and React

Malhar Lathkar

Apress®

Modern Django Web Development: With Channels, DRF, GraphQL, and React

Malhar Lathkar (iD)
Nanded, Maharashtra, India

ISBN-13 (pbk): 979-8-8688-1471-6   ISBN-13 (electronic): 979-8-8688-1472-3
https://doi.org/10.1007/979-8-8688-1472-3

Managing Director, Apress Media LLC: Welmoed Spahr
Acquisitions Editor: James Robinson-Prior, Divya Modi
Development Editor: James Markham
Coordinating Editor: Jacob Shmulewitz

Cover designed by eStudioCalamar

Distributed to the book trade worldwide by Springer Science+Business Media New York, 1 New York Plaza, New York, NY 10004. Phone 1-800-SPRINGER, fax (201) 348-4505, e-mail orders-ny@springer-sbm.com, or visit www.springeronline.com. Apress Media, LLC is a Delaware LLC and the sole member (owner) is Springer Science + Business Media Finance Inc (SSBM Finance Inc). SSBM Finance Inc is a **Delaware** corporation.

For information on translations, please e-mail booktranslations@springernature.com; for reprint, paperback, or audio rights, please e-mail bookpermissions@springernature.com.

Apress titles may be purchased in bulk for academic, corporate, or promotional use. eBook versions and licenses are also available for most titles. For more information, reference our Print and eBook Bulk Sales web page at http://www.apress.com/bulk-sales.

Any source code or other supplementary material referenced by the author in this book is available to readers on GitHub (https://github.com/Apress). For more detailed information, please visit https://www.apress.com/gp/services/source-code.

If disposing of this product, please recycle the paper

It's been a great privilege to have learned from many exceptional teachers, who taught from the heart and not just the book.

I dedicate this work to all of them.

Table of Contents

About the Author

Malhar Lathkar brings over 35 years of experience as an independent software developer, entrepreneur, author, trainer, and mentor. Though formally trained in electronics at the postgraduate level, he has successfully transitioned into the profession of software training and development as a self-taught expert.

A passionate educator at heart, Malhar has positively impacted the careers of countless students and professionals worldwide, particularly in the technologies related to Python and Java. He actively collaborates with various EdTech companies as a subject matter expert, contributing to the design of high-quality training programs.

He is a recognized author with works featured by prominent publishing houses, including his 2023 FastAPI book with Apress. Malhar also provides corporate training. He is frequently invited to conduct workshops and deliver technical talks to students in various institutions.

Beyond his professional pursuits, Malhar enjoys Indian classical music and is an avid sports enthusiast.

About the Technical Reviewer

 **Rajiv Tulsyan** is an accomplished Solutions Architect with a distinguished career spanning over two decades, marked by a proven track record in architecting distributed systems and driving enterprise-level technology road maps on a global scale. His expertise encompasses a spectrum of skills, from designing and building accelerators to a deep understanding of SOA, event-driven, and Microservices event-based architectures. Rajiv's mastery extends to cloud technologies, including Hybrid Cloud Architecture and managed services, coupled with proficiency in Java, Kubernetes, Docker, and API gateway technologies. As a Solutions Architect, he is currently steering the design of architecture strategies for large-scale application deployments, showcasing his commitment to scalable, resilient, and innovative solutions. Rajiv's career journey reflects not only technical acumen but also leadership and a passion for developing technical talent, positioning him as a luminary in the ever-evolving landscape of technology.

With an academic background featuring an MS in Consulting Management from BITS Pilani, India, and an MCA in Computer Application from MDU Rohtak, Rajiv Tulsyan has seamlessly blended theoretical knowledge with practical application throughout his career. From leading a medium-sized Integration Architecture practice at Software AG to heading the B2B Practice and Knowledge Management Practice, Rajiv's management experience is as robust as his technical expertise. His commitment to excellence is underscored by certifications such as WebMethods 9.0 Certified ESB Developer, WebMethods Certified BPM Developer, and TOGAF 9.2: Enterprise Architecture, positioning him as a thought leader in the field. Rajiv Tulsyan's career stands as a testament to his dedication to pushing the boundaries of technology and fostering an atmosphere of technical excellence.

Acknowledgments

My previous work *High-Performance Web Apps with FastAPI*, published by Apress (Springer Nature) in 2023, has been well received. I am deeply grateful to them for their continued support. It is a privilege to partner with a distinguished brand like Apress. I thank the editorial team for entrusting me with another opportunity to share my knowledge through this book.

This book would not have been possible without the invaluable contributions of many individuals. First and foremost, I extend my heartfelt gratitude to James Robinson-Prior and Divya Modi – both highly skilled editors – for their support, guidance, and feedback during the various stages of the process of finalizing the draft of this book.

I would also like to express my sincere appreciation to Rajiv Tulsyan (the technical reviewer) for his expert insights and invaluable suggestions to make the content as authentic as possible.

Murlimohan Kanagala has been a close friend for almost three decades. Frequent constructive interactions with him have always been immensely helpful in my journey as a developer, author, and educator. I take this opportunity to acknowledge his support.

Treading an offbeat career path is never easy, unless you have a strong support system of friends and family. I can't resist thanking my wife, Jayashree, for being with me through the good and bad times.

Finally, sincere thanks from the bottom of my heart to my students, colleagues, and collaborators.

Introduction

Django is by far the most preferred Python framework for developing data-driven web applications. Over the period, it has evolved to become a powerful full-stack framework, growing and expanding its capabilities for building asynchronous solutions, APIs, and real-time applications.

This book aims to equip the reader with the core concepts of Django and to highlight new facets and best practices of web application development with Modern Django. It emphasizes features such as Channels for the implementation of the WebSocket protocol, DRF for building REST APIs, using Graphene and Strawberry for GraphQL APIs, and developing a frontend app with React JS.

How This Book Is Arranged

This book comprises ten chapters. They are organized into two distinct parts.

The first part deals with the basics of Django development, describing the MVT architecture of Django with a lot of practical, real-world examples.

Chapter 1 (Django Basics) sets the ball rolling by explaining the concepts of web development. It introduces Python's asyncio module for asynchronous processing and gives an overview of the Django framework.

Chapter 2 (Django: First Steps) guides you through the installation of Django and creating your first Django application. It also gives a detailed explanation of Django's Admin interface.

Chapter 3 (Django ORM) deals with an important aspect of Django's MVT architecture – models. You will learn how to use Django Shell, model fields, and their types and the relationships.

Chapter 4 (Django Templates) covers the View component of Django's architecture. You will learn about various template tags, different types of views, and the static assets.

Chapter 5 (Django: Using Databases) is aimed at enabling you to work with a wider range of databases. You will use SQLAlchemy ORM and different libraries that let you use MongoDB as a backend to your Django application.

In the second part, more advanced features of Django and various apps in the Django ecosystem are discussed.

Chapter 6 (Advanced Django) will cover features such as messaging, authentication, and security. It also discusses how to build and include reusable apps such as the Django Debug Toolbar.

Chapter 7 (REST API with Django) helps you to explore the powerful features of Django REST Framework to build robust REST APIs with Django.

Chapter 8 (GraphQL with Django) explains the basics of GraphQL protocol and discusses how to use Graphene and Strawberry packages for building GraphQL API with Django.

Chapter 9 (WebSockets with Django) takes a detailed look at the WebSocket protocol and its implementation in Django with the Django Channels app.

Chapter 10 (ReactJS with Django) teaches you to use ReactJS to build frontend clients for your Django-based REST, GraphQL, and WebSocket APIs.

Thus, this book, *Modern Django Web Development*, will be a comprehensive guide that covers all the aspects required for creating successful and easy-to-use Django web applications.

CHAPTER 1

Django Basics

Introduction

Even after more than a decade and a half since the release of its earliest version, Django is still the most popular web framework of Python developers. The enduring relevance of Django can be attributed to its continuing evolution by incorporating modern trends in the web development technology. The latest version of Django (Django 5.0), released in December 2023, also includes a number of new features that enhance Django's versatility, scalability, and maturity and provide a cleaner architecture.

Before embarking upon our journey to learn to develop Modern Django-based web applications, let us refresh some of the fundamental concepts of web development. This chapter covers the following topics:

- Fundamentals of HTTP

- HTTP methods

- CGI

- WSGI

- wsgiref package

© Malhar Lathkar 2025
M. Lathkar, *Modern Django Web Development*,
https://doi.org/10.1007/979-8-8688-1472-3_1

- What is a web framework?

- MVC vs. MVT

- Asynchronous processing

- ASGI

- Overview of Django

Fundamentals of HTTP

Let us start with HTTP (**Hypertext Transfer Protocol**), since it is the backbone of any data exchange over the World Wide Web. It is an application layer protocol built on top of a TCP connection. The HTTP follows a client-server communication model, wherein an HTTP client (generally a web browser) opens a connection with the server and initiates a request for a certain resource to be served to it.

The web application hosted on the HTTP server accepts the request, processes it, and sends back an appropriate response. The web application interacts with a database and may use certain static resources such as images and documents to formulate the response.

On receiving the server's response, it is rendered by the client, and the connection it has opened is either used for further requests or it is closed. Thus, the request-response cycle, as depicted in Figure 1-1, drives the HTTP communication.

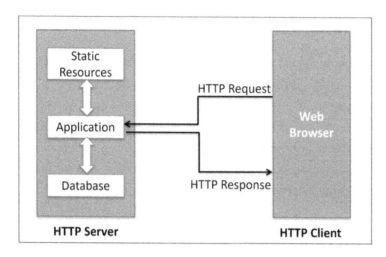

Figure 1-1. *Request-response cycle*

Apart from the metadata about the identity of the client (such as the IP address, the language, the user agent, etc.), the HTTP request has two important constituents: the URI of the required resource on the server and the action to be performed on the resource expressed in the form of HTTP verbs like **GET**, **POST**, **PUT**, **DELETE**, etc. We shall learn more about them in the next section.

The HTTP response, on the other hand, includes either the requested resource or an error message, along with a status code indicative of the fate of the request (whether successfully processed, required resource couldn't be found, request declined by the server, etc.)

HTTP is a stateless protocol, which means that the HTTP server doesn't hold on to any identity of the client it had requested to connect. However, techniques such as cookies and sessions help the developer to provide an enhanced user experience.

HTTP Methods

An aspect of the HTTP request that a web application developer has to deal with the most is the HTTP methods (also called verbs), as it indicates the action the application must take on the request data. In a typical web application, requests with the POST, GET, PUT, and DELETE methods are processed. These methods ask a new resource to be created, retrieve one or more resources, modify the contents of resources, and remove specified resources from the server, respectively.

POST Method

An HTTP request with the POST verb indicates that the client wants a new resource to be created on the server. Obviously, it will need certain data to form the said resource object. Usually, the request body is populated with the data filled in an HTML form. In other words, the client uses an HTML form with its method attribute set to POST. On successful creation of a new resource, the server responds by sending a message with **201** status code.

GET Method

Every HTTP request is a GET request by default. It expects the server to render one or more resources in its HTTP response. The server intimates the content type (plain, HTML, media, JSON, etc.) along with the success status code (**200 OK**). In case of failure to process the request, the status code is **400** (Bad Request) or **404** (Not Found).

PUT Method

Often, the client requests an existing resource on the server to be modified, attaching the updated data. The PUT verb conveys this intention to the server. Again, the server responds with a status code (**200 OK**) for success or **404** (Not Found) for failure.

DELETE Method

The client's request to remove one or more resources altogether from the server comes with the DELETE verb. The possible status codes are **200 OK** for successful processing of the request and **404** Not Found in case of failure.

It is important to know about two characteristics of the HTTP methods. They are idempotency and safety.

The HTTP method is said to be **idempotent** if making several identical requests has the same effect on the server as making a single request. Only the POST method is not idempotent, as sending a POST request again creates another resource. All others (GET, PUT, and DELETE) are idempotent.

The safety of an HTTP method refers to whether or not it alters the state of the server. In this respect, the GET method is safe, as it only performs retrieval. The PUT and DELETE methods are idempotent but unsafe. The POST method is neither idempotent nor safe.

HTTP defines a few additional request methods as well – such as **PATCH**, **HEAD**, **OPTIONS**, **TRACE**, and **CONNECT**. However, they are very rarely employed in a typical web application; hence, they find just a passing mention here.

CGI

While the **World Wide Web** (WWW) in its early stages was just a collection of static web pages, soon various technologies came about to make it more dynamic and interactive. CGI (**Common Gateway Interface**) was one of the earliest tools in this direction. The CGI is a set of standards recommended for an HTTP server software. Programs in languages such as C/C++, PHP, Python, and Perl are stored on the server and executed on the client's request. These programs, called CGI scripts, generate the output in HTML format, which the server sends as a response to the client. The use of Python for web development was primarily as CGI.

A simple Python CGI script served to the browser client is shown in Figure 1-2.

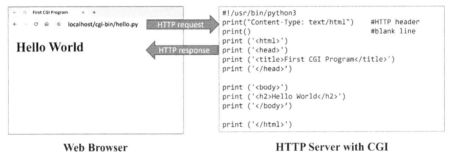

Figure 1-2. *Python as CGI script*

However, the world quickly moved away from CGI because of its major drawback that it treats each connection request as a new process, consuming a large memory and thereby resulting in poor performance.

One could achieve better results with the **mod_python** extension installed on the Apache web server. However, with many Python-based web frameworks coming up, along with many web server platforms in addition to Apache (IIS, Nginx, lighttpd, etc.), the need for a simple and a uniform interface between Python applications and the web software was felt.

Having a standard interface makes it easy to use an application that supports WSGI with a number of different web servers. This thought led the Python community to the proposal of WSGI.

WSGI

The process of having a standardized interface in place for web servers and Python-based web applications started with raising a PEP – which stands for **Python Enhancement Proposal** – bearing a number 333 in the year 2003 (and later updated by PEP 3333 in 2010). This proposal is known as WSGI (**Web Server Gateway Interface**) and recommends a set of specifications for the web servers and web application frameworks for Python.

In a typical web application, there is a server, a certain middleware object, and the web application itself. As per WSGI specifications, the workflow between these components should be as follows.

As a request from the HTTP client (web browser) is received, the WSGI-enabled server invokes a WSGI application object by passing two arguments to it. These arguments are

> **environ**: A dictionary-like object that includes key-value pairs corresponding to different server and environment variables and their values.

> **start_response**: The application object invokes this callback function to begin the HTTP response of the server, with appropriate status codes and response headers.

The WSGI application object may be a function, a method, or a callable object. It must return an iterator consisting of a single byte string.

The following Python function (Listing 1-1) acts as a simple WSGI application that returns a Hello World string as the response.

Listing 1-1. WSGI Hello World

```python
def wsgiapp(environ, start_response):
    """Basic WSGI application object"""
    status = '200 OK'
    response_headers = [('Content-type', 'text/plain')]
    start_response(status, response_headers)
    return ['Hello world!\n']
```

Figure 1-3 shows the schematics of a WSGI architecture.

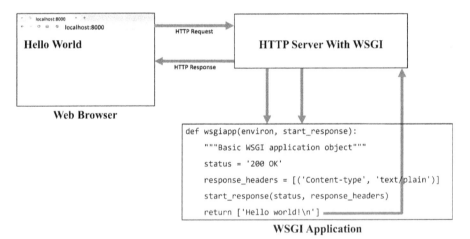

Figure 1-3. *WSGI*

wsgiref Package

To help Python web developers to add WSGI support to a web server, the Python's standard library comes with a reference implementation of WSGI specifications. The wsgiref package has been a part of the standard library since Python's version 2.5 onward.

The wsgiref.simple_server module is a handy implementation of a threaded HTTP server that serves WSGI applications on a given host and a port. The make_server() method of the simple_server class returns an instance of WSGI server.

```
wsgiref.simple_server.make_server(host, port, app)
```

You need to call the serve_forever() method of the server object so that it starts listening to the incoming requests. This module also has a demo_app() function. It is a WSGI application object that, when invoked, prints a Hello World message, along with the list of environment variables.

Save the following Python code (Listing 1-2) as main.py and run it to serve the demo_app on port 8000 of the localhost.

Listing 1-2. WSGI demo_app

```python
from wsgiref.simple_server import make_server, demo_app
server = make_server('', 8000, demo_app)
server.serve_forever()
```

Open a new window of your favorite browser and use http://localhost:8000 as the URL. The browser displays the Hello World text, followed by a long list of environment variables.

```
Hello world!

ALLUSERSPROFILE = 'C:\\ProgramData'
APPDATA = 'C:\\Users\\user\\AppData\\Roaming'
CHOCOLATEYINSTALL = 'C:\\ProgramData\\chocolatey'
CHOCOLATEYLASTPATHUPDATE = '133449782501759075'
COMMONPROGRAMFILES = 'C:\\Program Files\\Common Files'
COMMONPROGRAMFILES(X86) = 'C:\\Program Files (x86)\\
Common Files'
COMMONPROGRAMW6432 = 'C:\\Program Files\\Common Files'
COMPUTERNAME = 'GNVBGL3'
```

```
COMSPEC = 'C:\\WINDOWS\\system32\\cmd.exe'
CONTENT_LENGTH = ''
CONTENT_TYPE = 'text/plain'
DRIVERDATA = 'C:\\Windows\\System32\\Drivers\\DriverData'
EFC_14456 = '1'
GATEWAY_INTERFACE = 'CGI/1.1'
HOME = 'C:\\Users\\user'
HOMEDRIVE = 'C:'
HOMEPATH = '\\Users\\user'
```

. . .

. . .

Let us use our own Hello World app instead of the pre-installed demo_ app. Save and run the following code (Listing 1-3) as main.py.

Listing 1-3. Hello World WSGI

```python
from wsgiref.simple_server import make_server

def wsgiapp(environ, start_response):
    host=environ.get('HTTP_HOST')
    start_response("200 OK", [("Content-type", "text/html")])
    ret = [("<h2>Hello World App on WSGI Server Running at
    :{}</h2>".format((host)).encode("utf-8"))]
    return ret

server = make_server('localhost', 8000, wsgiapp)
server.serve_forever()
```

The details of the host name and the port number of the web server are read from the HTTP_HOST header available in environ object. The web browser shows the output as shown in Figure 1-4 when it visits the URL http://localhost:8000.

Figure 1-4. *WSGI app*

Apart from the `simple_server`, the `wsgiref` package also provides a set of utilities for handling WSGI environment variables and response headers. It also includes a validation tool, static type checkers, and the handler classes for implementing WSGI servers and gateways.

You can extend the functionality of the WSGI application beyond merely displaying a Hello World message, such as presenting web forms for the user to submit the response, performing database operations based on the input data, and rendering well-formatted results to the user. However, building these features in a raw Python code will be cumbersome, and what is more, with increasing complexity, the solution will be hit with maintenance and scalability issues.

This is where the web frameworks (also called web application frameworks) come into the picture. A Python developer has a number of web frameworks to choose from so as to build a robust and scalable application that also saves on development time. Django is one of the most widely used frameworks. Let us first try to understand in brief how a framework works.

What Is a Web Framework?

In its most generic meaning, the term "framework" stands for a conceptual structure consisting of objectives, rules, and constraints that acts as a guide to build a certain product or solve a given problem. In the context of application software development, a framework is a set of libraries that provide a generic functionality needed for a certain type of application. It also performs most of the frequently needed low-level tasks and presents a basic working template application, in which the developer can include additional functionality to fine-tune to build the software that fulfills the requirements.

Thus, a software framework is more of an abstract template or a skeleton of all the necessary building blocks of a certain application. The control flow of the application is already pre-decided. The developer only has to plug in the business logic into the blocks. Hence, it results in rapid and scalable development.

Web application framework is one of the types of software application frameworks, the others being

- GUI frameworks

- Game development frameworks

- Testing frameworks

- Machine learning frameworks

- Scientific computing frameworks, etc.

A web application development also involves building its ergonomic frontend, with HTML, CSS, and JavaScript technologies. Frontend frameworks (also called client-side frameworks) encapsulate these technologies to facilitate rapid UI development. React and Angular are popular examples of frontend frameworks. The server-side frameworks, on the other hand, mainly deal with the application logic and the database interaction. The term "web framework" generally refers to the server-side or backend frameworks such as Django.

As mentioned earlier, one can, of course, develop a web-based application without using a framework (such as Django), but the network-related operations involved (such as request handling, state management, etc.) have to be explicitly coded, and it involves a lot of effort, which can be substantially more than the actual application logic. A web application framework, on the other hand, lets the developer concentrate on the application functionality by providing a standard platform to build and deploy the application. Thus, a web framework facilitates rapid application development.

The features offered by a web application framework may vary depending on the scope and the nature of its target application. Some frameworks are called full stack frameworks. These frameworks are equipped with all the tools required to develop a fairly comprehensive application. The term "Batteries Included" is often used to describe them. Django, the subject matter of this book, is a full stack framework. The other category is microframeworks. They are minimalistic and lightweight in nature, with only the essential features. You can, of course, plug in additional libraries to enhance the scope of the application.

Some of the common tasks handled by a typical web framework are

- **User management**: An interface that handles user registration, verifies their identity, and manages roles and privileges.

- **URL mapping**: Modern web apps serve their resources to their users based on the composition of the URL requested by them. One of the important tasks of a framework is to map request URLs to specific resources or views to structure the application's code.

- **File uploads**: Most web apps let their users upload images, documents, and other media on the server. The frameworks handle this type of task very seamlessly.

13

- **Database interaction**: Web applications are invariably data-driven. The framework facilitates interaction with a backend database and performs CRUD operations as and when needed.

- **API services**: This feature allows other applications or services to interact with the application's data and functionality in a controlled manner.

MVC vs. MVT

The **Model-View-Controller** (MVC) is a popular software design pattern that aims to divide application logic into three interconnected layers. These layers in the MVC approach have clearly defined roles as follows:

> **Controller**: The user requests are intercepted by the controller. It coordinates with the View layer and the Model layer to send the appropriate response back to the client.

> **Model**: The model is responsible for data definitions, processing logic, and interaction with the backend database.

> **View**: The view is the presentation layer of the application. It takes care of the placement and formatting of the result and sends it to the client as the application's response.

Figure 1-5 shows the MVC architecture.

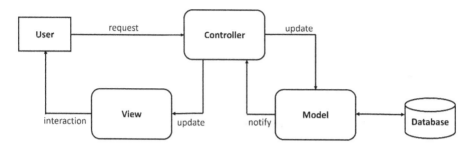

Figure 1-5. *MVC architecture*

Although the MVC pattern is traditionally used in desktop GUI development, many web application frameworks also employ this pattern.

The MVT (**Model-View-Template**) pattern is a slight variation of MVC. While the Model layer in MVT has a similar role to play as in MVC, the View layer in MVT is in fact the one that undertakes the processing logic, and the Template is the presentation layer, performing the role of View in MVC.

Django adapts the MVT approach. In addition to the Model, View, and Template, there's another important stage in Django's architecture. It is called URL dispatcher. In fact, the URL dispatcher mechanism is equivalent to Controller in the MVC architecture. The interaction between components of the MVT pattern is depicted in Figure 1-6.

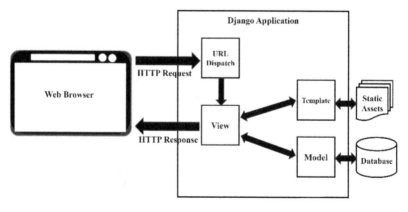

Figure 1-6. *MVT pattern*

15

When the server receives a request in the form of client URL, the dispatcher matches its pattern with the predefined patterns and routes the flow of the application toward its associated view.

Asynchronous Processing

Early versions of Django (before Django version 3.1) supported a synchronous execution, which is implemented by WSGI-compliant web servers, such as Apache. Since then, Django has incorporated support for writing asynchronous views. Django applications can now perform nonblocking IO operations and concurrent processing. This coincided with the induction of the `asyncio` module in Python's standard library.

As against in a multithreading, where the main thread opens multiple threads of operation and the CPU coordinates their execution by a certain scheduling algorithm, in the asynchronous approach, only a single thread runs but it has the ability to move on to a next task while the current task is being processed.

In asynchronous processing, an asynchronous function voluntarily yields to another function when it reaches an event or a condition so that by the time the result from the other function is obtained, the original function can attend some other operations.

Asynchronous processing is done over a single thread, unlike in a multithreaded process. It is called cooperative multitasking, as its function pauses its execution and relinquishes control to other functions. It improves the overall performance by optimizing the system resources.

asyncio Module

The two newly added keywords – async and await – and the induction of the `asyncio` module in the standard library brought the asynchronous support to Python. Normally, when a function is called, it blocks the execution till its execution is completed. To define a nonblocking function, it is defined with the `async` keyword before the def keyword. The asynchronous functions are called coroutines.

While a normal Python function is defined as

```
def syncHello():
    print ("Hello World")
```

the coroutine (asynchronous function) is defined as

```
async def asyncHello():
    print ("Hello World")
```

When prefixed with the async keyword, it returns a coroutine object and is not invoked like a normal Python function. Instead, it is passed as an argument to the `run()` function (refer to Listing 1-4) defined in the `asyncio` module.

Listing 1-4. Coroutine

```
import asyncio

async def asyncHello():
    print ("Hello World")

asyncio.run(asyncHello())
```

The coroutine so defined is an awaitable function. When one coroutine is called from another with the `await` keyword, the first function pauses its execution and yields to the other, till the other completes its run.

The following Python code (Listing 1-5) has two coroutines. The asyncHello() function sleeps for two seconds before printing the Hello World message. Note that the sleep() function in the `asyncio` module is also an awaitable function. The `main()` coroutine repeatedly pauses every time the `asyncHello()` coroutine is invoked.

Listing 1-5. Async Hello World

```
import asyncio
import time

async def asyncHello():
    await asyncio.sleep(2)
    print("\tHello World")

async def main():
    for i in range(1, 4):
        print ("Iteration:", i)
        print(f"\tstarted at {time.strftime('%X')}")
        await asyncHello()
        print(f"\tfinished at {time.strftime('%X')}")

asyncio.run(main())
```

The output shows how cooperative multitasking takes place between the two coroutines.

```
Iteration: 1
    started at 00:02:11
    Hello World
    finished at 00:02:13
Iteration: 2
    started at 00:02:13
    Hello World
    finished at 00:02:15
Iteration: 3
    started at 00:02:15
    Hello World
    finished at 00:02:17
```

ASGI

The classical WSGI interface is not suitable for modern web protocols such as WebSocket. To take advantage of the async capabilities of Python (added since version 3.5 onward), a new set of specifications have been developed. This is called **Asynchronous Server Gateway Interface** (ASGI). The asgiref module is a reference implementation of ASGI. It is not a part of Python's standard library and hence needs to be installed manually. Also, the asgiref module doesn't come with a development server (the wsgiref module has an HTTP server in the form of simple_server object). Hence, we also need to install an ASGI server module such as Uvicorn or Daphne.

To install asgiref and Uvicorn, use the PIP utility:

```
pip3 install asgiref
pip3 install uvicorn
```

The ASGI application is an asynchronous callable (**coroutine**) that takes three parameters: send, receive, and scope.

The send and receive parameters are asynchronous callables that enable the application to send and receive event messages to and from the client, respectively. The scope parameter is a dict containing details of a specific connection provided by the server, such as the protocol, headers, etc.

The minimal ASGI Hello World application to be run with the Uvicorn server is given below. Save the following code (Listing 1-6) as **main.py**.

Listing 1-6. ASGI Hello World

```python
import uvicorn

async def app(scope, receive, send):
    await send({
        'type': 'http.response.start',
        'status': 200,
```

19

```
        'headers': [
            [b'content-type', b'text/html'],
        ],
    })

    await send({
        'type': 'http.response.body',
        'body': b'<h2>Hello World App on ASGI Server</h2>',
    })
if __name__ == "__main__":
    uvicorn.run("main:app", port=5000, log_level="info")
```

Run the above Python script and visit http://localhost:5000/ to get the ASGI app running in the browser (Figure 1-7).

Figure 1-7. *ASGI app*

For Django version 3.1 and above, the asgiref library is a core dependency. It makes Django add ASGI features like asynchronous workflows and nonblocking I/O operations in the application to achieve better performance and scalability. One of the main features of asgiref is the SyncToAsync wrapper, which allows the synchronous code in asynchronous context without any rewrite. ASGI is thus a superset of WSGI specifications.

Modern Django apps such as **Channels** and **Django REST Framework** rely heavily on ASGI for handling WebSocket connections, asynchronous background tasks, etc.

Overview of Django

The preceding sections of this chapter presented a brief review of some important foundational aspects that would help the learner understand the concepts, the design philosophy, and the architecture of the Django framework with more clarity. It is now time to know more about the Django framework itself.

As mentioned earlier, Django has been around for close to two decades. It is the most preferred tool for Python web developers. First developed in 2005 by **Adrian Holovaty** and **Simon Willison**, the Django project is being maintained by the **Django Software Foundation**. In the plethora of Python web frameworks, Django stands out because of the following features.

Batteries Included

"The web framework for perfectionists with deadlines" – this is the tagline of Django. Django is considered to be a full-stack web application framework. The Django package is bundled with all the necessary components required to build a full-fledged web application. Django has its own templating system (**Django Template Language**), object relation model (**Django ORM**), and regex-based URL dispatcher. Unlike the other microframeworks, you don't need to install any other libraries for these core activities.

Utility Apps

The Django package is also bundled with a number of applications for general-purpose consumption. The `contrib` package provides a robust admin and authentication system, built-in security mechanism to prevent CSRF and SQL injection attacks, and much more.

Scalability

Django uses a "shared-nothing" architecture. It is designed to accommodate additional hardware – such as database servers, caching servers, or web/application servers at any point of the lifetime of a web application. It separates the components such as its database layer and application layer very cleanly.

Documentation and Support

For an open source project, Django has very excellent and comprehensive documentation. Besides, Django has a large and active community of developers. A lot of resources such as books, tutorials, articles, and forums are available for an aspiring Django developer. The significant user base of Django includes some well-known organizations such as Instagram, Mozilla, Disqus, etc.

It may be noted that Django is considered as an opinionated framework. While this has certain advantages such as a cleaner and consistent code that is easier to maintain, it has a steeper learning curve as compared to many of the other frameworks. Also, it is not flexible enough to let the user choose the tools other than those bundled with the Django package.

Summary

This chapter aims to refresh some of the fundamental concepts of web application and web frameworks. With specific reference to Python's web frameworks, the role of WSGI and ASGI has been explained in this chapter.

The stage is now set for us to explore the Django framework and the associated tools in the Django ecosystem. In the next chapter, we shall write our first Django application and also get acquainted with Django's admin interface.

CHAPTER 2

Django: First Steps

As compared to some of the other, simpler Python-based web frameworks, to get started with Django is a little difficult. This is mainly because it follows a fairly rigid process of building an app. Django is also very particular about the project structure and the nomenclature. Its extensive features and the batteries included approach make Django an opinionated framework, and hence, it has a steeper learning curve as compared to others.

Precisely for this reason, it is important we spend enough time to understand how different components of a Django app work and their interplay. This chapter navigates you through the seemingly tricky early stages.

This chapter explains the following topics:

- Install Django

- Set up the Django project

- Adding an app

- Define views

- Mapping a view to URL

- Serving web pages

- Django admin site

© Malhar Lathkar 2025
M. Lathkar, *Modern Django Web Development*,
https://doi.org/10.1007/979-8-8688-1472-3_2

Install Django

Django is an open source Python package. Obviously, you need to have Python installed on your computer. In the case of Linux, most of the distributions today come with Python3 bundled with them. However, different versions of Django need specific versions of Python. For Django versions 4.x and 5.x, the minimum Python version needed is Python 3.8. The Ubuntu Desktop 22.04 LTS distribution, for example, comes with Python 3.10 preinstalled, which is fine for installing Django 4 as well as Django 5. The Django 4.2.x series is the last to support Python 3.8 and 3.9 versions.

However, it is recommended that you use the latest release of each Django series and the latest Python version. As of December 2023, Python 3.12.1 is the latest version, and Django 5.0.1 is the latest Django version.

In the case of Windows 10 or Windows 11, Python is not pre-installed. So you need to download the installer of the latest version and run it. (Make sure that the Python installation directory is added to the PATH environment variable).

With this first step done, let us proceed to the installation of Django. The preferred way of installing Django (as also any Python package) from the official Python package repository is to use PIP utility. Python also recommends using isolated environments (also called virtual environments) rather than system-wide installation of packages. The venv module facilitates creating and managing the virtual environment.

Installation on Ubuntu

The PIP utility as well as the venv module are not a part of Python software on Ubuntu distributions. Hence, it has to be installed with the help of Ubuntu's APT package manager. Use the following command in the Ubuntu terminal:

```
sudo apt install python3-pip
```

To add venv to Python's library, use the following command:

```
sudo apt install python3-venv
```

We shall now create a virtual environment and install Django in it. To begin with, create a new directory workspace inside the user's home. Enter the directory and create a virtual environment with its name as djenv:

```
mkdir workspace
cd workspace
~/workspace$ python3 -m venv djenv
```

This will create another directory (djenv) inside the workspace. The virtual environment will have the directory structure shown in Figure 2-1.

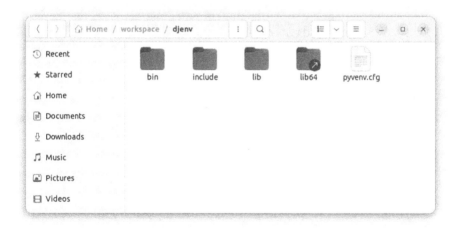

Figure 2-1. *Python virtual environment*

The bin directory contains a copy of Python executable, PIP utility, as well as a script to activate the environment. Figure 2-2 shows the contents of the bin directory.

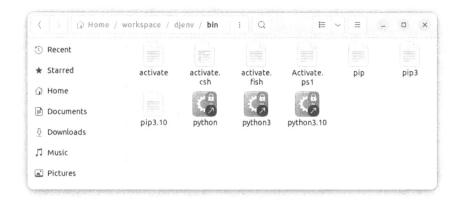

Figure 2-2. *Virtual environment scripts*

Activate the virtual environment with the following command:

~/workspace$ source djenv/bin/activate

The name of the environment now appears on the left of the prompt.

(djenv) malhar@ubuntu:~/workspace$

Now we can install Django inside this virtual environment with the following command:

(djenv) malhar@ubuntu:~workspace$ pip3 install django>4.2

The default Django version in the Ubuntu repository may not be the latest one. Hence, we have asked the version greater than 4.2 (which is 5.0.1) to be installed.

Along with Django, certain other packages are also installed. The list of all the packages in the environment is obtained by the pip freeze command.

(djenv) malhar@ubuntu:~/workspace$ pip3 freeze
asgiref==3.7.2
Django==5.0.1
sqlparse==0.4.4
typing_extensions==4.9.0

To double-check the correct installation of Django, start the Python interpreter, import Django, and check its version.

```
(djenv) malhar@ubuntu:~/workspace$ python3
Python 3.10.12 (main, Nov 20 2023, 15:14:05) [GCC 11.4.0]
on linux
Type "help", "copyright", "credits" or "license" for more
information.
>>> import django
>>> django.__version__
'5.0.1'
```

The installation adds a Django-admin command-line utility in the bin folder of the virtual environment, as shown in the Figure 2-3.

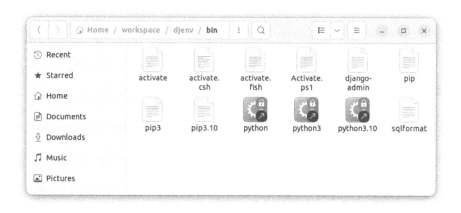

Figure 2-3. *django-admin utility*

The django-admin utility has been provided to perform many administrative tasks such as project creation and management, creating the skeleton of a typical Django app, starting the Django development server, and many more. We shall shortly use this utility for building our first Django app.

27

Installation on Windows

The procedure for installation of Django on Windows is almost similar. On Windows, the Python executable and the utilities for package installation (PIP) and activation of the virtual environment (activate.bat) are placed in the scripts subfolder of the virtual environment folder (djenv). Figure 2-4 displays the contents of the scripts directory.

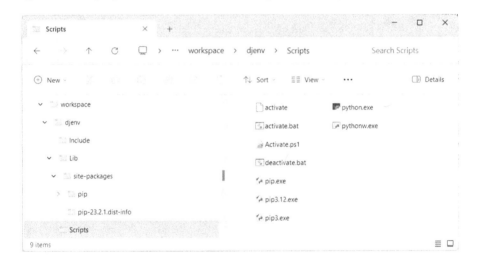

Figure 2-4. *Python virtual environment in Windows*

To activate the virtual environment on Windows, run the following command in the command prompt window (here it is assumed that the virtual environment djenv is created inside the C:\workspace folder):

```
C:\workspace>djenv\scripts\activate
```

The name of the virtual environment appears on the left of the command prompt. You can install Django with the same command as in the case of Ubuntu.

```
(djenv) C:\workspace>pip3 install Django
```

Set Up the Django Project

Django has been developed with the objective of providing a tool for building a complex, robust, modular, and scalable web-based application. An enterprise application may have multiple submodules (Django calls them as apps), and they may be interacting with each other. They can even share certain resources and parameters. A project in Django controls the common features of its apps. It is essentially a high-level structure of your entire application. A project is a hierarchical structure of folders and files that holds all the essential components like database configuration, Django-specific options, and application-specific settings.

As mentioned earlier, a command-line utility called `django-admin` is made available along with the installation of Django. This utility helps you perform different actions. The very first use of this utility is to create a project structure. Django's recommended way is to run the `startproject` command with the `django-admin` utility.

In your OS terminal, ensure that you are in the workspace directory, and run the following command to create a Django project with the name **firstproject**:

```
(djenv) C:\workspace>django-admin startproject firstproject
```

This will create a file structure inside the workspace directory as shown in Figure 2-5.

```
└──firstproject
        manage.py

        └──firstproject
                asgi.py
                settings.py
                urls.py
                wsgi.py
                __init__.py
```

Figure 2-5. *Django project structure*

There are two folders named **firstproject** in the figure. The outer one acts as the root of your project. The inner directory of the same name is a Python package (as is evident by the fact that it has the `__init__.py` file). Django auto-generates a file (`settings.py`) defining the default values of a number of parameters such as installed apps, database configuration, URL dispatcher, etc. We shall come to know more about different configuration settings later in this chapter, and also as we go along. There are a few more Python modules also in the inner project package folder:

> **settings.py**: We have talked a little about this earlier. Django creates this script with certain default values of various parameters such as database connection, URLCONF path, location of templates and static assets, etc. You may want to add or modify the settings as required.

> **urls.py**: This module is called URLCONF. Django uses this script to locate the view that matches with the request URL. The urlpatterns of all the apps are registered with the URLCONF of the project.

> **wsgi.py**: This module uses the project's settings and returns a WSGI application object. Any WSGI-compatible server can use this object to serve the application.

> **asgi.py**: From version 3.2 onward, Django supports ASGI specifications. The module is the entry point for ASGI-compatible web servers such as Uvicorn or Daphne to serve your project.

Let us turn to the Python script in the top-level root folder – `manage.py` file. Think of it as a local copy of the django-admin command-line utility. All the administrative tasks (that `django-admin` can perform) can also be done with the `manage.py` script. In fact, using `manage.py` is

30

more convenient especially if you are dealing with a single project. If the application involves multiple Django projects, the django-admin utility is more suited.

For now, we want to check whether the project we have just created (**firstproject**) works. Use the manage.py script to start Django's built-in development server with the following command. Ensure that the current directory of your command-line console (Command prompt in Windows, or the terminal in Linux) is the top-level root project folder.

```
(djenv) C:\workspace\firstproject>python manage.py runserver
```

In the terminal, you should see an activity log similar to this:

```
System check identified no issues (0 silenced).

You have 18 unapplied migration(s). Your project may not work
properly until you apply the migrations for app(s): admin,
auth, contenttypes, sessions.
Run 'python manage.py migrate' to apply them.
February 02, 2024 - 23:40:27
Django version 5.0.1, using settings 'firstproject.settings'
Starting development server at http://127.0.0.1:8000/
Quit the server with CTRL-BREAK.
```

Ignore the migrations-related warning for now, and note that the server has started. Head over to your favorite browser, and enter the URL http://127.0.0.1:8000/ and see if it shows the output as in the Figure 2-6.

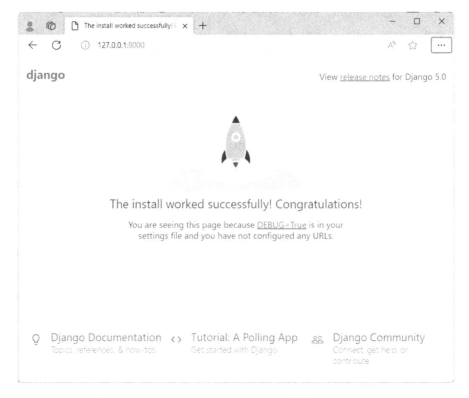

Figure 2-6. *The Django server runs successfully*

If everything goes well, you should see the above display. The caption itself is self-explanatory.

The Django project can be served without the built-in Django development server. Since Django is a WSGI-compatible framework, the simple_server defined in the wsgiref package is capable of serving it. As mentioned earlier, the wsgi.py module from the project's Python package returns a WSGI application object. The following code serves the Django project as a pure WSGI application:

```
import firstproject.wsgi as ws

from wsgiref.simple_server import make_server
server = make_server('localhost', 8000, ws.application)
server.serve_forever()
```

To run a Django application in ASGI-compatible mode, we need an ASGI web server, as it is not bundled with Python's standard library. The Daphne package is an ASGI server, optimized for Django's asynchronous features.

Let us install the Daphne package first.

```
(djenv) C:\workspace>pip3 install daphne
```

The asgi module in Django's project package defines the ASGI application object. Daphne has a simple command-line interface to launch the server and serve the application:

```
(djenv) C:\workspace\firstproject>daphne firstproject.
asgi:application
```

With the project structure successfully created, we are now good to go ahead and create a Django app in it.

Django App

The Django project is a complete web application whose functionality may have multiple submodules. In Django parlance, the submodules are called apps. Thus, a Django project may have one or more apps. On the other hand, an app may be a part of one or more projects. In that sense, a Django app is an entirely stand-alone application capable of becoming a part of a bigger project.

Think of an e-commerce website of a company dealing in electronic products as an example of a Django project, wherein its various components such as products, customers, and orders are handled by individual apps. The project facilitates the transactions between the apps.

If built with its reusability in mind, any of the apps can be added to another project. To extend the example, the product app can be included in the e-learning marketplace website as well.

In the previous chapter, we learned that Django uses the MVT approach. In fact, it is the app (not so much the project) that implements the MVT architecture. The project primarily acts as the URL dispatcher, as we shall come to know shortly.

A Django app is a Python package. The app package folder with some auto-generated modules is created by the startapp command.

```
(djenv) C:\workspace\firstproject>python manage.py startapp
firstapp
```

This command is run while the current directory is the project root. The app package is created alongside the project app, under the project root directory, as in the Figure 2-7.

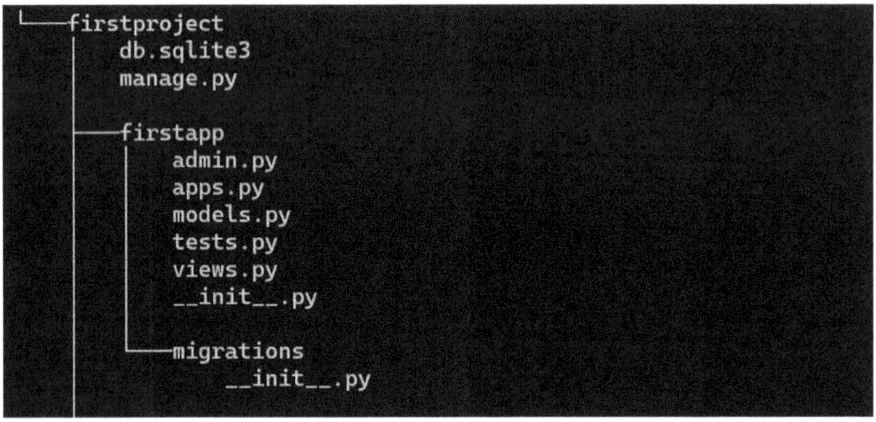

```
└──firstproject
        db.sqlite3
        manage.py

    ├──firstapp
        │   admin.py
        │   apps.py
        │   models.py
        │   tests.py
        │   views.py
        │   __init__.py
        │
        └──migrations
                __init__.py
```

Figure 2-7. Django app structure

Add an App

After the app folder with the above structure is created, it must be included in the project. When we create a project with the startproject command, the project's default settings are stored in the settings.py module. Django also installs certain utility apps such as the admin app, the session management app, etc.; the list is available in the INSTALLED_APPS settings. Open the settings.py file and include this app (**firstapp**) at the end of the list.

```
# Application definition

INSTALLED_APPS = [
    'django.contrib.admin',
    'django.contrib.auth',
    'django.contrib.contenttypes',
    'django.contrib.sessions',
    'django.contrib.messages',
    'django.contrib.staticfiles',
    'firstapp',
]
```

Define Views

As mentioned earlier, the View layer in Django's MVT architecture is where the processing logic is defined. A view is a Python function or a class that has been assigned the job to process the incoming request and formulate an appropriate response to be returned to the client. The startapp command auto-generates a views.py module, which is more or less empty (there is a solitary import statement) to begin with.

Let us plan to add two view functions. We want that the index() function should be invoked when the user's request URL is http://localhost:8000/firstapp/, and it should return a Hello World message.

The other view function about() should render a message such as "Know more about this app", in response to the URL http://localhost:8000/firstapp/about/.

The Django server provides the HttpRequest object as an argument to a view function, which returns an object of HttpResponse class (defined in the django.http module).

Add the functions shown in Listing 2-1 in the views.py file.

Listing 2-1. views.py

```
from django.http import HttpResponse

def index(request):
    return HttpResponse("<h2>Hello, World. This is the home
    page of FirstApp.</h2>")

def about(request):
    return HttpResponse("<h2>Know more about FirstApp.</h2>")
```

Define urlpatterns

The URL pattern is a mapping of a view to its desired request URL. Typically, the urlpatterns are defined in a urls.py module in the app package folder. This file doesn't exist by default, so we need to create a new one with this name. The path() function defined in the django.urls module creates the association of a URL route with the view function.

```
path(route, view, kwargs=None, name=None)
```

The route argument is a string representing the URL pattern. The string contains the tailing path_info part of the URL, excluding the hostname and the prefix. For example, in the URL http://localhost:8000/firstapp/about/, **firstapp** is the prefix after the hostname; hence, the route argument is "**about/**".

The view argument is the name of the function in the views.py module. The "about/" route is to be mapped to the views.about() function.

36

The name argument, though optional, should be provided as it proves useful in forming named urlpatterns (we shall learn more about this feature later).

Create a new Python module named urls.py and save the code shown in Listing 2-2 in it.

Listing 2-2. urls.py (in app)

```python
from django.urls import path
from . import views

urlpatterns = [
    path("", views.index, name="index"),
    path("about/", views.about, name="about"),
]
```

Update URLCONF

The urls.py module in the project package is referred to as URLCONF. It includes the urlpatterns of all the installed apps in the project. When a client request is received, Django locates a matching view function from the registered patterns. We need to include the urlpatterns of the app (firstapp/urls.py) in the URLCONF of the project (firstproject/urls.py). The include() function from the django.urls module does this job. Listing 2-3 shows the updated urlpatterns list.

Listing 2-3. urls.py (in project)

```python
from django.contrib import admin
from django.urls import path, include

urlpatterns = [
    path("firstapp/", include("firstapp.urls")),
    path('admin/', admin.site.urls),
]
```

The **'admin/'** route has been registered in the list of patterns by default. We shall discuss this later in this chapter.

So we have done everything that is required to serve our app. Start the Django server, and visit http://localhost:8000/firstapp/ to get the Hello World message displayed in the browser.

Change the URL to http://localhost:8000/firstapp/about/, and the browser displays the output as shown in Figure 2-8.

Figure 2-8. *Django app route*

Path Parameters

We know that the Django server provides the **HttpRequest** object as a mandatory argument to a view function. However, you can declare a view with additional parameters that can be fetched from the urlpatterns.

Let us define a **user()** function as a view in our app, with name as a string parameter. The function inserts the received string in the Welcome message to be returned as the response.

```
def user(request, name):
    return HttpResponse(f"<h2>Hello, {name}. Welcome to the
    home page of FirstApp.</h2>")
```

This function needs to be mapped with a URL route user/ in the app's URL pattern list. This route needs to have a variable part corresponding to the parameter of the view function and must be put inside angular brackets < and > for Django to capture the value and pass to the function.

In this case, as the URL route should be user/<name>/ and mapped with the views.user function, add the following pattern (shown in bold) in the app's URL pattern list:

```
from django.urls import path
from . import views
urlpatterns = [
    path("", views.index, name="index"),
    path("about/", views.about, name="about"),
    path("user/<name>/", views.user, name="user"),
]
```

Make the changes in both the modules – views.py and urls.py – and start the server. Use the URL http://localhost:8000/firstapp/user/Kevin and check if the response in the browser is as in the Figure 2-9.

Figure 2-9. *Path parameters in URL*

At times, you may need to pass the path parameters of some other types. By default, the parameter inside the angular brackets is of str type. For other types, the appropriate path converter prefix must be included. For example, it should be <int:userID> to let Django interpret the parameter as an integer.

Here's the list of the path converters recognized by Django:

> **str**: Matches any non-empty string. In the above example, we could have written <str:name>; however, it is the default if a converter isn't included in the expression.

39

int: To read an integer parameter from the URL, use int: inside the angular brackets, for example, `<int:userID>`. Any non-negative integer may be present.

slug: A slug is a string that can only include characters, numbers, dashes, and underscores. In this case, a string consisting of ASCII letters or numbers plus the hyphen and underscore characters that identifies a particular page on a website. For example, `<slug:post_title>`.

uuid: This converter matches a formatted UUID. As a convention, to prevent multiple URLs from mapping to the same page, dashes must be included and letters must be lowercase.

path: This converter matches any non-empty string, including the path separator, '/', so as to allow you to match against a complete URL path rather than a segment of a URL path as with str.

In the forthcoming chapters, we shall be using these path converters in the formation of urlpatterns.

Serving Web Pages

The view function returns its response in the form of an `HttpResponse` object, with a string as its content. In addition, other HTTP headers may be included in the constructor. By default, the **Content_Type** header is `text/html`. Hence, any HTML tags included in the response string will be accordingly parsed by the browser. You can, of course, set it to any other type, such as `application/json` if you wish to formulate a JSON response (usually in the case of APIs).

Instead of passing raw HTML strings, Django allows to serve an HTML page as the response. A very handy render() function, defined in the django.shortcuts module, is used for the purpose. Django can render a static web page as well as a web page in which a dynamic content can be inserted, such a page being called as a template.

To render a web page, the Django server checks if the page is available in any of the directories in the DIRS attribute of the TEMPLATES setting. Conventionally, the template folder under the project root folder is the place where templates are put. The project root folder is referred to by BASE_DIR.

Create a directory named templates under the project root, locate the TEMPLATES section in the settings.py file, and set the DIRS attribute as shown in Listing 2-4.

Listing 2-4. settings.py (TEMPLATES section)

```
TEMPLATES = [
    {
        'BACKEND': 'django.template.backends.django.
        DjangoTemplates',
        'DIRS': [BASE_DIR/'templates'],
        'APP_DIRS': True,
        'OPTIONS': {
            'context_processors': [
                'django.template.context_processors.debug',
                'django.template.context_processors.request',
                'django.contrib.auth.context_processors.auth',
                'django.contrib.messages.context_processors.
                messages',
            ],
        },
    },
]
```

Inside the templates folder, save the HTML script shown in Listing 2-5 as index.html.

Listing 2-5. index.html

```html
<html>
<body>
<h2>Hello, World. This is the home page of FirstApp.</h2>
</body>
</html>
```

To render this page as the response of index view, modify its definition in views.html as in Listing 2-6.

Listing 2-6. views.py

```python
from django.shortcuts import render

def index(request):
    return render(request, 'index.html')
```

Run the server again and visit the index route in your browser. Now, the contents of index.html are displayed.

In the above code, the render() function is called. The first argument passed to this function is the HttpRequest object that the view receives from the server. The contents of the HTML page (the second argument) is returned as the HttpResponse.

The render() function can also have a third argument called context. It is a dictionary object, whose values are inserted in the template tags placed inside the HTML code. Django has an elaborate template system, with which data from sources such as databases can be inserted to generate dynamic web pages. We have a complete chapter on all the powerful features of Django Template Language, later in this book.

Admin Site

A fully customizable, automatic admin interface is one of the most powerful features of Django. However, it should be only used as an organization's internal management tool. The admin app is automatically added to the project as a result of the startproject command.

The admin interface depends on the django.contrib.admin app. You'll find it in the **INSTALLED_APPS** section of the settings.py (along with its dependencies).

```
INSTALLED_APPS = [
    'django.contrib.admin',
    'django.contrib.auth',
    'django.contrib.contenttypes',
    'django.contrib.sessions',
    'django.contrib.messages',
    'django.contrib.staticfiles',
]
```

The startproject template also includes the admin app in the URLCONF of the project. The default code in the urls.py file in the project package folder is shown in Listing 2-7.

Listing 2-7. urls.py (in project)

```
from django.contrib import admin
from django.urls import path

urlpatterns = [
    path('admin/', admin.site.urls),
]
```

The pre-installed apps use database tables to store and retrieve information. We need to create the database tables necessary for these apps. Run the `migrate` command to use the models in these apps and build their respective table structure. We shall learn more about migration in a subsequent chapter.

Django uses a SQLite database by default. You'll find db.sqlite3 created in the project root folder. Django can be configured to use any other type of database (such as MySQL), for which we will have to modify the database configuration in the project's setting module. For now, we shall stick to SQLite database.

In fact, `migrate` is a `django-admin` command. However, we shall execute it with the `manage.py` script as follows:

```
(djenv) D:\workspace\firstproject>python manage.py migrate
```

The console shows a log similar to the following:

```
Operations to perform:
  Apply all migrations: admin, auth, contenttypes, sessions
Running migrations:
  Applying contenttypes.0001_initial... OK
  Applying auth.0001_initial... OK
  Applying admin.0001_initial... OK
  . . .
  Applying sessions.0001_initial... OK
```

The required tables are thus created. You need at least one user to be able to use the admin panel. A user is an object of the User class found in the `django.contrib.auth.models` module. Use the `createsuperuser` command as follows:

```
(djenv) C:\workspace\firstproject>python manage.py
createsuperuser
```

You will be asked to furnish the following details:

```
Username (leave blank to use 'mlath'): admin
Email address: admin@example.com
Password: ********
Password (again): ********
The password is too similar to the username.
This password is too short. It must contain at least 8
characters.
This password is too common.
Bypass password validation and create user anyway? [y/N]: y
Superuser created successfully.
```

Now, we can launch the Django development server and open the admin site at the URL http://localhost:8000/admin/. Your browser should display a login screen as in the Figure 2-10.

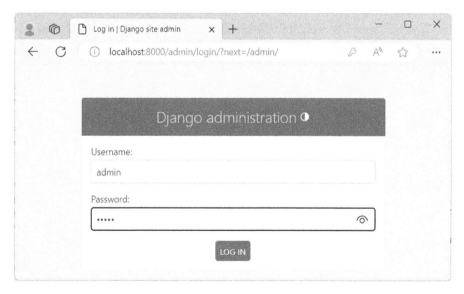

Figure 2-10. *Login screen of the admin site*

Enter the login credentials of the superuser we just created to get to the home page of the admin site (refer to the Figure 2-11).

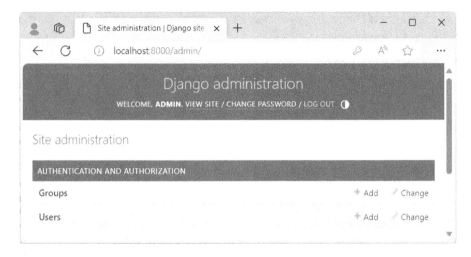

Figure 2-11. *Home page of the admin site*

To add a new user, click the + symbol in the Users row. An interface as shown in the Figure 2-12 opens up. Enter username and password for the new user.

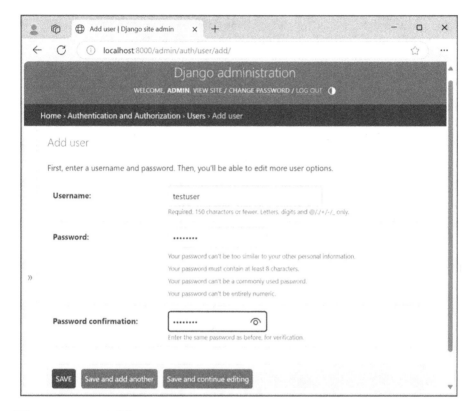

Figure 2-12. *Add a user*

A user belongs to any of the following types:

> **superuser**: A user object that can log into the admin site and possesses permissions to add/change/delete other users as well as perform CRUD operations on all the models in the project, through the admin interface itself.

> **staff**: The User object has an `is_staff` property. When this property is set to True, the user is able to log in to the Django admin site. However, a staff user doesn't automatically get the permission to create,

47

read, update, and delete data in the Django admin;
it must be given explicitly. The superuser is a staff
user by default.

active: All users are marked as active by default.
However, a user may be marked as inactive if
its authentication fails or has been banned for
some reasons. A normal active user (without staff
privilege) is not authorized to use the admin site.

Check/uncheck the boxes as shown in Figure 2-13 to make the user a
superuser, staff, or just an active user.

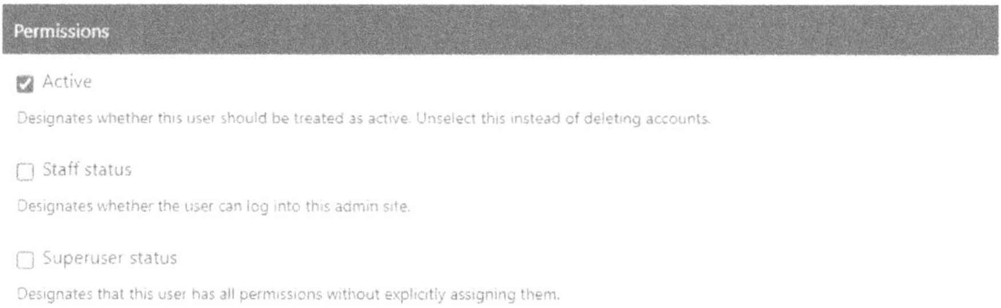

Permissions

☑ Active
Designates whether this user should be treated as active. Unselect this instead of deleting accounts.

☐ Staff status
Designates whether the user can log into this admin site.

☐ Superuser status
Designates that this user has all permissions without explicitly assigning them.

Figure 2-13. *User permissions*

A superuser has all the privileges to add a new user, grant or revoke
permissions to other users, create and grant roles to a group of users, etc.

Django has a built-in Python `shell` that helps in performing the same
user management tasks with this command-line interface that we have
learned to perform with the help of the admin site.

To invoke the Python shell, use the following command:

```
python manage.py shell
```

Against the Python prompt, import the User class and call its
`create_superuser()` function. Give the username, email, and password
parameters.

```
>>> from django.contrib.auth.models import User
>>> usr=User.objects.create_superuser('manager', 'manager@abc.
com', 'pass123')
>>> usr.save()
```

With the create_user() function, create a normal user.

```
>>> from django.contrib.auth.models import User
>>> usr=User.objects.create_user('testusr', 'test@abc.com',
'pass123')
```

To enable logging in to the admin site with this newly created user, set its is_staff property to True.

```
>>> usr.is_staff=True
>>> usr.save()
```

This shell inside the Django environment is an extremely useful tool with the ability to execute Python code and interact with your project directly. It may be used for different purposes such as testing models, inspecting data in your database, and, in general, experimenting with Python code within the context of your project.

We shall be dealing with the admin site later in this book when we learn about authentication and authorization.

Summary

This chapter explained how to build a basic Django project and an app. In this chapter, we also learned how the admin interface of a Django site works and how to create users with web as well as shell interface.

In the next chapter, we shall explore the Model layer of Django architecture. We shall learn how to configure a database and perform migrations.

CHAPTER 3

Django ORM

In the previous chapter, we discussed the View layer of the Django application. We learned how to write views and how to map URL routes to them. In this chapter, we shall learn about the Model layer – the second component of Django's MVT (Model, View, and Template) architecture.

Large, complex, and dynamic web-based applications are always data driven. The application invariably uses a certain database backend for data storage and retrieval. Instead of interacting with the database with raw SQL queries, Django recommends handling the database through an abstraction layer having Python objects called models. By the end of this chapter, you will be able to write models, perform migrations to build databases representing the models, and perform CRUD operations through the model object.

In this chapter, the following topics will be covered:

- DB-API

- ORM

- Database configuration

- Model class

- Migrations

- Django admin shell

© Malhar Lathkar 2025
M. Lathkar, *Modern Django Web Development*,
https://doi.org/10.1007/979-8-8688-1472-3_3

- CRUD operations
- Model field types
- Model relationships

DB-API

The Python Database API (DB-API) is a collection of specifications recommended to be implemented by the database access modules for any relational database. Python modules acting as interface for respective relational databases – such as `mysqldb` or `mysqlclient` for MySQL, `psycopg` for PostgreSQL, etc. – use the same set of classes, objects, and functions as defined in DB-API. The standard library bundled with Python distribution includes the sqlite3 module, which is a reference implementation of DB-API, and is meant to be used with the SQLite database.

SQLite is a lightweight, file-based, serverless database. Python's standard library readily provides built-in support for working with it in the form of sqlite3 module. In fact, a Django project set up with the `startproject` template is configured to use the SQLite database by default.

To interact with a database, the first step is to establish a connection and obtain a connection object.

```
import sqlite3
conn=sqlite3.connect("mydata.sqlite3")
```

Next, we need to obtain a cursor object that acts as a handle to the database. The cursor object is responsible for executing all the SQL queries that perform CREATE, RETRIEVE, UPDATE, and DELETE operations (popularly known by the acronym **CRUD**).

```
cur=conn.cursor()
```

All we need to do now is call the execute() method of the cursor object and pass a string representing a valid SQL query to it.

For example, the code in Listing 3-1 creates a Books table with a given field structure in the mydata.sqlite3 database.

Listing 3-1. Create table

```
import sqlite3

conn=sqlite3.connect("mydata.sqlite3")
cur=conn.cursor()

qry='''
CREATE TABLE IF NOT EXISTS Books (
   id INTEGER (10) PRIMARY KEY,
   title STRING (50),
   author STRING (20),
   price INTEGER (10),
   publisher STRING (20)
   );
'''

cur.execute(qry)
conn.close()
```

The database is created in the current working folder and can be verified with any SQLite viewer app (Figure 3-1).

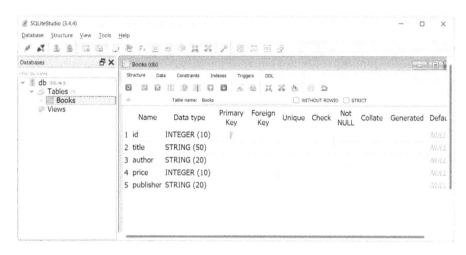

Figure 3-1. *Table in SQLite*

Let us also add a few test records in the Books table using the GUI provided by the viewer app itself (refer to Figure 3-2).

Figure 3-2. *Books table*

This database can be easily accessed in a Django view function. We need to pass a SELECT query to the execute() method of the cursor object from the sqlite3 module.

Add a new function in the views.py module to fetch the records from the Books table (refer to Listing 3-2). The resultset of the SELECT query is rendered as the response to the client.

Listing 3-2. books view

```
import sqlite3

def books(request):
    conn=sqlite3.connect("db.sqlite3")
    cur=conn.cursor()
    qry = "SELECT * FROM Books"
    cur.execute(qry)
    books=cur.fetchall()
    return HttpResponse(str(books))
```

You also need to map this view to a URL route. This is done by appending the following path() expression in the urlpatterns list of the app. The new route is shown in bold letters in Listing 3-3.

Listing 3-3. Update urlpatterns

```
urlpatterns = [
    path("", views.index, name="index"),
    path("about/", views.about, name="about"),
    path("books/", views.books, name="books"),
]
```

You may also provide another view to fetch a specific record whose id is captured from the URL route as a path parameter.

In the views.py module, add a new book() view, as shown in Listing 3-4. It has two arguments; one of course is the request object. The second argument is id, which Django provides by parsing the mapped

URL route. The SQL query is a prepared statement that substitutes the value of id received from the URL dispatcher in the SELECT statement. The record returned by the fetchone() method of the cursor is rendered as the response.

Listing 3-4. book view

```
def book(request, id):
    conn=sqlite3.connect("db.sqlite3")
    cur=conn.cursor()
    qry = "SELECT * FROM Books WHERE id=?"
    cur.execute(qry, (id,))
    book=cur.fetchone()
    return HttpResponse(str(book))
```

This time, the URL route to be mapped with this view has a trailing integer path parameter. Update the urlpatterns list in the urls.py module as shown:

```
urlpatterns = [
    path("", views.index, name="index"),
    path("about/", views.about, name="about"),
    path("books/", views.books, name="books"),
    path("book/<int:id>/", views.book, name="book"),
]
```

These two view functions fetch one or all the records from the table. Likewise, the other CRUD operations can be implemented easily. It basically involves passing an appropriate SQL query string to the execute() method.

However, we shall not pursue this approach of handling databases with the DB-API functionality any further. Instead, we shall find how Django's preferred method of employing **Object-Relational Mapper** (ORM) for the database interaction works.

What Is ORM?

Working with the relational databases with the DB-API-compliant modules has two issues. One of course, is that you as a Python developer should also be proficient in the syntax and construction of various SQL queries. The second issue is more about the programming paradigm mismatch between Python and SQL. The nomenclature of type system in SQL is not at all similar to Python. Apart from numeric and string types, other types have no equivalent counterparts in Python. Python uses objects with attributes of different types. SQL, on the other hand, doesn't support object-oriented programming.

To elaborate this mismatch, consider the Python class definition in Listing 3-5.

Listing 3-5. Books class

```
class Books:
    def __init__(self, id, title, author, price, publisher):
        self.id = id
        self.title = title
        self.author = author
        self.price = price
        self.publisher = publisher
```

Let there be an object of the Books class:

```
b1 = Books(1, "Decoupled Django", "Gagliardi", 3874, "Apress")
```

To store this object in the Books table of the above SQLite database, we need to unpack the attributes of this object need to be manually to equivalent SQL types, and construct the SQL query string argument for the execute() method.

```
cur.execute("INSERT INTO Books VALUES (?,?,?,?,?)",\
            (b1.id, b1.title, b1.author, b1.price, b1.publisher))
```

On the other hand, when the execute() method is provided with a SELECT query string, it returns a resultset. Each row in the resultset is a dictionary of fields and their values. You will have to populate the Book object by parsing the dictionary into the object's attributes.

```
cur.execute("select * from Books WHERE author=?",("
Gagliardi",))
row=cur.fetchone()
b1=Books(row['id'], row['title'], row['author'], row['price'],
row['publisher'])
```

Such a manual conversion between Python object attributes and SQL data types is extremely cumbersome. Moreover, things become messy when you are required to modify the class attributes. Instead, if you could work only with the objects and leave its interaction with the database to some handler, things would become extremely convenient, scalable, and easier to maintain. The **Object-Relational Mappers** are meant to perform exactly this task.

As the name suggests, the ORM API maps the object attributes with the structure of a table in a relational database. It may be noted that in the theory of RDBMS, the table is called a relation. Each object corresponds to a row in the mapped table, and each attribute of the object corresponds to a column in the table structure. Figure 3-3 illustrates how the ORM acts as an interface between a Python class and a database table.

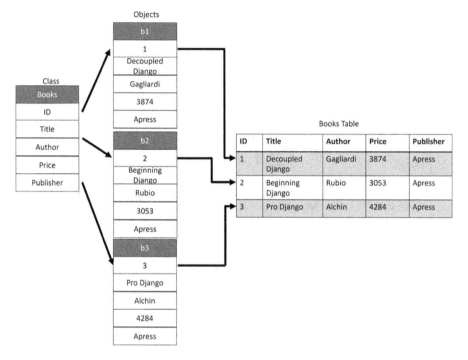

Figure 3-3. *Object-Relational Mapper*

There are a number of ORM libraries for Python that act as an object-oriented abstraction layer on top of the DB-API modules. Django has its own ORM, which is in fact used by the Django framework as a default for interacting with SQLite and the other relational databases, such as MySQL, PostgreSQL, etc. The other popular ORM libraries are SQLAlchemy, SQLObject, Peewee, and more.

To add a database support to your Django application, you need to undertake the following steps.

Define a Model

Define a class with its attributes matching with the desired structure of a table in the relational database of your choice. In Django terminology, such a class is called model and subclasses the Model class defined in the `django.db.models` module. A Django app may have more than one model. Their definitions are placed in the models.py module, which the `startapp` command automatically creates inside the app folder.

You should find the models.py file, virtually empty, in the **firstapp** package folder. Let us define a Book model (as in Listing 3-6) whose attribute structure matches with the field structure of the Books table to be created in the backend database.

Listing 3-6. Book model

```
from django.db import models

# Create your models here.

class Book(models.Model):
    id = models.IntegerField(primary_key=True)
    title = models.CharField(max_length=50)
    author = models.CharField(max_length=50)
    price = models.IntegerField()
    publisher = models.CharField(max_length=50)

    class Meta:
        db_table = "books"
```

The `Meta` subclass is completely optional. It basically adds a certain metadata of the model. Here, we are setting the `db_table` property. When this model structure is translated to the table in the database, Django uses this name. If not specified, Django uses the name of the model class itself as the table name.

Note that each attribute is an object of one of the Field classes, defined in the django.db.models module. We shall learn more about the field types later.

Database Configuration

Choose the database for your Django project. The Django project set up with the startproject command is configured to use the SQLite database as the backend. You can find the DATABASES section in the settings.py module of the project, as shown in Listing 3-7.

Listing 3-7. DATABASES settings

```
DATABASES = {
    'default': {
        'ENGINE': 'django.db.backends.sqlite3',
        'NAME': BASE_DIR / 'db.sqlite3',
    }
}
```

Django has built-in support for other databases like MySQL, Oracle, and PostgreSQL in addition to SQLite. To choose any of these types, you will need to set the respective backend database engine. For instance, change the ENGINE property to 'django.db.backends.mysql' if you intend to employ a MySQL database. You may have to provide additional information about the hostname, port, username, password, etc., in the database configuration settings. A typical database configuration for MySQL database looks like the one shown in Listing 3-8.

Listing 3-8. MySQL settings

```
DATABASES = {
    'default': {
        'ENGINE': 'django.db.backends.mysql',
        'NAME': 'mydatabase',
        'USER': 'root',
        'PASSWORD': '',
        'HOST': 'localhost',
        'PORT': '3306',
    }
}
```

For now, let us keep the database configuration to its default choice of a SQLite database.

Next, we need to ensure that the Django app is added to the list of INSTALLED_APPS in the `settings.py` file.

```
INSTALLED_APPS = [
    # pre-installed apps,
    'firstapp',
]
```

Run Migrations

We are now in a position to translate the model attribute structure to the corresponding table structure in our designated SQLite database. Django uses the mechanism of migration to propagate the models into the database schema.

The migration-related commands are executed with the `manage.py` script. Remember we had already run the migrate command? It was to create the tables from the models in the pre-installed apps. For example, we created a superuser and a normal user. These have been stored in the **auth_user** table. Now that we have added a new app in the project, we need to run the migrations again.

First step is to run the `makemigrations` command. That helps Django detect if there have been new models added, or any existing models modified.

```
(djenv) C:\workspace\firstproject>python manage.py
makemigrations
Migrations for 'firstapp':
  firstapp\migrations\0001_initial.py
    - Create model Book
```

Django has found out that a new model has been defined, and it needs to be propagated. To view the SQL equivalent statements internally executed while performing migrations, run the `sqlmigrate` command:

```
(djenv) C:\workspace\firstproject>python manage.py sqlmigrate
firstapp 0001
BEGIN;
--
-- Create model Book
--
CREATE TABLE "books" ("id" integer NOT NULL PRIMARY KEY,
"title" varchar(50) NOT NULL, "author" varchar(50) NOT NULL,
"price" integer NOT NULL, "publisher" varchar(50) NOT NULL);
COMMIT;
```

Finally, update the database schema by executing the above SQL query by running the `migrate` command:

```
(djenv) C:\workspace\firstproject>python manage.py migrate
Operations to perform:
  Apply all migrations: admin, auth, contenttypes, firstapp,
  sessions
Running migrations:
  Applying firstapp.0001_initial... OK
```

Register Model with Admin Site

Open the database with the SQLite viewer app to confirm if the Books table has been created. However, you won't see the Books table on the Admin site of your project. To be able to administer your model, you need to register it with the admin site.

Open the `admin.py` module available in the app package folder. Import the Book model, and register the same as in Listing 3-9.

Listing 3-9. admin.py

```
from django.contrib import admin

# Register your models here.
from .models import Book

admin.site.register(Book)
```

Go to the Site administration page by logging in with the superuser credentials. The Books model will now be visible as shown in Figure 3-4.

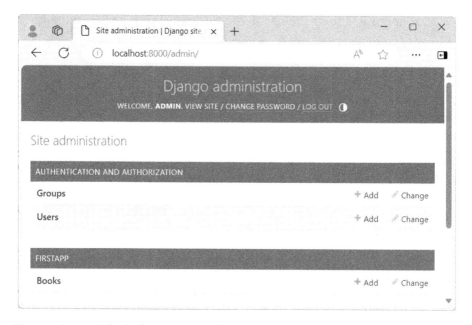

Figure 3-4. *Admin home page showing the Books model*

Django Admin Shell

One of the very powerful but often underused features of the Django framework is its ability to interactively access the models, the database, and other components of a Django project from inside a Python shell. When invoked, the Django admin shell imports the parameters and settings of your current project, and you can handle its resources, especially the models and the database, from the Python prompt.

To invoke the Django shell, run the manage.py script from the command prompt:

```
(djenv) C:\workspace\firstproject>python manage.py shell
```

This opens a Python shell, with the settings of your project already imported.

```
Python 3.12.0 (tags/v3.12.0:0fb18b0, Oct  2 2023, 13:03:39)
[MSC v.1935 64 bit (AMD64)] on win32
Type "help", "copyright", "credits" or "license" for more
information.
(InteractiveConsole)
>>>
```

The Django shell provides easy access to the Object-Relational Mapper (ORM) so that you can directly interact with the database and perform the CRUD operations on the database by calling the corresponding methods defined in the model class.

Add Objects

Let us start by importing the Book model (which we have defined in the earlier section) in the Django shell.

```
>>> from firstapp.models import Book
```

Go ahead and declare an object of the Book class:

```
>>> b1 = Book(1, "Decoupled Django", "Gagliardi", 3874,
"Apress")
```

This object naturally resides in the memory. To save its data into the table mapped with the table during the migration process, you need to explicitly call its save() method.

```
>>> b1.save()
```

If you go back to the home page of the admin site, the Books model (note that Django's admin interface displays the plural form of the model name), which was empty earlier, now shows the newly added Book object.

Instead of declaring an object and then calling its save() method, you can use a convenience method, create(), available to the QuerySet class. Let us add a couple of books with the help of the create() method.

```
>>> b2 = Book.objects.create(id=2, title="Beginning Django",
author="Rubio", price=3053, publisher="Apress")
>>> b3 = Book.objects.create(id=3, title="Pro Django",
author="Alchin", price=4284, publisher="Apress")
```

Retrieval

Ok, so we now have three objects in the Books model. How do we retrieve them – something that the SQL SELECT query does? The Django model class has a Manager attribute. Django adds a Manager with the name objects to every Django model class.

```
>>> type(Book.objects)
<class 'django.db.models.manager.Manager'>
```

The all() method of the Manager class returns the QuerySet consisting of all the objects in the model.

```
>>> Book.objects.all()
<QuerySet [<Book: Book object (1)>, <Book: Book object (2)>,
<Book: Book object (3)>]>
```

To fetch a single object (corresponding to a single row in the mapped table), you may also use the get() method from the Manager class.

```
>>> Book.objects.get(id=2)
<Book: Book object (2)>
```

Note that the get() method must retrieve only a single instance. If multiple records match the query specified within the get() method, this will result in a "MultipleObjectsReturned" error.

The QuerySet object is a list of objects. However, the above result is not quite meaningful, as it hardly reveals anything about the attributes. Hence, we shall add a __str__() method (as in Listing 3-10) in the Book model.

Listing 3-10. Book model updated

```
from django.db import models

# Create your models here.

class Book(models.Model):
    id = models.IntegerField(primary_key=True)
    title = models.CharField(max_length=50)
    author = models.CharField(max_length=50)
    price = models.IntegerField()
    publisher = models.CharField(max_length=50)

    class Meta:
        db_table = "books"

    def __str__(self):
        return "Title : {} Author : {} Price : {}".format(self.
        title, self.author, self.price)
```

Note that the __str__() is Python's magic method that returns a string version of an object. Check the output of all() method now:

```
>>> Book.objects.all()
<QuerySet [<Book: Title : Decoupled Django Author : Gagliardi
Price : 3874>, <Book: Title : Beginning Django Author : Rubio
Price : 3053>, <Book: Title : Pro Django Author : Alchin
Price : 4284>]>
```

Or you can even iterate through the QuerySet object:

```
>>> for i in Book.objects.all():
...     print(i)
...
Title : Decoupled Django Author : Gagliardi Price : 3874
Title : Beginning Django Author : Rubio Price : 3053
Title : Pro Django Author : Alchin Price : 4284
```

Search

We can perform a search for objects within the given model. Recall that similar action is performed by SELECT FROM with the WHERE clause query in SQL. The search criteria are specified as a filter() method of the QuerySet.

This statement returns the book with ID=2.

```
>>> Book.objects.all().filter(id=2)
<QuerySet [<Book: Title : Beginning Django Author : Rubio Price
: 3053>]>
```

You can apply Field lookup operators as the parameters in the filter() method. Some of the lookup criteria are

> **contains**: Equivalent to LIKE in SQL

> **range**: Equivalent to BETWEEN in SQL

> **gte** (greater than or equal to): Equivalent to
> >= in SQL

> **lte** (less than or equal to): Equivalent to <= in SQL

Here are some example uses of these operators:

```
>>> Book.objects.all().filter(price__gte=4000)
<QuerySet [<Book: Title : Pro Django Author : Alchin
Price : 4284>]>
>>> Book.objects.all().filter(price__range=(3500, 4500))
<QuerySet [<Book: Title : Decoupled Django Author : Gagliardi
Price : 3874>, <Book: Title : Pro Django Author : Alchin
Price : 4284>]>
>>> Book.objects.all().filter(title__contains="Django")
<QuerySet [<Book: Title : Decoupled Django Author : Gagliardi
Price : 3874>, <Book: Title : Beginning Django Author : Rubio
Price : 3053>, <Book: Title : Pro Django Author : Alchin
Price : 4284>]>
```

Updating the Objects

Django ORM makes modifying one or more attributes of one or more objects in a model super easy. The object Manager provides an update() method. The method accepts a variable number of keyword arguments, each specifying the new value of an attribute. Under the hood, the update() method executes the SQL UPDATE query

For example, you may want to change the name of the publisher in all the records from Apress to Springer:

```
>>> Book.objects.all().update(publisher="Springer")
```

This is equivalent to the SQL UPDATE query as

```
UPDATE Books SET publisher="Springer"
```

Or increase the price of each book by 100. Here, we import the F() function from the django.db.models module. It represents the value of a given model field. Hence, F('price') gives the value of the price field, which we can use in an expression to compute the new price.

```
>>> from django.db.models import F
>>> Book.objects.all().update(price=F('price')+100)
```

Check the effect of these statements in the admin interface, a SQLite viewer, or even by retrieving all() objects in the Django shell itself.

You can combine the filter() method along with update() to modify the attributes of only those objects that satisfy the given criteria.

As an afterthought, you've decided to roll back the increase with price>4000. Run the following statement for the purpose:

```
>>> Book.objects.filter(price__gte=4000).
update(price=F('price')-100)
```

Finally, removing one or more objects (and, in turn, rows from the table) is done with the delete() method. Understandably, you will always call this method along with a filter, else all the records will be removed. You can also use the get() method to delete a single instance.

As an example, we shall remove an object with ID=1:

```
>>> Book.objects.get(id=1).delete()
```

The Django admin shell thus gives a convenient access to the Django ORM. It's a very handy tool to test and debug database interactions without the need to modify the Django project. We will in fact use all these CRUD methods (add(), filter(), update(), etc.) programmatically inside Django's views throughout the subsequent chapters of this book.

Model Field Types

While a Django model is a regular Python class, the behavior of its attributes is very unique. As mentioned above, it subclasses the Model class in the `django.db.models` module. The fields are the most crucial part of the model definition. An attribute in a model class is a class attribute (an attribute outside any of the instance methods) and is an instance of an appropriate Field class. In the example used here, the attributes title, price, etc., are the instances of `CharField` and `IntegerField`. Django ORM provides a number of other field types to choose from.

Here is the interesting (and intriguing) part. If title, author, price, etc., are the class attributes, how is it that each instance of Book class (each book) has a different value title, author, or price, which is what an instance attribute does?

Let us create a new Book object:

```
>>> id=4
>>> title = "A new Django Book"
>>> author = "Django Expert"
>>> price = 2000
>>> publisher = "Springer Nature"
>>> b1 = Book(id, title, author, price, publisher)
```

The parameters passed to the constructor are regular Python types – the variables id and price are integers and title, author, and publisher variables are of str type – and not the Field types of the class attributes. And there is no explicit __init__() constructor either that initializes instance attributes like self.title. So what is happening here?

The Django ORM handles this paradox in a very peculiar manner. As mentioned above, the class attributes of the model serve as the blueprint of the table to be created when the migration is performed. When you declare an instance of the model, Django stores the data in an internal structure of its own and only maps this structure with the field structure whenever you call the API methods such as create(), save(), update(), or delete().

That brings us to the various field types that Django ORM provides. As per the Django documentation, there are more than two dozen field classes, the subclasses of an abstract Field class. The field types, employed in most use cases, are as follows.

CharField

Easily the most common type, normally used to store string attributes such as name, title, etc. For fairly large sized text, you can use the TextField type. Usually, an additional argument – max_length – is given to the CharField constructor:

```
title = models.CharField(max_length=50)
```

While the value in the given CharField is a Python string, when migrated to the database, the corresponding field becomes a VARCHAR or equivalent data type supported by the corresponding database product. The TextField attribute is mapped to SQL's TEXT field type.

IntegerField

The attributes intended to store integer values such as EmployeeID, RollNo, etc., are defined to be of IntegerField type in a model. BigIntegerField (64-bit integer), SmallIntegerField, AutoField, etc., are the other field types in the category. If you want to set a certain field to be a primary key in the mapped table, you can pass a primary_key argument and set it to True.

```
id = models.IntegerField(primary_key=True)
```

You can, of course, set any field as the primary key of the module. On the database side, `IntegerField` is translated as INT, INTEGER, or any such field type supported by the database you use.

FloatField

A float Python object, which is a floating-point number, can be stored in an attribute of `FloatField`. Examples can be salary, price, etc.

```
salary = models.FloatField()
```

A `FloatField` is conveniently mapped to FLOAT or DOUBLE field types in SQL.

BooleanField

This type of model attribute is also frequently employed, usually to store bool type values (true or false). For example, you may want to provide an attribute – isebook – to indicate whether a book is available in ebook format or not.

```
isebook = models.BooleanField()
```

Most of the RDBMS products (MySQL, PostgreSQL, etc.) have a BOOLEAN field type, to which the `BooleanField` model attribute is mapped against.

DateField

Python stores the date in the `datetime.date` object. The corresponding model attribute in Django is `DateField()`. This attribute type is often required in a model definition, for example, date of birth, date of appointment, date of publication, etc.

```
publication_date = models.DateField()
```

As you would expect, this type of model attribute is translated to the DATE type of SQL, when migrated.

Apart from the above, there are several other Field types in Django. We shall use them later, if and when required.

We can see that a certain ORM type represents a corresponding Python data type. On the other hand, the ORM type is mapped to a corresponding SQL type upon migration. Table 3-1 comes handy for understanding the relation between Python types, ORM types, and SQL types.

Table 3-1. *Django ORM types*

Python Type	ORM Type	SQL Type
str	CharField or TextField	VARCHAR or TEXT
integer	IntegerField, BigIntegerField, AutoField	INT, INTEGER, BIGINT
float	FloatField, DecimalField	FLOAT, DOUBLE, DECIMAL
bool	BooleanField	BOOLEAN
date, time	DateField, DateTimeField	DATE, TIMESTAMP

Types of Relationships

Let us have a brief recap of some of the key concepts of the RDBMS. In a relational database, a relation is a table that represents an entity. The attributes of the entity are the columns in the table, and each row is an instance of the entity. One of the columns in a table is constrained to have a unique value and is said to be the primary key of the table.

In Figure 3-5, the Products table is designed to have the ProductID column as the primary key. Similarly, in another Customers table, CustomerID is its primary key.

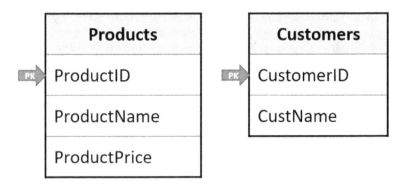

Figure 3-5. *Products and Customers tables with primary key*

When the primary key of one table appears as one of the fields in another table (which may have its own primary key), then it is called the foreign key. The Invoices table shown in Figure 3-6 has CustomerID as a field (or column) that refers to the CustomerID of the Customers table, and hence, it is a foreign key. Similarly, the ProductID column in the Invoices table is another foreign key as it refers to the primary key of the Products table.

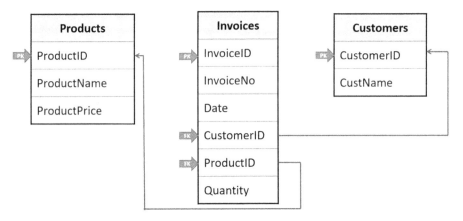

Figure 3-6. *Invoices table with foreign keys*

Based on the foreign keys, the tables can be joined. We can fetch the name of the customer of a given invoice number, retrieve the price of the product purchased, and compute values like tax. The idea behind designing related tables is to avoid data redundancy (unnecessary repetition of same data in many rows) and ensure data integrity.

Imagine that instead of the unique productid in the Invoices table, a longish name of product field is used; it will have to be entered every time a customer buys it – and it may introduce some typo errors. Similarly, if a product whose ID is referred to in the Invoices table is removed from the Products table, the other details of the product such as its price will not be available.

Relational databases have a mechanism to prevent the deletion of primary key if it is being used in the related table, so that the data integrity is intact.

Since the Django models are mapped to the corresponding tables in the database, you can define such relationships between the two model fields also. Three types of relationships exist:

- One to one

- One to many

- Many to many

One-to-One Relationship

If, for each primary key in one model, there exists only one record in the other related model, the two models are said to have a one-to-one relationship.

Let us take an example of a college model and a principal model. A college can have only one principal, and the other way round, one person can be a principal of only one college.

The college model can be described as in Listing 3-11.

Listing 3-11. College model

```
class College(Model):
    CollegeID = models.IntegerField(primary_key = True)
    name = models.CharField(max_length=50)
    strength = models.IntegerField()
    city=models.CharField(max_length=50)
```

While defining the Principal model, we need to provide the CollegeID field as the foreign key to indicate the person with the given ID is the principal of which college. To express this relationship, the foreign key field must be of a special field type – OneToOneField. The first parameter should be the table to which the foreign key refers to, and the second option specifies what should happen in case the associated object in the primary model is deleted. The on_delete option should be one of the following values:

- CASCADE: Deletes the object containing the ForeignKey.

- PROTECT: Prevents deletion of the referenced object

- RESTRICT: Prevents deletion of the referenced object by raising RestrictedError

Let us defined the Principal model with the field structure as in Listing 3-12.

Listing 3-12. Principal model

```
class Principal(models.Model):
    id = models.IntegerField(primary_key=True)
    name = models.CharField(max_length=50)
    qualification = models.CharField(max_length=50)
```

```
CollegeID = models.OneToOneField(
        College,
        on_delete=models.CASCADE
        )
```

One-to-Many Relationship

In a one-to-many relationship, one object of a model can be associated with one or more objects of another model. A case in point is that of a teacher qualified to teach a subject, but there may be more than one teacher in a college who can teach the same subject.

The Subject model is as explained in Listing 3-13.

Listing 3-13. Subject model

```
class Subject(models.Model):
    Subjectcode = models.IntegerField(primary_key = True)
    name = models.CharField(max_length=30)
    credits = models.IntegerField()
```

The Teacher model (Listing 3-14) has its own primary key. Its foreign key – Subjectcode – establishes one-to-many relationship with the Subject model.

Listing 3-14. Teacher model

```
class Teacher(models.Model):
    TeacherID = models.IntegerField(primary_key=True)
    name = models.CharField(max_length=50)
    qualification = models.CharField(max_length=50)
    subjectcode=models.ForeignKey(
            Subject,
            on_delete=models.CASCADE
                )
```

Many-to-Many Relationship

In a many-to-many relationship, multiple objects of one model can be associated with multiple objects of another model.

Let us redefine the relationship between the subject and teacher models in the above example. Assuming that the college has more than one teacher who can teach the same subject, additionally, a teacher can teach more than one subject as well. So there is a many-to-many relationship between the two.

Django implements this with the ManyToManyField type. Let us use it in defining the Subject model.

The Teacher model is straightforward (refer to Listing 3-15).

Listing 3-15. Teacher model updated

```
class Teacher(models.Model):
    TeacherID = models.IntegerField(primary_key=True)
    name = models.EmailField(max_length=50)
    qualification = models.CharField(max_length=50)
```

The design of the Subject model class (as in Listing 3-16) reflects the many-to-many relationship.

Listing 3-16. Subject model updated

```
class Subject(models.Model):
    Subjectcode = models.IntegerField(primary_key = True)
    name = models.CharField(max_length=30)
    credits = models.IntegerField()
    teacher = models.ManyToManyField(Teacher)
```

Let us migrate these models to construct corresponding tables in the underlying SQLite database.

```
(djenv) C:\workspace\firstproject>python manage.py
makemigrations firstapp
Migrations for 'firstapp':
firstapp\migrations\0002_subject_teacher.py
    - Create model Subject
     - Create model Teacher
```

To have a look at the SQL queries that will be indirectly executed by Django ORM, run the sqlmigrate command:

```
(djenv) C:\workspace\firstproject>python manage.py sqlmigrate
firstapp 0002_subject_teacher
BEGIN;
--
-- Create model Subject
--
CREATE TABLE "firstapp_subject" ("Subjectcode" integer NOT NULL
PRIMARY KEY, "name" varchar(30) NOT NULL, "credits" integer
NOT NULL);
--
-- Create model Teacher
--
CREATE TABLE "firstapp_teacher" ("TeacherID" integer NOT NULL
PRIMARY KEY, "name" varchar(50) NOT NULL, "qualification"
varchar(50) NOT NULL);
--
-- Add field teacher to subject
--
```

```
CREATE TABLE "firstapp_subject_teacher" ("id" integer NOT
NULL PRIMARY KEY AUTOINCREMENT, "subject_id" integer NOT
NULL REFERENCES "firstapp_subject" ("Subjectcode") DEFERRABLE
INITIALLY DEFERRED, "teacher_id" integer NOT NULL REFERENCES
"firstapp_teacher" ("TeacherID") DEFERRABLE INITIALLY DEFERRED);
CREATE UNIQUE INDEX "firstapp_subject_teacher_subject_id_
teacher_id_abb3b881_uniq" ON "firstapp_subject_teacher"
("subject_id", "teacher_id");
CREATE INDEX "firstapp_subject_teacher_subject_id_00acbe0f" ON
"firstapp_subject_teacher" ("subject_id");
CREATE INDEX "firstapp_subject_teacher_teacher_id_0d8af8b3" ON
"firstapp_subject_teacher" ("teacher_id");
COMMIT;
```

Finally, run the migrate command.

```
(djenv) C:\workspace\firstproject>python manage.py migrate
Operations to perform:
  Apply all migrations: admin, auth, contenttypes, firstapp,
  sessions
Running migrations:
  Applying firstapp.0002_subject_teacher... OK
```

Thus, three new tables (firstapp_subject, firstapp_teacher, and firstapp_subject_teacher) will be created in the SQLite database (db. sqlite3) in the project root folder.

Summary

In this chapter, we have learned an important aspect of the Django framework that is also at the center of the entire Django application, namely, models. We started with Python's DB-API, discussed its drawbacks, and explained the concept of ORM. We learned how to define models and how to perform migrations. We also learned to perform CRUD operations on the models from within the Django Shell.

In the end, we discussed the field types and the types of relationships between the models. In the next chapter, we shall deal with the third organ of Django's MVT architecture – templates – and learn how to render dynamic web pages by populating the templates with the data from the models.

CHAPTER 4

Django Templates

The templates are the presentation layer of a Django web app. Django is a data-driven web framework. Its elaborate templating mechanism makes it very easy to merge the data from sources such as databases with the static HTML to generate dynamic web pages.

This chapter takes a detailed look at the powerful features of Django's Template Language. Let us discuss the following topics in this chapter:

- Template object

- render() function

- Template context

- Template variables

- Tags

- Form templates

- Class-based views

- Generic views

- Static assets

- Template inheritance

© Malhar Lathkar 2025
M. Lathkar, *Modern Django Web Development*,
https://doi.org/10.1007/979-8-8688-1472-3_4

Template Object

The word "template" generally refers to a blueprint or a skeleton of a certain product, with a fixed design interspersed with one or more placeholders for inserting variable components. Many word-processing and presentation software provide ready-to-use templates for quickly preparing documents such as resumes, certificates, flyers, meeting agenda, etc. To prepare a resume, for example, you can select a template of your desired design. The layout, the headings, the fonts and colors, etc., are pre-formatted with placeholders for the variable information. You just fill up the required details such as name, address, experience, etc., in the appropriate places provided in the template.

In the context of a web framework such as Django, a template is essentially a web page, with its static HTML content intermittently populated with template markups. Django uses its own templating system, known by the name **Django Template Language** (DTL). It defines a set of symbols and keywords that are used in a template web page. The template engine – a tool that uses certain context data – reads the template code, interprets the tags in it, and replaces them with the corresponding data from the context provided.

Figure 4-1 depicts the functioning of a template engine.

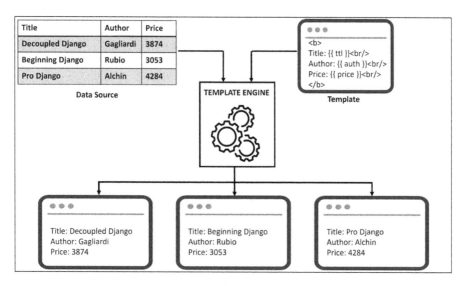

Figure 4-1. *Template engine*

The templating mechanism is controlled by certain parameters set in the settings module (*settings.py*). The TEMPLATES section sets the choice of template backend, the location of templates, etc.

Typically, the TEMPLATES section of the settings module of a Django project created by the startproject command reads as in Listing 4-1.

Listing 4-1. Templates settings

```
TEMPLATES = [
    {
        'BACKEND': 'django.template.backends.django.
        DjangoTemplates',
        'DIRS': [BASE_DIR/'templates'],
        'APP_DIRS': True,
        'OPTIONS': {
            'context_processors': [
                'django.template.context_processors.debug',
                'django.template.context_processors.request',
```

```
            'django.contrib.auth.context_processors.auth',
            'django.contrib.messages.context_processors.
            messages',
        ],
    },
  },
]
```

By default, Django uses the Django Template Engine for template processing. Its functionality is provided in the DjangoTemplates class. This class is defined in the django.template.backends.django module. The DIRS parameter is a list of directories where you will put your templates, i.e., web pages. If you want Django to search for the templates in multiple directories, put them in the order of preference. By default, it is an empty list, but the convention is to use the templates directory under the BASE_DIR, i.e., the parent project folder.

Django also lets you use the **jinja2** template engine instead of its default. If you wish to use it, set the BACKEND parameter to django.template.backends.jinja2.Jinja2 class.

We know that any view function formulates an HttpResponse from a Python string that may have various HTML tags, to be returned to the user, as in the index() function (Listing 4-2).

Listing 4-2. index view

```
from django.http import HttpResponse

def index(request):
    return HttpResponse("<h2>Hello, World.</h2>")
```

If we want to render the Hello message that contains a name passed as an argument to the view function (such as Hello John), we can use any of Python's string substitution methods (such as the f-string, or the format() function) to insert the name argument and then return the response. Add a user() view function as in Listing 4-3:

Listing 4-3. user view with parameter

```
def user(request, name):
    return HttpResponse(f"<h2>Hello, {name}.</h2>")
```

Even if the response is completely static, passing a lengthy string that represents a hard-coded HTML string as the view response is not feasible. Ideally, we would like a separately constructed web page to be used by the view function to formulate its response. The Template object performs precisely this task.

Django loads the given web page by invoking the get_template() method of the django.template.loader class to obtain the Template object.

```
template=loader.get_template("index.html")
```

Here, index.html is a simple Hello World web page, situated in the BASE_DIR/templates folder. If required, this object is manipulated to insert a certain context data (we shall discuss this aspect in the next section). The render() method of the Template object returns a string with the context data substituted at the appropriate placeholders in the HTML script.

```
string = template.render(context, request)
```

Currently we don't have any placeholders in index.html, nor do we have any context to be filled. The view function (Listing 4-4) then passes it as its response.

Listing 4-4. Rendering template

```
def index(request):
    template=loader.get_template("index.html")
    context = {}
    return HttpResponse(template.render(context, request))
```

render( ) Function

A collection of various convenience functions, defined in the django. shortcuts module, includes a render() function that really is a shortcut for rendering a template. Instead of loading the template, inserting context data in the DTL markups inside the HTML, and returning the HttpResponse, using the render() function is the all-in-one alternative. You need to pass an HTTP request object and the template web page as the mandatory arguments.

```
render(request, template_page)
```

Let us change the index() view function as shown in Listing 4-5.

Listing 4-5. render() function

```
from django.shortcuts import render

def index(request):
    return render(request, 'index.html')
```

Optionally, you can pass the context data as a Python dictionary object, the content_type of the response (which is text/html by default), and the status code to the render() function.

Template Context

As mentioned earlier, the Django Template Language substitutes variable data at the appropriately marked placeholders inside the HTML script. So it is much like the f-string processing in Python, where a variable surrounded by the curly brackets is substituted by its value. The only difference is you have to use double curly brackets to mark a template variable. Hence, in our *index.html* template page (refer to Listing 4-6), put {{ name }} to insert the name argument at the runtime.

Listing 4-6. Template web page

```
<html>
<body>
<h2>Hello, {{ name }}.</h2>
</body>
</html>
```

The values to be substituted in all the template variables in the HTML script come from the Context object that you need to pass to the render() function. Django builds the Context object from a Python dictionary, with its keys corresponding to the template variable names. The template engine, during the processing of the template, fills the place of the variable with the corresponding value in the dictionary. So the call to the render() function will be

```
render(request, template, context)
```

We have already defined a user() view function that takes name as a path parameter. So start the server and go to the URL http://localhost:8000/firstapp/user/John. The browser should now show a **Hello John** message.

The context argument for the render() function is a dictionary, with each key being the template variable. The name of the template variable follows the usual convention – having alphabets, digits, or an underscore. The template variable may also have a dot character.

Its value may be a singular Python object (string, or a numeric), a list, a dict, or even an object of any Python class.

We can use the index to access a specific element. If the context object is

```
context = {"subjects": ["Phy", "Che", "Maths"]}
```

91

then to render the 0th element in the template, use

```
{{ subjects[0] }}
```

If it is a dictionary as

```
context = {"subjects": {"Phy": 60, "Che":70, "Maths":80}}
```

the template variable to be used to display the marks of "Phy" subject should be

```
{{ subjects["Phy"] }}
```

The dot (.) operator is used in the name of a template variable as a lookup for a certain attribute of an object. Let us say we pass a Teacher object as the context:

```
context = { "teacher": Teacher(id = 1, name = "Anand Bose",
subject = "Data Science", qualification = "ME, Ph.D")}
```

in which case, to show the name of the teacher in the template output, the name of the template variable should be

```
{{ teacher.name }}
```

Template Tags

The Django Template Language lets you do a lot more than just outputting the context data in the response. It provides various tags that add enhanced processing of the context, such as conditional formatting, iterating over a collection, etc. The tags related to template inheritance are extremely important in ensuring that the pages have a uniform look and feel. We shall discuss the concept of template inheritance in the next chapter.

The template tags are put inside the symbols {% and %}:

```
{% tag <additional parameters> %}
```

{% if %} Tag

To incorporate conditional processing inside the template, DTL has {% if %}, {% elif %}, {% else %}, and {% endif %} tags.

Just like the if statement in Python, the {% if %} tag evaluates a variable, and if it is "true", the contents of the subsequent block are output. Each {% if %} tag must have a closing {% endif %} tag. In between, there may be one or more {% elif %} tags and an {% else %} tag.

```
{% var1 %}
    Expression1
{% elif var2 %}
    Expression2
{% else %}
    Expression3
{% endif %}
```

Let us put the {% if %} tag to some realistic use. Earlier, we had defined the Book model. Let us add a new Boolean field – ebook (as in Listing 4-7) – to indicate whether the book is available in ebook format or not. The newly added field is shown in boldface.

Listing 4-7. Book model – modified

```
class Book(models.Model):
    id = models.IntegerField(primary_key=True)
    title = models.CharField(max_length=50)
    author = models.CharField(max_length=50)
    price = models.IntegerField()
    publisher = models.CharField(max_length=50)
    ebook = models.BooleanField(default=True)
```

The default value of this field as True means that all the books are available in ebook format. As we have modified the model, we need to go through the process of migration as below:

```
python manage.py makemigrations firstapp
python manage.py migrate
```

Out of the book objects in the model, let us update the book with ID=2 and set its ebook attribute to False, indicating that it is not available in ebook format.

```
python manage.py shell
>>> from firstapp.models import Book
>>> b1 = Book.objects.get(id=2)
>>> b1.ebook=False
>>> b1.save()
```

Next, let us define a book() view as in Listing 4-8, that retrieves a Book object with the given ID as the path parameter and pass it as the context to a *book.html* template.

Listing 4-8. book view

```
def book(request, id):
    book = Book.objects.get(id=id)
    context = {'book' : book}
    return render(request, 'book.html', context)
```

The *book.html* (Listing 4-9) template simply outputs the attributes of the retrieved book, such as the title, author, etc. Additionally, it checks if the ebook attribute is True or False and renders a conditional response.

Listing 4-9. book.html

```
<html>
<body>
    <h2 style = "text-align: center;">Title: {{ book.
    title }}</h2>
    <br>
                    <p><b>ID:</b> {{ book.id }}</p>
                    <p><b>Author:</b> {{ book.author }}</p>
                    <p><b>Price:</b> {{ book.price}}</p>
                    <p><b>Publisher:</b> {{ book.
                    publisher }}</p>
                    {% if book.ebook %}
                    <p><b>Available as Ebook?: </b> Yes</p>
                    {% else %}
                    <p><b>Available as Ebook?: </b> No</p>
                    {% endif %}
                    <hr>
</body>
</html>
```

To wire up the book() view with the route that passes the ID parameter, add this path to the urlpatterns in the app's URLCONF.

```
path("book/<int:id>/", views.book, name="book"),
```

With these steps completed, start the server, and check the browser display (Figure 4-2) for **"book/2"** endpoint.

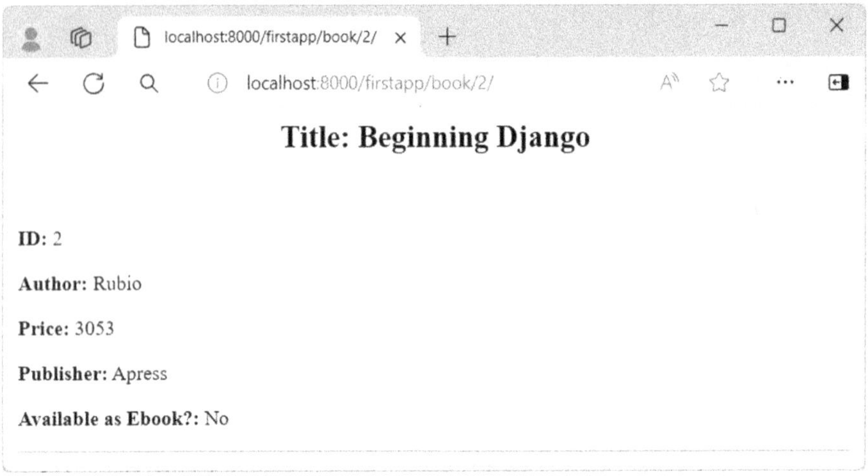

Figure 4-2. *{% if %} tag*

Try and check the same for any other book that has its ebook attribute as True.

{% for %} Tag

The for tag is employed in a template when the context variable is a collection of objects and you want to iterate over the collection. The syntax of Django's for template tag is similar to the for statement in Python, except that every {% for %} must have a corresponding {% endfor %} tag.

```
{% for object in collection %}
{{ object }}
{% endfor %}
```

Unlike Python, the DTL doesn't use uniform indents to mark a block. Hence, the endfor tag marks the end of the for loop. Same thing applies to the use of {% endif %} with each {% if %}. There may be one or more HTML expressions or other template tags in between. For example, you may want to use the {% if %} . . . {% endif %} construct inside the for loop.

The following view function sends a list as the context to a given template:

```
def langs(request):
    context = {"langs" : ["Python", "Java", "C++"]}
    return render(request, 'template.html', context)
```

We employ a {% for %} . . {% endfor %} pair of tags in the template code (Listing 4-10) to display the list of languages as the response.

Listing 4-10. for – endfor tag

```
<ul>
        {% for lang in langs %}
                <li>{{ lang }}</li>
        {% endfor %}
</ul>
```

Django outputs the list when the browser is pointed to the URL route list/ (it needs to be mapped to the langs() view in the *urls.py* module as discussed earlier).

- Python

- Java

- C++

Let us use the {% for %} tag to display the list of books. Add the books() view. It passes the collection of Book objects to the *list_books.html* template (Listing 4-11).

Listing 4-11. books view

```
from django.shortcuts import render
from .models import Book
def books(request):
    books = Book.objects.all()
    context = {'books': books}
    return render(request, 'list_books.html', context)
```

The {% for %} tag in Listing 4-12 processes a Book object at a time and renders its attributes in one iteration.

Listing 4-12. list_books.html

```
<html>
<body>
    <h2 style = "text-align: center;">List of Books</h2>
    <br>
            {% for book in books %}
                    <p><b>Title:</b> {{ book.title }}</p>
                    <p><b>Author:</b> {{ book.author }}</p>
                    <p><b>Price:</b> {{ book.price}}</p>
                    <p><b>Publisher:</b> {{ book.
                    publisher }}</p>
                    <hr>
            {% endfor %}

</html>
```

You need to map the books() view to the **"books/"** route by appending a new path to the urlpatterns list.

```
path("books/", views.books, name="books"),
```

The URL http://localhost:8000/firstapp/books/ now displays the list of books as shown in Figure 4-3.

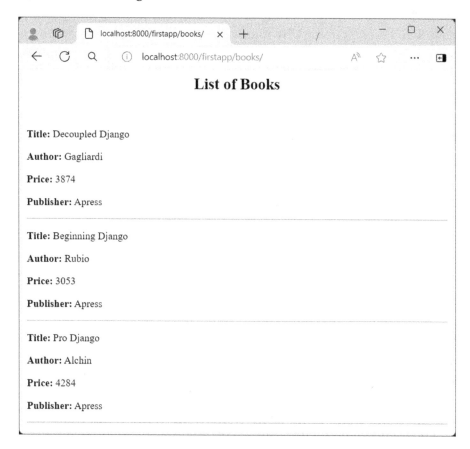

Figure 4-3. *Using loop in template*

Out of the various other template tags in DTL, we shall discuss the {% block %} and {% extends %} tags when we discuss the "Template Inheritance" section.

Form Templates

The view functions defined so far in this chapter are invoked when the user visits their corresponding URL routes with the HTTP GET request, which retrieves one or more resources from the server. The books() view retrieves a list of books, and the book() view retrieves a book whose ID matches with the ID parameter it parses from the URL. To add a new resource (in this case, a new book) or to update any existing resource, we need to send a POST request, along with the data to add or update.

An HTML form collects the data from the user in appropriate input elements (such as text box, radio buttons, drop-downs, etc.) and sends it to a function on the server that parses the request data and uses it to add/update a book.

Django offers a robust form rendering API that makes it very convenient to construct a form with elements matching with the types of fields in the model definition and validate the data entered by the user before performing any action such as adding a new object or updating an existing object.

HTML Form

Let us start by designing a simple HTML form that accepts inputs for the fields in the Book model that we have already defined. As mentioned above, the method attribute of the form should be set to POST. When submitted, the form data is sent to a view function addbook(), which is the action attribute of the form. We have four text input elements for the fields in the Book model (title, author, price, and publisher). The HTML script below is saved as bookform.html (Listing 4-13) in the templates folder.

Listing 4-13. bookform.html

```html
<form action="/firstapp/addbook/" method="post">
    {% csrf_token %}
    <p><label for="ttl">Title: </label>
    <input id="ttl" type="text" name="title"></p>
    <p><label for="auth">Author's name: </label>
    <input id="auth" type="text" name="author"></p>
    <p><label for="price">Price: </label>
    <input id="price" type="text" name="price"></p>
    <p><label for="pub">Publisher: </label>
    <input id="pub" type="text" name="publisher"></p>
    <input type="submit" value="OK">
</form>
```

Note the use of the {% csrf_token %} tag inside the <form> .. </form> code. This tag is Django's mechanism against the CSRF attacks.

CSRF is an acronym for Cross-Site Request Forgery. It is the most common type of security attack on a website. The attacker utilizes this type of vulnerability and forces the user (even if they have an authenticated access) to perform certain actions that eventually turn out to be harmful for them.

Django installs a middleware called CsrfViewMiddleware (this can be found in the lists of installed MIDDLEWARE in the settings module). It provides a handy solution to prevent CSRF attacks.

When a user visits the Django application, it generates a token and stores it as a cookie in the client's machine. The {% csrf_token %} tag in the HTML form code renders a hidden field with the name "csrfmiddlewaretoken".

```
<input type="hidden" name="csrfmiddlewaretoken"
value="S9tIMDKsbtbhbKhmr1BXsO7k2znSPIQkvkq
fH4IqVre5mOdSfUuAyEYbtlzetnkZ">
```

As the user submits the form, the server checks if it has this token field and its value is the same as the cookie value. If it doesn't match, the further processing of the form is terminated, thereby avoiding any unwanted action.

The above HTML form is really a static template, without any variable component. To render this form, add a view function – getbook() – in the *views.py* module (as in Listing 4-14).

Listing 4-14. getbook view

```
def getbook(request):
    context={}
    return render(request, "bookform.html", context)
```

Make sure that this view is mapped to a URL route by updating the urlpatterns list in the *urls.py* module:

```
path("getbook/", views.getbook, name="getbook"),
```

You will get a basic HTML form rendered on your browser (Figure 4-4).

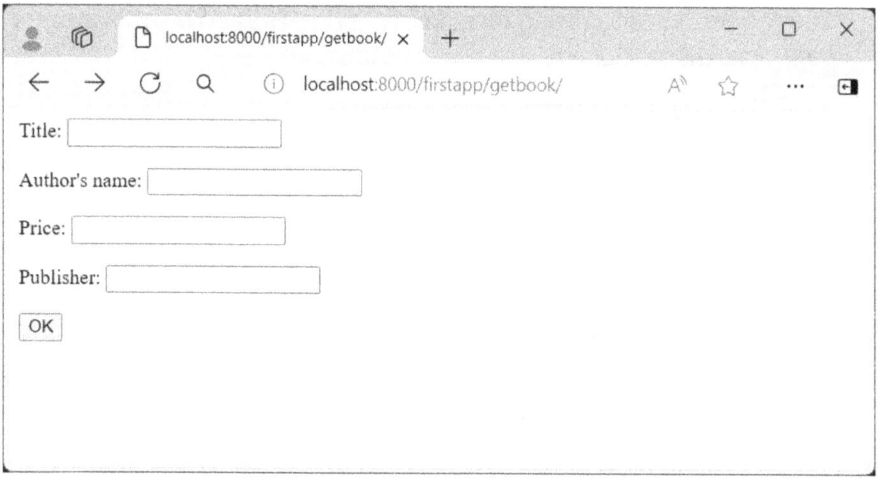

Figure 4-4. *HTML form*

Form Class

The HTML form as above works well, especially in relatively simpler cases (we can improve its design by applying appropriate CSS styles). For more complex situations though, especially where the models are related (one-to-one or one-to-many) and for models with fields of more advanced type, the form design becomes difficult. We also need to validate the data before processing. The modern HTML5 form fields do present certain basic client-side validations; form handling of a certain higher level is required.

The Form class (defined in the django.forms module) and various types of form fields provide an effective form design and validation mechanism.

Define a subclass of django.forms.Form class. Its object renders an HTML form. The class attributes of the Form class are the objects of appropriate form field classes, all inherited from the django.forms.fields.Field class. The form field types are very much similar to the model field types. For example, the forms.CharField corresponds to the models.CharField, whereas the forms.BooleanField corresponds to the models.BooleanField.

The properties of a certain form field are determined by one or more of the following attributes:

> **required**: A Boolean parameter indicating if a value to this field is needed. If true, and the field is empty, it raises the validation error with the **'This field is required.'** Message.

> **label**: A text to be associated when the field is rendered.

> **initial**: You can specify the initial value to use when rendering this field.

> **widget**: Each field uses a default HTML element when it is rendered. For example, a CharField is rendered as a text input element. However, if you wish to provide a TextArea element, use the widget property.

So let us declare a BookForm class and define the form fields that reflect the Book model. Add the script (as in Listing 4-15) in the *forms.py* module in the app package folder.

Listing 4-15. forms.py

```python
from django import forms

class BookForm(forms.Form):
    title = forms.CharField(label="Title ", max_length=50)
    author = forms.CharField(label='Author ', max_length=50)
    price = forms.IntegerField(label='Price ')
    publisher = forms.CharField(label = 'Publisher ',
    max_length=50)
    ebook = forms.BooleanField(initial=True)
```

The getbook() view (refer Listing 4-16) passes an object of this form as a context to the *bookform.html* template.

Listing 4-16. getbook view with Form object

```
def getbook(request):
    form = BookForm()
    context={'form' : form}
    return render(request, "bookform.html", context)
```

In the previous example, the *bookform.html* script rendered the hard-coded HTML form elements. Instead, we now want the Django form to be rendered.

The Django Template Language renders each form field attribute as its associated HTML widget. For example, the title attribute

```
title = forms.CharField(label="Title ", max_length=50)
```

is rendered on the browser as

```
<label for="id_title">Title:</label>
<input type="text" name="title" maxlength="50" required
id="id_title">
```

However, Django outputs the field elements in one of the following predefined outputting styles:

> **{{ form.as_div }}**: Renders the form as a series of <div> elements, with each <div> containing one field.

> **{{ form.as_p }}**: Renders the form as a series of <p> tags, with each <p> containing one field.

{{ **form.as_ul** }}: Renders the form as a series of <li> tags, each containing one field. It does not include the <ul> and </ul> tags surrounding a sequence of <li> .. </li> tags.

{{ **form.as_table** }}: Renders the form as an HTML table, with each field and its label in one row. Again, the enclosing <table> and </table> tags are not included, you need to explicitly provide them in the template code.

Moreover, Django does not include the <form> and </form> tags or an <input type="submit"> tag too. You have to include them too in the template code.

So let us modify the *bookform.html* (Listing 4-17) template that renders the form in the form of an HTML table.

Listing 4-17. bookform.html – rendering form as a table

```
<form action="/firstapp/addbook/" method="post">
    {% csrf_token %}
    <table>
    {{ form.as_table }}
    </table>
    <input type="submit" value="OK">
</form>
```

The user is presented with a tabular layout of all the fields as in Figure 4-5.

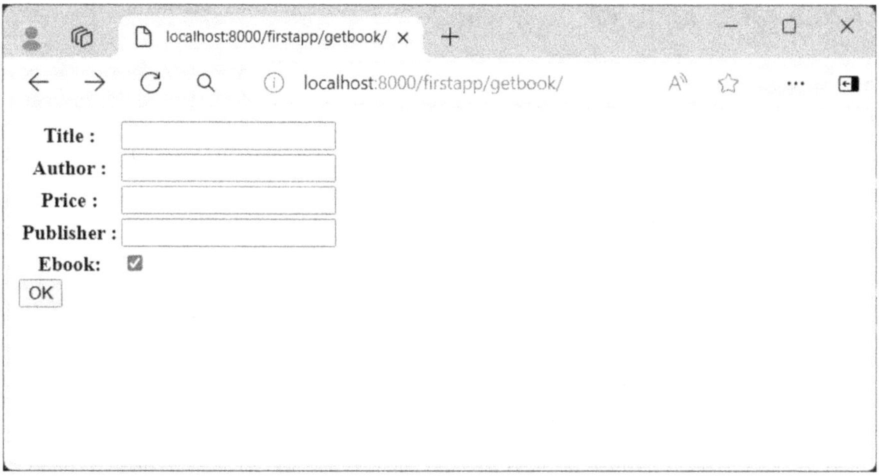

Figure 4-5. *The Form class*

When a user fills the data and submits the form, the browser is directed to the **"addbook/"** route. Let us first wire this URL route to the addbook() view. Update the app's urlpatterns list by adding a new path:

```
path("addbook/", views.addbook, name="addbook"),
```

What does the addbook() function (refer to Listing 4-18) do?

First, it checks if the request method is POST. If yes, the form instance is populated with the form data (available in the request.POST dict object).

To validate the form, call its is_valid() method. Django applies all the built-in validations with the fields and returns True if it passes the validation.

If the form is found to be valid, extract the validated values of each field. The cleaned_data attribute of the form returns a dictionary of the clean values.

Instantiate an object of the Book model, and call its save() method.

Add the function shown in Listing 4-18 in the *views.py* module.

Listing 4-18. addbook view with POST request

```
def addbook(request):
    if request.method == 'POST':
        form = BookForm(request.POST)
        if form.is_valid():
            data = form.cleaned_data
            ttl = data["title"]
            auth = data["author"]
            pr = data["price"]
            pu = data["publisher"]
            b1 = Book(title=ttl, author=auth, price=pr,
            publisher=pu)
            b1.save()
            return HttpResponse("<h2>Book added successful-
            ly</h2>")
```

ModelForm

The *django.forms* module also includes a handy ModelForm class that provides a simpler and even more convenient approach to rendering a form based on the given model's field structure. Instead of manually defining the field attributes that match with the model's structure, you just have to set the model attribute. Django automatically generates the form fields that match with the type of model attributes. With the fields attribute, you can also specify which fields do you want to accept the user inputs for. Setting

```
fields = "__all__"
```

populates the form with all the fields. You can also specify only those fields you require in the form

```
fields = ["f1", "f2",..]
```

or exclude one or more fields from the list:

```
exclude = ["f1", "f2",..]
```

Listing 4-19 shows our BookForm class based on the ModelForm class.

Listing 4-19. ModelForm class

```
from django import forms
from .models import Book
class BookForm(forms.ModelForm):
    class Meta:
        model = Book
        fields = "__all__"
```

We don't need to change our *bookform.html* template, or the getbook() view. The addbook() view becomes even simpler, as in Listing 4-20. After performing the validation, the form data is automatically mapped to a model object; just call the save() method of the form to save the object itself.

Listing 4-20. addbook view to save the ModelForm

```
def addbook(request):
    if request.method == 'POST':
        form = BookForm(request.POST)
        if form.is_valid():
            form.save()
            return HttpResponse("<h2>Book added
            successfully</h2>")
```

Finally, we need a form to let the user change values of one or more fields of an object. While it should be similar to the bookform generated by the ModelForm class, we don't want the input elements to be empty. Instead, they should be populated by the existing values of the object to be updated.

This can be done by specifying the instance attribute in the constructor of the ModelForm class. Let us say we wish to update the details of a book written by a certain author, and we would pass the name of the author as a path parameter to the getbook() function. So the getbook() function should have the signature as

```
getbook(request, author)
```

Now the URL that will invoke this view will have to be like **"getbook/ xyz"**. Hence, this requires a change in the URL mapping. Modify the urls. py module and add a string path parameter to the URL pattern.

```
path("getbook/<author>", views.getbook, name="getbook"),
```

The getbook() view accepts the author parameter from the URL. Inside the function, we need to locate the object with the given author. This object is then set as the instance property for the ModelForm constructor:

```
b1 = Book.objects.get(author=author)
form = BookForm(instance=b1)
```

Accordingly, change the code for the getbook() view function in the *views.py* module as in Listing 4-21.

Listing 4-21. getbook view showing pre-populated ModelForm

```
from .forms import BookForm

def getbook(request, author):
    b1 = Book.objects.get(author=author)
    form = BookForm(instance=b1)
    context={'form' : form}
    return render(request, "bookform.html", context)
```

Rest of the things being the same, start the Django server, and visit the **"getbook/Rubio"** URL route to see that the form (as in Figure 4-6) is populated with the corresponding object.

Figure 4-6. *ModelForm populated with object*

You can now change any of the fields and submit the form. The addbook() function, as explained before, will update the current object.

Class-Based View

Using Python functions in Django's View layer is an established practice right from its early versions. In 2008, Django introduced the feature of class-based views. A view class, inherited from the django.views.View class, offers better control and flexibility compared to the traditional function-based views. A class-based view provides the advantages like better organization and code reusability.

One of the difficulties with the approach of using Python functions as views is that you either have to write different functions for handling each type of HTTP request (GET, POST, etc.) or use conditional branching code inside a single view function.

The View subclass, on the other hand, allows you to define separate methods for each type of request inside it. You don't have to provide a separate route for handling each type of request. All you need to do is to define a get() method to handle a GET request and a post() method in the same class that responds to the POST request.

The view function in Listing 4-22 does conditional processing of a GET or POST request.

Listing 4-22. Function-based view with conditional request handling

```
def myfunction(request):
    if request.method=="GET":
        #view logic to handle GET request
        return HttpResponse("response to GET request")

    if request.method=="POST":
        #view logic to handle POST request
        return HttpResponse("response to POST request")
```

In the new class-based view approach (Listing 4-23), the view class has separate methods for each request.

Listing 4-23. View class example

```
from django.views import View
class MyView(View):
    def get(self, request):
        #view logic to handle GET request
        return HttpResponse("response to GET request")

    def post(self, request):
        #view logic to handle POST request
        return HttpResponse("response to POST request")
```

However, Django's URL resolver sends the request and path parameters to a callable function, not a class. To get around this, the View class has an as_view() class method that returns a method corresponding to the request type. Hence, we need to map the URL with the class.as_view() parameter in the path() function to build the urlpatterns list.

```
path("myview/",MyView.as_view(), name="myview")
```

Let us elaborate on this usage further. The MyView class defines a get() method that renders a template that contains a simple HTML form with an input element as name and posts it back and a post() method that retrieves the name entered by the user.

Listing 4-24 shows the *mytemplate.html* web page.

Listing 4-24. mytemplate.html

```
<html>
    <body>
        <form action="" method="POST">
            {% csrf_token %}
            <p><label for="nm">Name: </label>
            <input id="nm" type="text" name="name"></p>
            <input type="submit" value="OK">
        </form>
    </body>
</html>
```

and, the View class (refer Listing 4-25):

Listing 4-25. MyView class

```
class MyView(View):
    def get(self, request):
        return render(request, "mytemplate.html", {})
```

```
def post(self, request):
    name=request.POST['name']
    return HttpResponse(name)
```

The **name/** URL route is defined in the urlpatterns list with

```
path("name/",MyView.as_view(), name="name")
```

You can easily implement the form handling mechanism with the view class by adopting a similar approach that we used in the preceding section.

Generic Views

The introduction of class-based views is seen as a robust alternative to the function-based views. To make the web development, especially the task of writing the view logic, even simpler, various special-purpose generic view classes have been designed. These views are targeted toward a specific type of view logic. For example, the TemplateView class is specially designed to make the template rendering virtually a one-statement code. All the generic views have to be used as the base class, and you need to subclass the appropriate generic view. There are generic display classes, generic classes that help in performing CRUD operations, etc.

Let us learn about some of the frequently used generic views.

TemplateView

Of all the generic views, the TemplateView is the simplest. It renders the given template, optionally populating it with the context data collected locally or from the URL parameters. The TemplateView class is defined in the django.views.generic.base module. You need to subclass it and set its template_name attribute.

```
from django.views.generic.base import TemplateView
class IndexView(TemplateView):
    template_name = "index.html"
```

Make sure that the above view class is properly mapped to a URL in the app's URLCONF.

```
path("", IndexView.as_view(), name="index"),
```

The *index.html* is a simple Hello World script, without any variables. If, however, it does have to render a variable, the template uses the context returned by the get_context_data() method in the class (refer to Listing 4-26). Let us override this method in the above class and pass a template variable "name" to *index.html*.

Listing 4-26. TemplateView class

```
class IndexView(TemplateView):
    template_name = "index.html"

    def get_context_data(self, **kwargs):
        context = {"name" : 'John'}
        return context
```

Edit the *index.html* script (Listing 4-27) to include the template variable in the Hello message.

Listing 4-27. index.html for TemplateView

```
<html>
    <body>
        <h2> Hello {{ name }}</h2>
    </body>
</html>
```

We might want to pass the name as a path parameter in the URL. That is done by changing the URL mapping in the *urls.py* module, as done below:

```
path("<name>", IndexView.as_view(), name="index"),
```

Instead of assigning some hard-coded value to the context variable, let us read it from the keyword arguments (Listing 4-28).

Listing 4-28. TemplateView with kwargs

```
from django.views.generic.base import TemplateView
class IndexView(TemplateView):
    template_name = "index.html"

    def get_context_data(self, **kwargs):
        context = {"name" : self.kwargs['name']}
        return context
```

One should use the TemplateView especially to render templates with a certain static content or having very little context. For more complex requirements, such as rendering a form that collects the data for creating a new object, or updating it, Django provides other special-purpose generic views such as CreateView, UpdateView, etc.

CreateView

As the name suggests, this generic view provides an easier alternative to create a new object, as compared to the function-based view that we used earlier in this chapter. We created a ModelForm, rendered it as an HTML form with a POST method with a template, and saved the form data as an object after validation. This entire process is performed in a very concise manner by the subclass of CreateView.

The two mandatory attributes to be defined are the name of the model (we'll use the Book model) and the list of fields to be rendered on the form. By default, Django builds a model form with the name of the model, followed by _**form** as a suffix. In our case, it will be **book_form**. You can change the suffix if you want, or set the template_name property to a specific form template, instead of the default. Listing 4-29 includes the CreateView subclass that renders the ModelForm template.

Listing 4-29. CreateView

```
from django.views.generic import CreateView
class BookCreateView(CreateView):
    model = Book
    fields = "__all__"
    template_name = 'book_create_form.html'
    success_url = '../books/'
```

The success_url attribute is the URL route to which the browser is redirected after successfully creating a new object.

Since we have defined the template_name, you need to provide the same, much like the ModelForm template (Listing 4-30), except that the form is posted to the same URL as the one that renders the form.

Listing 4-30. ModelForm template for CreateView

```
<html>
    <body>
        <form method="post">
            {% csrf_token %}
            <table>
            {{ form.as_table }}
            </table>
```

117

```
            <input type="submit" value="OK">
        </form>
    </body>
</html>
```

As one would imagine, the BookCreateView class has to be mapped to a URL route in the URLCONF of the app by updating the urlpatterns list:

```
from firstapp.views import BookCreateView
urlpatterns += [path("newbook/", BookCreateView.as_view(),
name="newbook")]
```

A visit to the **"newbook/"** URL displays the entry form. When the user submits the same with valid data entered in it, the browser is directed to the view that displays a list of all the books, including the newly added book.

UpdateView

This is one of the generic view classes that allows you to update the contents of an existing object. Django selects the object to be updated, based on its primary key, or a slug field. To pass the primary key of the object, add the following URL route in the urls.py module:

```
urlpatterns += [path("update/<int:pk>", BookUpdateView.as_
view(), name="update")]
```

As in the case of the CreateView, you need to set the model property (Book model in our case) and the list of fields to appear in the update form template. In the example below, the UpdateView subclass uses the same template that we used earlier, with the CreateView code. An HTML form, pre-populated with the values of an object corresponding to the primary key passed from the URL, will appear.

In Listing 4-31, the success_url attribute is set to **"../books/"** so that after the object is updated, the list of books appears, showing the modifications done.

Listing 4-31. UpdateView

```
from django.views.generic.edit import UpdateView
class BookUpdateView(UpdateView):
    model = Book
    fields = '__all__'
    template_name = "book_create_form.html"
    success_url = "../books/"
```

The **"update/2"** URL route shall display the details of the corresponding objects, giving an opportunity to change the values. Submitting the form runs the UPDATE query in the background and returns to the page showing the list of books.

DeleteView

The DeleteView class is another generic base view. As the name implies, its purpose is to delete a given object from the model. The selection of an object for deletion is based on its primary key or a slug, as in the case of the UpdateView. Additionally, Django lets you select the object to be deleted by overriding the get_object() method.

Sometimes, using the primary key for the purpose of deleting objects may not be convenient, especially when the primary key doesn't exactly tell you the serial number of the object in the collection. Instead, we would like to identify the object with another attribute like author (refer to Listing 4-32). Let us configure the URL route to pass the name of the author as the path parameter and map it with the DeleteView.

```
from firstapp.views import BookDeleteView
urlpatterns += [path("delete/<author>", BookDeleteView.as_
view(), name="delete")]
```

The BookDeleteView class overrides the get_object() method to select the object corresponding to the author's name passed from the URL.

Listing 4-32. DeleteView

```
from django.views.generic.edit import DeleteView
class BookDeleteView(DeleteView):
    model = Book
    template_name = "book_confirm_delete.html"
    success_url = "../books/"

    def get_object(self):
        return Book.objects.get(author=self.kwargs['author'])
```

We need to provide a template to be used by this view to perform this operation. In the *book_confirm_delete.html* template (Listing 4-33), a POST form asks for confirmation from the user, giving them the chance to cancel the operation.

Listing 4-33. book_confirm_delete.html

```
<html>
<body>
 <form method="post">
    {% csrf_token %}
    <h2> {{ object.title }} By {{ object.author }}</h2>
    <p>Are you sure you want to delete ?</p>
```

```
    <input type="submit" value="Confirm"> <a href="../
    list/"><input type="button" value="Cancel" /></a>
</form>
</body>
</html>
```

When the delete operation is successfully executed, the browser is directed to the view that lists out all the remaining books. Try entering the URL as **"delete/xyz"** (where xyz is the author's name) and check the behavior.

The form opens up with Confirm and Cancel buttons (Figure 4-7). Hitting cancel takes the browser to the list page. Confirm page also displays the list, but with the object deleted.

Figure 4-7. *Template for DeleteView*

Django also has a couple of generic views for two of the most common requirements: a view that displays the attributes of a single attribute (DetailView) and a view that renders the list of selected objects (ListView).

DetailView

Most web applications need a feature that displays one or more than one attribute of a single object from the model, for example, the book() view that we had used earlier. It displays the details of a book of a given id, read from the path parameter in the URL. The DetailView class performs the same task, in a much more elegant manner.

Once again, one essential attribute of the subclass of the DetailView generic view class is the name of the model (the Book model). This class also has a template_name_suffix property that defaults to _detail, which means that it assumes that the name of the template that displays the object details is *model_detail.html*. You may set any other string as the suffix, or even specify any other template_name (as in Listing 4-34). We are going to use the same template (book.html) as in the earlier example.

Listing 4-34. DetailView class

```
from django.views.generic.detail import DetailView
class BookDetailView(DetailView):
    model = Book
    template_name = "book.html"
```

The DetailView subclass identifies the object to be processed, depending on the path parameter that is a primary key, or a slug field. We shall pass the primary key (pk) as the path parameter in the URL route to map the BookDetailView.

```
from firstapp.views import BookDetailView
urlpatterns += [path("show/<int:pk>", BookDetailView.as_view(),
name="show")]
```

Go to the browser (with the Django server running) and visit the **"show/2"** URL route. The details of the book with primary key=2 will be displayed.

ListView

This view performs the role of the books() function – a function-based view explained earlier. It collects the queryset comprising of all the objects in a model. By default, a subclass of ListView class (Listing 4-35) looks for a template set as the value of the template_name property (*list_books. html*). The get_context_data() method builds the context required for the template.

Listing 4-35. ListView class

```
from django.views.generic.list import ListView
class BookListView(ListView):
    model = Book
    template_name = "list_books.html"

    def get_context_data(self, **kwargs):
        books = Book.objects.all()
        context = {'books': books}
        return context
```

As always, wire up the as_view() method of the above view class to the **"list/"** URL route by updating the app's URLCONF module.

```
urlpatterns += [path("list/", BookListView.as_view(),
name="list")]
```

The template code (Listing 4-36) renders the object collection in an HTML table, with each row having buttons displaying the detailed view, the update view, and the delete view of the respective object when clicked.

Listing 4-36. list_books.html

```
<h2 style = "text-align: center;">List of Books</h2>
    <br>
    <div style="overflow-x: auto;">
        <p><a href="../newbook"><input type="button"
        value="Add New" /></a></p>
```

```
<table>
  <tr>
        <th>Title</th>
        <th>Author</th>
        <th>Price</th>
        <th>Details</th>
        <th>Update</th>
        <th>Delete</th>

  </tr>
    {% for book in books %}
    <tr>
            <td> {{ book.title }}</td>
            <td> {{ book.author }}</td>
            <td> {{ book.price}}</td>
            <td> <a href="../show/{{ book.id }}">
            <input type="button" value="Detail" />
            </a></a></td>
            <td> <a href="../update/{{ book.id }}">
            <input type="button" value="Update" />
            </a></td>
            <td><a href="../delete/{{ book.author }}">
            <input type="button" value="Delete" />
            </a></td>
    </tr>
    {% endfor %}
  </table>
</div>
```

The URL http://localhost:8000/firstapp/list displays the list of books as shown in Figure 4-8.

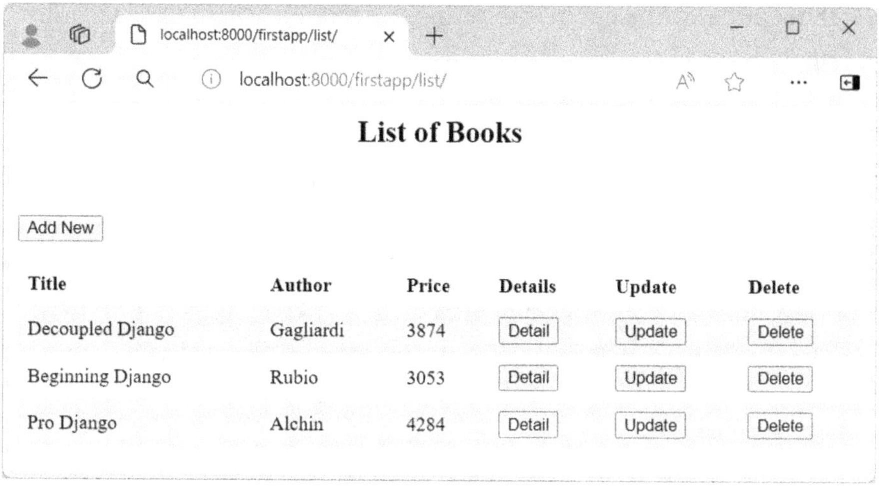

Figure 4-8. *Table template for ListView*

You can experiment with the functionality of the Add New, Update, and Delete buttons. The HTML code shown above uses some CSS styling, which you can find out in the source code in the book's repository.

Static Files

A web application framework such as Django mainly handles dynamic content. However, many times the dynamic websites do need to serve additional files such as images, JavaScript, or CSS. In Django, these files are referred to as static files. The default project template installs the `static-files` app (`django.contrib.staticfiles`), which manages the static files in a Django project.

To use the static assets in a project, we should ensure that the following configurations are in place.

If not already present in the settings.py module, set the STATIC_URL parameter.

```
STATIC_URL = 'static/'
```

This tells Django to look for the static files in the **app/static** folder (a folder named as static in the app's package folder). However, your project might also have certain static assets located outside the app folder. In that case, you can define a list of directories (STATICFILES_DIRS) to be searched by Django to locate the static files.

```
STATICFILES_DIRS = [
 BASE_DIR / "static",
 ]
```

When you are using the local Django server for running the application (with the **runserver** command), it is in the DEBUG mode by default. Django serves the static assets either from the app/static folder or the folders in the STATICFILES_DIRS list.

When you decide to launch a Django-powered web application, the development environment is not recommended. You need to host it on a web server such as Apache, Nginx, etc., in the settings and define STATIC_ ROOT as the absolute path of a folder where all collected static files will be placed. The normal practice is to designate the static folder under the BASE_DIR (the parent project folder) for the purpose.

```
STATIC_ROOT = os.path.join(BASE_DIR, 'static')
```

At the time of deployment, make sure that this folder collects all the static files in the app/static folder as well as from the folders in STATICFILES_DIRS. This is ensured by running the management command – collectstatic:

```
python manage.py collectstatic
```

For now, though, we are sticking with the development environment (with DEBUG=True in the settings module). Hence, all the static files in the examples under this topic are assumed to be placed in the **firstapp/ static** folder.

To begin with, load the static template tag from the staticfiles app.

```
{% load static %}
```

The {% static %} template tag takes the relative path to your static file as an argument. In a normal HTML, we use the <img src> tag to display an image:

```
<img src = "django.png ">
```

On the other hand, to include the image stored in the static directory of your app, you'd use

```
<img src="{% static 'django.png' %}">
```

Going a step ahead, to render the image whose name has been passed to a template in a context, you'd use

```
<img src="{% static '' %} {{filename}}">
```

How do we include a CSS file? A **.css** file is also treated as a static asset, hence placed in the static folder. In a normal HTML code, the syntax of including a CSS file is

```
<link rel="stylesheet" type="text/css" href="styles.css" />
```

But here, we want to include it as a static file. Provide its relative path to the {% static %} tag in the **href** attribute.

```
<link rel="stylesheet" type="text/css" href="{% static 'style.
css' %}">
```

Here is a simple example. We want to display the text in a **<h2>** tag, such that it is placed horizontally in the center of the page. The required styling is put in *style.css* (Listing 4-37), and the file is placed in the static folder.

Listing 4-37. style.css

```
h2 {
    text-align: center;
    }
```

We shall refer to this stylesheet in the template code as in Listing 4-38.

Listing 4-38. Including css file

```
<body>
        {% load static %}
        <link rel="stylesheet" href="{% static 'style.css' %}">
        <h2>Hello World!</h2>
    </body>
```

When rendered, the test will follow the text alignment as horizontally centered.

Files with JavaScript code are also static files for Django. Using the same principle, we can include a .js file in a template. The JS scripts are usually loaded in the **<head>** section of the HTML script:

```
<head>
        {% load static %}
        <script src="{% static 'script.js' %}"></script>
    </head>
```

Let us now implement the concepts of how to handle the static assets with a few use cases.

Image As Static Asset

We have already seen how the DetailView works. The BookDetailView example explained earlier presents the attributes of a book with the given primary key. Let us modify the structure of the Book model (refer to Listing 4-39) by adding a CharField (coverimg) that stores a string containing the name of the image file that represents the cover page of the book.

Listing 4-39. Book model modified

```
class Book(models.Model):
    id = models.AutoField(primary_key=True)
    title = models.CharField(max_length=50)
    author = models.CharField(max_length=50)
    price = models.IntegerField()
    publisher = models.CharField(max_length=50)
    ebook = models.BooleanField(default=True)
    coverimg = models.CharField(max_length=50)

    class Meta:
        db_table = "books"
```

Since we have modified the model structure, we must run the migrations. Use the UpdateView to add the image names in the coverimg field of each object.

We don't need to make any changes to the code of the BookDetailView class. We shall, however, modify its template – *books.html.*

We are interested in displaying the cover image alongside the detailed view. The main **<div>** tag in the **<body>** section of the page has two adjacent **<div>** tags. On the left, we use the **<img>** tag to insert the static image with the {{ book.coverimg }} variable, and inside the right **<div>**, we output the other book attributes. Listing 4-40 gives the updated template code.

Listing 4-40. books.html – display static image

```
<html>
<body>
    <div>
        <div style="float:left;width:45%;">
            {% load static %}

            <img src="{% static '' %}{{book.coverimg}}">
        </div>
        <div style="float:right;width:45%;" >
                    <p><b>ID:</b> {{ book.id }}</p>
                    <p><b>Author:</b> {{ book.author }}</p>
                    <p><b>Price:</b> {{ book.price}}</p>
                    <p><b>Publisher:</b> {{ book.publisher }}
                    </p>
                    {% if book.ebook %}
                    <p><b>Available as Ebook?: </b> Yes</p>
                    {% else %}
                    <p><b>Available as Ebook?: </b> No</p>
                    {% endif %}
                    <hr>
        </div>
    </div>
</body>
</html>
```

The detailed view of the book with ID=2 will appear as shown in Figure 4-9.

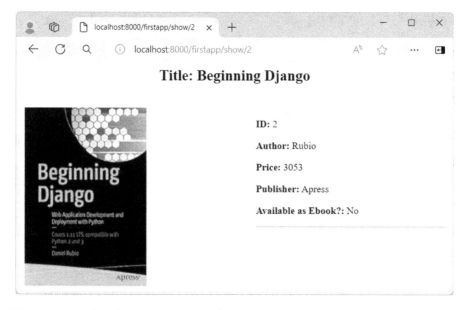

Figure 4-9. *Static image example*

CSS and JavaScript

The objective of the example in this section is to display a list of clickable **<div>** tags, each populated by the {{ book.title }} variable. Below each of these **<div>** tags, a hidden **<div>** tag is inserted that displays an unordered list of the other attributes of the book. To make the title holder **<div>** element clickable, a JavaScript function – myfunction() – is registered with its onclick() event.

The myfunction() function receives the id of the <div> clicked, finds its next sibling (which happens to be the one containing the attributes such as author, price, etc.), and toggles its display style between block and none (block will hide the element, and none will display it).

Save the following function in script.js (refer Listing 4-41) and put the file in the **static/** folder.

Listing 4-41. JavaScript function to hide/display the <div> tag

```
function myfunction(id) {
    var x=document.getElementById(id+id);
    if (x.style.display === "none")
    x.style.display = "block";
  else
  x.style.display = "none";
  }
```

We shall also use certain CSS rules for the **<div>** tag that holds the title. These CSS rules are stored in the style.css file, which is inside the **static/** folder.

Listing 4-42 shows how both the static assets are loaded in the **<head>** section of the template.

Listing 4-42. Loading static assets

```
<head>
        <meta name="viewport" content="width=device-width,
        initial-scale=1">
        {% load static %}
        <script src="{% static 'script.js' %}"></script>
        <link rel="stylesheet" href="{% static 'style.css' %}">
    </head>
```

Listing 4-43 shows the template code responsible for rendering the clickable titles.

Listing 4-43. aboutbooks.html

```
    {% for book in books %}
    <div id = "item-{{ book.id }}" class="collapsible"
    onclick="myfunction(this.id)">
        {{ book.title }}
```

```
    </div>
     

        <div style="display:none; font-size: 20px;">
         <ul>
            <li><b>ID:</b> {{ book.id }}</li>
            <li><b>Author:</b> {{ book.author }}</li>
            <li><b>Price:</b> {{ book.price}}</li>
            <li><b>Publisher:</b> {{ book.publisher }}</li>
                {% if book.ebook %}
            <li><b>Available as Ebook?: </b> Yes</li>
                {% else %}
            <li><b>Available as Ebook?: </b> No</li>
                {% endif %}
         </ul>
        </div>

    {% endfor %}
```

Lastly, we need a view that renders this template. Add an aboutbooks() view (Listing 4-44).

Listing 4-44. aboutbooks view

```
def aboutbooks(request):
    books = Book.objects.all()
    context = {'books': books}
    return render(request, 'aboutbooks.html', context)
```

Register the **"aboutbooks/"** URL route mapped to it in the urlpatterns, as we have done throughout this chapter.

Visit the **"aboutbooks/"** URL route, and it displays the list of titles (Figure 4-10). Click on any of them to show/hide the corresponding details.

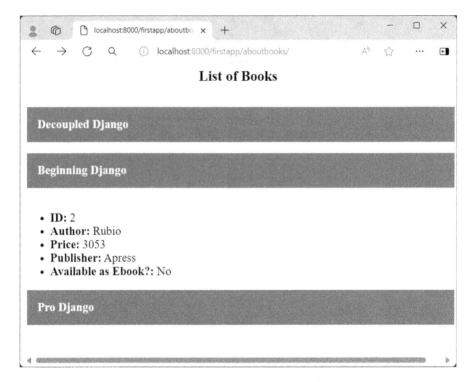

Figure 4-10. *Using JavaScript in Django template*

Django's collection of generic views includes a few others such as FormView, ReDirectView, as well as a few generic date views. Discussion of these views has been kept outside the scope of this book. Interested readers can go through the official documentation of Django.

Template Inheritance

As a Python developer, you must be familiar with the term "inheritance" wherein a class extends the functionality of an existing class. Django Template Language borrows a lot of terminology from Python – such as variables, conditionals, and loops. Similarly, in Django, a template can also be inherited, you'll soon learn how.

Any web application is likely to have many web pages, some static ones and others dynamically rendered templates. Obviously, you would like each page to have a uniform appearance, i.e., similar color scheme, fonts, same header and footer on each page, etc.

As a simple example, consider a Django application with three views: home, about, and login – each rendering a template index.html, about. html, and login.html. It is desired to have a navbar on each page with links to others and a footer with a copyright message.

One way is to put the navbar code and the footer on each page, which is obviously not ideal. A better approach would be to have the navbar code in top.html and footer in bottom.html and use the {% include %} tag in each of the templates.

{% include %} Tag

The include tag simply loads the contents of one template into another. The include keyword inside the tag is followed by a string representing the template to be included:

```
{% include "template.html" %}
```

Normally, the templates in a Django application are placed in the BASE_DIR/templates folder. The template to be included should also be in this folder; however, its path can be mentioned relatively or in absolute terms.

Assuming that the index() view function is supposed to render the index.html template as shown in Listing 4-45.

Listing 4-45. index view

```
from django.shortcuts import render
def index(request):
    return render(request, 'index.html')
```

This page simply displays the text "This is Home page". However, we want a navbar and a footer to be displayed. For this, first create top.html and bottom.html and then include them in index.html, as in Listing 4-46.

Listing 4-46. Top and bottom templates

```
#top.html
<nav>
    <ul>
        <li><a href="{% url 'home' %}">Home</a></li>
        <li><a href="{% url 'about' %}">About</a></li>
        <li><a href="{% url 'login' %}">Login</a></li>
    </ul>
</nav>
#bottom.html
<footer>
    <p style="text-align: center;">&copy; 2025 All rights
    reserved.</p>
</footer>
```

Note that these two HTML files do not have the <html> and <body> tags as they will be appearing in the HTML code for index.html (in which these will be included).

While writing the HTML script of index.html, use the include tag to load top.html and bottom.html before and after its actual contents.

The navbar is stylized by an appropriate CSS code, made available in the style.css file placed in the static folder. The CSS code is not reproduced here; you may find the same in the book's repository.

Listing 4-47 shows the HTML script for index.html.

Listing 4-47. Including templates

```
{% load static %}
<!DOCTYPE html>
<html lang="en">
    <head>
        <link rel="stylesheet" type="text/css" href="{% static
        'style.css' %}">
    </head>
    <body>
        {% include 'top.html' %}
        <h1 style="text-align: center;">This is Home page</h1>
        {% include 'bottom.html' %}
    </body>
</html>
```

Make sure that the routes for the views are properly configured in the app's urls.py file (Listing 4-48).

Listing 4-48. urls.py

```
from django.urls import path
from . import views

urlpatterns = [
    path("", views.index, name="home"),
    path("about/", views.about, name="about"),
    path("login/", views.login, name="login"),
]
```

If all the above actions are implemented correctly, the index template should display a neat navbar and a footer as shown in Figure 4-11.

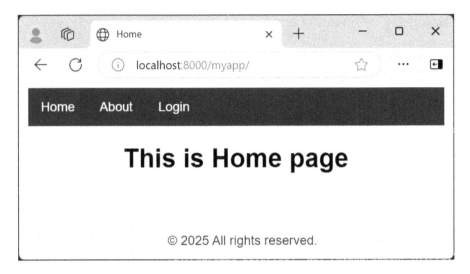

Figure 4-11. *Including another template*

You can go ahead and construct the other templates (about.html and login.html) on similar lines. However, you need to include the header and footer templates manually in each of them (and there may be many more templates in a more comprehensive application). This in fact is against DRY – one of the guiding principles of Django. This is where the other approach of using template inheritance comes in.

If you recall the principle of inheritance in Python (or any object-oriented language for that matter), the parent class defines one or more methods, which the child class may (or may not) override. As a result, when an object of the child class calls a method from its parent, it performs the process as per its overridden functionality (or the functionality defined in the parent class if it is not overridden). Inheritance in Django templates works much the same way.

The two important template tags in this context are {% extends %} and {% block %}.

{% block %} Tag

To implement template inheritance, you need to design the parent template that acts as a blueprint for the other templates. It will have certain static or fixed content that will be rendered as it is in the child templates. The navbar and the footer are such static parts. For the variable sections, you need to define the blocks. The block – endblock construct defines a block.

```
{% block block_name %}
. . .
{% endblock %}
```

For example, you define a base.html template to be used for inheritance, and you define a title block such as

```
{% block title %}
Title
{% endblock %}
```

When another template inherits this base.html with the help of the extends tag (explained next), it may or may not redefine the title block. The block tag in the parent template indicates to the template engine that a child template may override those portions of the template.

For our three-page application, we define the parent template as base. html as in the code in Listing 4-49.

Listing 4-49. Parent template (base.html)

```
<!DOCTYPE html>
<html lang="en">
    <head>
        <title>
            {% block title %}
```

```
            Title
            {% endblock %}
        </title>
    </head>
    <body>
        {% include 'top.html' %}
        <div class="content">
            {% block content %}
            {% endblock %}
        </div>
        {% include 'bottom.html' %}
    </body>
</html>
```

Note that there are two blocks in the code – one for the title and another for the content. The content block is empty. Hence, each child template must provide its content for such a dummy block.

{% extends %} Tag

The extends tag is used to establish inheritance between the child and the parent template. In the index.html template, the statement

```
{% extends 'base.html' %}
```

tells the template engine that it extends (inherits) the base template. When it is evaluated, the template engine will notice the block tags in base. html and replace those blocks with the contents of the child template.

Hence, the index.html code will now look like that shown in Listing 4-50.

Listing 4-50. Child template (index.html)

```
{% extends 'base.html' %}

{% block title %}
Home
{% endblock %}

{% block content %}
<h1 style="text-align: center;">This is Home page</h1>
{% endblock %}
```

Similarly, you can construct the about and login templates. Instead of just a text, we shall populate the content block in the login.html template with an HTML form (Listing 4-51).

Listing 4-51. Child template (login.html)

```
{% extends 'base.html' %}

{% block title %}Login{% endblock %}

{% block content %}
<div id="id01">
<form class="modal-content animate" action="" method="POST">
    {% csrf_token %}
    <div class="container">
    <label for="username"><b>Username</b></label>
    <input type="text" placeholder="Enter Username"
    name="username">
    <label for="password"><b>Password</b></label>
    <input type="password" placeholder="Enter Password"
    name="password">
```

```
    <input type="submit" value="Login">
    </div>
    </form>
</div>
{% endblock %}
```

The /login route thus renders a nicely stylized login form, shown in Figure 4-12. The CSS code for this purpose is available in the code repository.

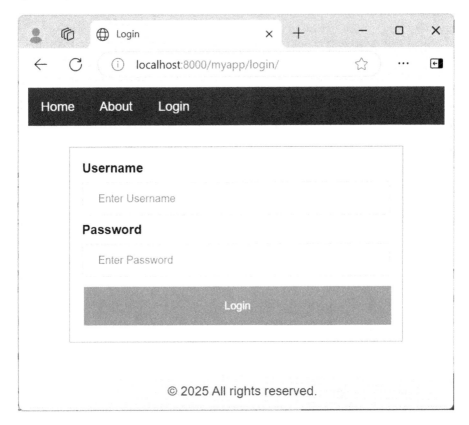

Figure 4-12. *Using template inheritance*

Thus, this powerful feature of template inheritance lets you maintain a consistent layout across your pages and makes it easier to update the common layout in one place.

Summary

Templates are the crucial component of Django's architecture. This chapter started with rendering a static template, and then we moved on to learn how to inject a context in the template. We learned about different template tags. Next, this chapter discussed the form templates – the HTML form and the ModelForm.

A substantial part of this topic discusses the generic views and how to build the templates for each generic view. We also learned about the static assets and how to load images, CSS, and JavaScript in the template code. Lastly, an important feature of Django – the template inheritance – has also been explained with a suitable example.

This chapter, along with the previous three chapters, forms the core of web development with Django. In the next chapter, we shall move one step ahead and learn to add important features in a Django app, such as state management, messaging, exception handling, etc.

CHAPTER 5

Django: Using Databases

As we learned earlier in this book, Django's ORM API is one of its standout features with which the database interaction becomes much more Pythonic, rather than having to execute raw SQL queries. However, it is too tightly coupled with the other features of the Django framework – such as the migrations, the admin interface, and more. There are other ORM libraries for Python, notably SQLAlchemy, SQLObject, etc., which are far more flexible. SQLAlchemy offers support for a wider range of databases and works well with other frameworks like Flask. Hence, if someone wants to port a Flask application to Django, is it possible to use SQLAlchemy with Django, and if yes, how? We shall find an answer to this in this chapter.

The Django ORM provides the abstraction layer for the relational (SQL-based) databases only. However, in today's world of real-life web applications, we need to handle a schema-less database such as MongoDB. In this chapter, we shall also explore how to use MongoDB in a Django application.

The topics to be discussed in this chapter include

- SQLAlchemy ORM

- Migrations with Alembic

- MongoDB

© Malhar Lathkar 2025
M. Lathkar, *Modern Django Web Development*,
https://doi.org/10.1007/979-8-8688-1472-3_5

- PyMongo

- MongoEngine

- Djongo

SQLAlchemy ORM

SQLAlchemy is a comprehensive SQL toolkit that has two components: SQLAlchemy Core and SQLAlchemy ORM. The Core part executes raw SQL queries with its own SQL Expression Language (SQEL). The Expression Language lets you interact with a relational database through the Python code. In a sense, it adds a bit of abstraction to the standard SQL queries. The ORM part is built upon the Core part. In principle, SQLAlchemy ORM is similar to the Django ORM we learned earlier in the book, as it too presents a high-level abstraction. However, there's a significant difference in their approach, as we shall shortly come to know.

SQLAlchemy communicates with almost any type of database (MySQL, Oracle, MS SQL Server, PostgreSQL, SQLite included) with a dialect system based on the corresponding DB-API-compliant module. As a result, if you intend to use a MySQL database, a Python module like pymysql must be available. The engine object that powers both the Expression Language constructs and the ORM uses the database-specific dialect and the connection pool. Figure 5-1 represents various constituents of SQLAlchemy.

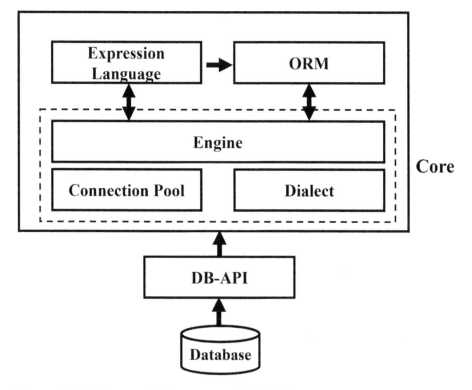

Figure 5-1. *Schematic diagram of SQLAlchemy*

SQLAlchemy adopts the data mapper pattern for implementing the abstraction. Django ORM, on the other hand, follows the active record pattern.

As we have seen, Django wraps the database table into a model class, and its single instance is tied to a single row. An in-memory object is added to the table as a row. Conversely, a single row is loaded as an object. When any of the attributes are updated, it also updates the row.

In the data mapper pattern used by SQLAlchemy, the data is transferred between a database table and its in-memory representation. Here, both the states are kept independent of each other. In other words, the object data is persisted only when it is explicitly committed.

Let us start by installing SQLAlchemy in the current Django virtual environment with the PIP utility.

```
(djenv) C:\workspace>pip3 install sqlalchemy
```

This will install the current version of the SQLAlchemy package, which is 2.0.29, as can be confirmed with the __version__ attribute.

```
>>> import sqlalchemy
>>> sqlalchemy.__version__
'2.0.29'
```

The latest version of SQLAlchemy is compliant with the features of modern Python like type annotations and asyncio.

Engine

As you must have understood from the above figure, you have to obtain the engine object as the first step to be able to use the ORM API. The Engine provides the connection to the database to be used and holds onto the connections inside of a connection pool for fast reuse. The create_engine() function that returns the engine object is called with the following syntax:

```
from sqlalchemy import create_engine
engine = create_engine(URL, **kwargs)
```

The first positional parameter is URL, which is a string indicating the database dialect and other connection credentials required, such as the username and the password.

SQLite is a file-based database, and Python's standard library has built-in support for it in the form of sqlite3 module. Hence, the URL parameter that returns the engine object for an in-memory SQLite database is

```
engine=create_engine('sqlite:///:memory:')
```

You can use an additional argument – echo=True – to the above constructor, which shows the equivalent SQL queries emitted by SQLAlchemy on the console.

You would prefer a persistent, file-based database, in which case the URL should be given as

```
engine =create_engine('sqlite:///db.sqlite3', echo=True)
```

For the other database variants, the URL parameter must include its dialect (database + module) in addition to the connection credentials. For example, if you intend to use a MySQL database and you have installed the pymysql module, the URL takes the following format:

```
engine = create_engine('mysql+pymysql://root@localhost/
mydatabase')
```

The above statement refers to the database named mydatabase on the MySQL server installed on the localhost and has root as the username with no password set.

Additional keyword arguments may be given; they may be specific to the engine, the dialect, as well as the connection pool.

Just to give another example, the URL for PostgreSQL database using the psycopg2 module looks like

```
engine = create_engine("postgresql+psycopg2://user:password@
localhost/dbname")
```

Table in SQLAlchemy Core

While using SQLAlchemy Core, you need to declare a Table object to be mapped with a corresponding database table, define its Column attributes, and add its metadata in a collection.

You need to declare a `MetaData` object first:

```
from sqlalchemy import MetaData
metadata = MetaData()
```

We can now declare a Table object as per the prescribed syntax:

```
from sqlalchemy import Table, Column, Integer, String
mytable = Table(
    dbtable, metadata,
    Column(col1, type, constraints),
    Column(col2, type, constraints),

    . . .,
)
```

The first parameter is the name of the table in the database. Each field is an object of `Column` class, for which its name, type, and other optional constraints such as primary key, secondary key, etc., are specified.

Let us create a SQLAlchemy table here that reflects the structure of the `Books` tabls used in the earlier chapter.

```
from sqlalchemy import MetaData
metadata = MetaData()

from sqlalchemy import Table, Column, Integer, String
book = Table(
    "Books", metadata,
    Column("id", Integer, primary_key=True),
    Column("title", String, nullable=False),
    Column("author", String, nullable=False),
    Column("price", Integer),
    Column("publisher", String)
)
```

There may be multiple Table objects in your application; the details of each of them are saved in the metadata object. Whenever its create_ all() method is called, SQLAlchemy emits the CREATE TABLE query for each Table.

```
metadata.create_all(engine)
```

Here is the console log:

```
INFO sqlalchemy.engine.Engine BEGIN (implicit)
INFO sqlalchemy.engine.Engine PRAGMA main.table_info("Books")
INFO sqlalchemy.engine.Engine [raw sql] ()
INFO sqlalchemy.engine.Engine PRAGMA temp.table_info("Books")
INFO sqlalchemy.engine.Engine [raw sql] ()
INFO sqlalchemy.engine.Engine
CREATE TABLE "Books" (
        id INTEGER NOT NULL,
        title VARCHAR NOT NULL,
        author VARCHAR NOT NULL,
        price INTEGER,
        publisher VARCHAR,
        PRIMARY KEY (id)
)
INFO sqlalchemy.engine.Engine [no key 0.00224s] ()
INFO sqlalchemy.engine.Engine COMMIT
```

Model

Conceptually, the model in SQLAlchemy serves the same purpose as the model in Django ORM. It is a Python class whose attributes are mapped with the fields of a table in the relational database.

151

The SQLAlchemy ORM API provides a façade around this complex procedure in the form of a `metaclass` named the `DeclarativeBase` class. A subclass of `DeclarativeBase` acts as a metadata container for all the models.

```
from sqlalchemy.orm import DeclarativeBase
class Base(DeclarativeBase):
    pass
```

A model is a class that inherits the Base class and establishes its mapping with a database table through its __tablename__ property.

```
from sqlalchemy.orm import mapped_column

class model(Base):
    __tablename__ = dbtable
    Col1 = mapped_column(type, constraints)
    Col2 = mapped_column(type, constraints)
    . . .
```

We use the `mapped_column`, an ORM-aware construct, to indicate an attribute that's mapped to a Core Column object.

Let us declare a SQLAlchemy ORM model that reflects the structure of the books table, used in the earlier examples. Add the following code in the `models.py` module in the app folder:

```
from sqlalchemy import Column, Integer, String

class Base(DeclarativeBase):
    pass

class Book(Base):
    __tablename__ = 'Books'

    id = mapped_column(Integer, primary_key=True, index=True)
    title = mapped_column(String(256))
```

```
author = mapped_column(String(256))
price = mapped_column(Integer)
publisher = mapped_column(String(256))
```

Since the Book class is inherited from the `DeclarativeBase`, which really is a metadata container, calling the `create_all()` method executes the CREATE TABLE BOOKS query (as we saw in the case of a Table object):

```
Base.metadata.create_all(engine)
```

As the echo parameter is set to True in the call to the `create_engine()` function, the console log shows the CREATE TABLE query being emitted, exactly the same as in the earlier case.

Session

How does SQLAlchemy synchronize the model with the SQL table? This is where the Session plays an important role. At a lower level of interaction, we open a connection with the database and execute SQL queries that perform CRUD operations (as we discussed in Chapter 3, section "DB-API"). As mentioned earlier, Django ORM uses the active record pattern, and hence, the effect of `create()`, `update()`, and `delete()` methods from the Manager class gets reflected in the database instantly. SQLAlchemy ORM uses the data mapper pattern, which needs an explicit instruction to add/update/delete a row corresponding to the object. The Session object performs exactly this role.

In the general sense of its meaning, the term "session" refers to the extent for which any interaction takes place. In the context of a database, the session starts when a connection is established and goes on till the connection is closed. In between, the user performs database-related actions – commonly known as CRUD operations.

In SQLAlchemy, you start the session either by creating an instance of Session class or with the help of the `SessionManager` factory. Any which way, the Session object requests for a connection resource from the Engine referring to the database in use.

Here's how we use the `SessionManager` factory:

```
from sqlalchemy import create_engine
engine = create_engine('sqlite:///db.sqlite3', echo=True)

from sqlalchemy.orm import sessionmaker
session = sessionmaker(bind=engine)
```

You may prefer to declare an object of Session class:

```
from sqlalchemy.orm import Session
session = Session()
```

This object is really a "holding zone" for all the ORM objects. Once you initialize an object of a model (subclass of `DeclarativeBase`), it has to be added to the session for it to be subsequently committed persistently to the database. On the other hand, you populate an ORM object with a row from the database table for it to be eventually updated or deleted.

We have declared a Book model earlier. Let us initialize a Book object, add it to the SQLAlchemy session, and commit the session.

```
b1=Book(id=1, title="Decoupled Django", author="Gagliardi",
price=3874, publisher="Apress")
session.add(b1)
session.commit()
session.close()
```

Python's preferred approach is to use the context manager that closes the session object at the end of the `with:` block. Also, the background interaction with the database is given the protection of Python's exception handling mechanism by placing the code inside the try: block. Here's a Django view function that adds a new Book object:

```python
def addbook(request):
    with Session(engine) as session:
        b1=Book(id=1, title="Decoupled Django",
        author="Gagliardi", price=3874, publisher="Apress")
        session.add(b1)
        session.commit()
        return HttpResponse("New Book added")
```

A more user-friendly approach would obviously be to get the object data from the user as an HTML form input and parse it to the model object, and then to be added to the session.

```python
def addbook(request):
    if request.method=="POST":
        with Session(engine) as session:
            data = request.POST
            ttl = data["title"]
            auth = data["author"]
            price = data["price"]
            pub = data["publisher"]
            b1 = Book(title=ttl, author=auth, price=price,
            publisher=pub)

            session.add(b1)
            session.commit()
            return HttpResponse("Record added")
    context={}
    return render(request, "bookform.html", context)
```

However, we cannot use Django's Form API (including the `ModelForm`) to render an HTML form that is automatically mapped to the model structure, as Django's Form is tied with the Django ORM only. Instead, you may look to use other server-side Form libraries (such as `WTForms`) as a replacement for Django Form. The discussion on `WTForms` is not a part of this book's scope. Interested readers may refer to the official documentation (`https://wtforms.readthedocs.io/`) and other resources on the Internet.

Alembic

As we learned earlier (in Chapter 3, section "Run Migrations"), the propagation of the initial definition of a model to the corresponding table in the database, as well as any subsequent changes in its structure, is handled by Django's migration-related commands. The migration mechanism also serves as an excellent tool for version control. Even though it is very easy to use, Django's migration is integrated tightly with Django's ORM. As such, it cannot be used if you intend to use any other ORM library (such as SQLAlchemy) apart from Django's own ORM.

Fortunately, SQLAlchemy has its own migration API called Alembic. Alembic is much more flexible as compared to Django migrations. Since SQLAlchemy supports a larger number of relational databases as compared to Django, the use of Alembic is essential if you intend to employ the SQLAlchemy ORM in your Django project.

In this section, we shall learn how to manage migrations of SQLAlchemy models with Alembic.

Let us start by installing Alembic in the same Django environment, in which we have earlier installed SQLAlchemy:

```
(djenv) C:\workspace>pip3 install alembic
```

From inside your Django project folder, run the following command to initialize Alembic:

```
alembic init alembic
```

This command places the file `alembic.ini` in the project directory (where the `manage.py` script, the app folder, and the SQLite database are present). Alembic uses different parameters initialized in this file to manage the migrations. Among others, the `sqlalchemy_url` parameter points to the database to be migrated. Since we are using the SQLite database, we need to edit the `alembic.ini` file and assign the database URL to this parameter:

```
sqlalchemy.url = sqlite:///./db.sqlite3
```

For other databases (such as MySQL or PostgreSQL), the parameter may be set in the following form:

```
sqlalchemy.url = driver://user:pass@localhost/dbname
```

The init command also creates a folder alembic in the same path, with the files `env.py` and `script.py.mako`, along with a README file in it.

script.py.mako is a Mako template file that is used to generate new migration scripts. Every new migration script is placed inside the versions folder.

To create a new database migration with the alembic revision command, it is recommended to use an optional -m flag to add a descriptive message:

```
alembic revision -m "create Book Table"
```

A new migration script will be created in the alembic/versions directory. Alembic assigns the file name to the migration script as a combination of a unique GUID-based revision number and the comment text. For example, the migration script could be named **4a525b80c4c9_create_book_table. py**. Figure 5-2 shows how typically the alembic folder populates.

```
alembic.ini
db.sqlite3
manage.py

alembic
    env.py
    README
    script.py.mako

    versions
        4a525b80c4c9_create_book_table.py
        7bd04b7040cf_add_year_field.py
```

Figure 5-2. *Schematic diagram of SQLAlchemy*

To propagate the model definitions from the migration script to the database, use the upgrade command (this serves the same purpose as the migrate command in Django ORM):

```
alembic upgrade head
```

Here, head refers to the latest migration script. The downgrade command reverts the database schema to its earlier version if one or more models or columns are dropped.

Alembic can also auto-generate migration scripts based on the current definitions of your SQLAlchemy models. To auto-generate, use the autogeneration feature; you need to edit the **env.py** script in the alembic folder and add the following statements to it:

```
from myapp.models import Book
target_metadata = [Book.metadata]
```

Use the following command:

```
alembic revision --autogenerate -m "Create Book Table"
alembic upgrade head
```

On the command prompt terminal, the following log is displayed:

```
INFO  [alembic.runtime.migration] Context impl SQLiteImpl.
INFO  [alembic.runtime.migration] Will assume non-
transactional DDL.
INFO  [alembic.runtime.migration] Running upgrade  ->
4a525b80c4c9, Create Book Table
```

You can now open the database and confirm if the Book table has been created. Alembic identifies the first migration script as base.

Let us modify the Book model by adding a new attribute and generate a new migration script. The Book model now looks like the following:

```python
from sqlalchemy import Column, Integer, String

class Base(DeclarativeBase):
    pass

class Book(Base):
    __tablename__ = 'Books'

    id = mapped_column(Integer, primary_key=True, index=True)
    title = Column(String)
    author = mapped_column(String(256))
    price = mapped_column(Integer)
    publisher = mapped_column(String(256))
    year_of_pub = mapped_column(Integer)
```

First, find out if the change necessitates a new migration script by running the alembic check command:

```
alembic check
New upgrade operations detected:[('add_column', None, 'Books',
Column('year_of_pub', Integer(), table=<Books>))]
```

Create a new migration script with the auto-generated command (add a suitable message):

```
alembic revision --autogenerate -m "add year field"
```

The new script with a unique revision number will be stored in the **versions** directory (e.g., 7bd04b7040cf_add_year_field.py), which will now be treated as head while running the upgrade command:

```
alembic upgrade head
```

We can also view the history of the migrations generated:

```
alembic history
4a525b80c4c9 -> 7bd04b7040cf (head), add year field
<base> -> 4a525b80c4c9, Create Book Table
```

To fall back to the status of the database to any of the earlier revisions, you can use the downgrade command. Our database has been updated to the latest migration script referred to as head. It can be reverted to a specific revision number. You can also perform relative upgrades or downgrades. To revert to the state of Book table before the year_of_pub column is added, use the following command:

```
alembic downgrade -1
INFO  [alembic.runtime.migration] Context impl SQLiteImpl.
INFO  [alembic.runtime.migration] Will assume non-
transactional DDL.
INFO  [alembic.runtime.migration] Running downgrade
7bd04b7040cf -> 4a525b80c4c9, add year field
```

Advantage of SQLAlchemy notwithstanding, there are a lot of limitations of using it with Django. As mentioned in the very beginning of this book, Django is an opinionated framework, not flexible enough to let the user choose the tools other than those bundled with the Django package. The models used in the apps bundled with Django (such as the admin app, the auth app, etc.) can be propagated only with the databases officially supported by Django (MySQL, Oracle, PostgreSQL, and SQLite). Hence, even if you choose to use other databases with the SQLAlchemy support, the built-in apps won't work with them.

There is an experimental **django-sorcery** package that does support the admin interface, but it is not compatible with the latest version of Django as well as SQLAlchemy.

Advent of NOSQL Databases

Relational databases (the likes of Oracle, SQL Server, MySQL, SQLite, etc.) are around for over seven decades and are still widely employed in all applications – big or small. However, they seem to fall short when it comes to handling flexible data models of modern real-time applications. The NOSQL databases came on the horizon in the early 2000s and since then are being increasingly used.

One of the main limitations of relational databases is that their design is based on tables having fixed schemas. NOSQL databases, on the other hand, are schema-less. This makes them more scalable as compared to SQL-based databases. The distributed architecture of NOSQL databases makes them more available and hence suitable for applications that need to handle huge amounts of data.

MongoDB is the most widely used NOSQL database. It is a document store database. There are other NOSQL databases as well – such as Amazon DynamoDB (a key-value store database), Cassandra (a wide-column store database), and others. In this chapter, we shall discuss how the MongoDB database is used as a database backend for Django-powered applications.

MongoDB

MongoDB is an open source, cross-platform, schema-less (NOSQL), document store (also called document-oriented) database. MongoDB has been developed by MongoDB Inc. (previously 10gen), an American software company in 2009. Its current stable version is 7.0.11.

A MongoDB database consists of one or more Collections. Each Collection is a document store. It is a collection of one or more Documents. Each Document is a JSON-like representation of field and value pairs. To be precise, MongoDB uses a Binary JSON (BSON) representation – a variant of JSON. Although a Collection contains Documents, each Document can have a variable number of field-value pairs. That's what schema-less means.

Compare this with a typical relational database that has one or more tables each with a fixed schema or structure. Each row in the table is a record with one or more columns as defined in the schema.

Thus, a Collection in MongoDB is analogous to the table in the relational database, and each BSON document to the record. The following figure offers a good comparison between the relational database and MongoDB.

Installation

You can use MongoDB mainly in two ways. One is to install the software locally on your machine, and the other is to use MongoDB Atlas.

Local Deployment

For local installation, MongoDB is available in two editions: Community edition and Enterprise edition. Both have the same developer features, but the Enterprise version provides additional operational and security features as well as advanced tools such as Ops Manager, BI Connector, and Enterprise Operator for Kubernetes.

To install MongoDB locally, download the installer software that is appropriate for your operating system from `https://www.mongodb.com/try/download/community` and follow the installation instructions.

While on a Windows machine, install MongoDB in the **D:\MongoDB** directory. Make sure that you also create a **\data\db** directory. Start the MongoDB server by running the `mongod` command:

```
D:\Mongodb\bin>mongod
```

If MongoDB has been properly installed, you should get the following message in the console log:

```
{"t":{"$date":"2024-06-16T00:23:36.251+05:30"},"s":"I",   "c":"
CONTROL",   "id":4615611, "ctx":"initandlisten","msg":"MongoDB
starting","attr":{"pid":18852,"port":27017,"dbPath":"D:/data/
db/","architecture":"64-bit","host":"GNVBGL3"}}
```

This indicates that the MongoDB server is listening at port 27017 of the localhost.

Atlas

Another way to use MongoDB is using its cloud-based service called MongoDB Atlas. You can easily deploy, operate, and scale MongoDB with Atlas.

Sign up and sign in to MongoDB to begin with by following the link `https://account.mongodb.com/account/login`, and create a free cluster with the provider of your choice.

Add your current IP address in the IP Access List (Figure 5-3).

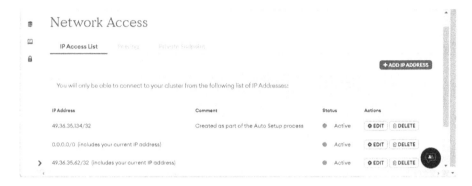

Figure 5-3. *Network access whitelist*

MongoDB Shell

You can interact with the server with the MongoDB Shell (similar to MySQL Shell, or SQL Plus for Oracle). You need to download and install Mongo Shell from `https://www.mongodb.com/try/download/shell`. Open another command terminal in its installation directory, and run the following command:

```
C:\Users\mlath\mongosh>mongosh
Current Mongosh Log ID: 666de3e6149d0383b990defd
Connecting to:          mongodb://127.0.0.1:27017/?directConnec
tion=true&serverSelectionTimeoutMS=2000&appName=mongosh+2.2.9
Using MongoDB:          7.0.4
Using Mongosh:          2.2.9

. . . .
test>
```

You can now perform the CRUD operations on a local database from within the MongoDB Shell.

To connect with the cluster with the MongoDB Shell, obtain the connection string as shown in Figure 5-4.

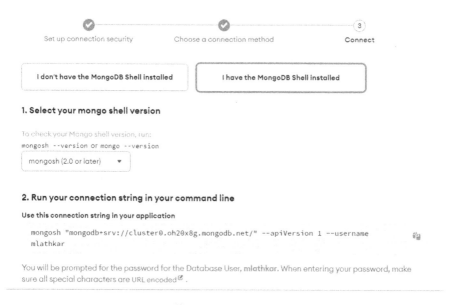

Figure 5-4. *Atlas connection string*

Paste the connection string into the command terminal. Enter the password when prompted.

```
C:\Users\mlath\mongosh>mongosh "mongodb+srv://cluster0.oh20x8g.
mongodb.net/" --apiVersion 1 --username mlathkar
Enter password: ********
Current Mongosh Log ID: 666dea805e7cda09d090defd
Connecting to:          mongodb+srv://<credentials>@cluster0.
oh20x8g.mongodb.net/?appName=mongosh+2.2.9
Using MongoDB:          7.0.11 (API Version 1)
Using Mongosh:          2.2.9

. . .
Atlas atlas-13zoim-shard-0 [primary] test>
```

You can execute MongoDB commands for CRUD operations; they are similar to SQL queries.

For instance, to create a new database:

```
test> use mydb;
switched to db mydb
```

A Collection is implicitly created when you insert a document. The insertOne() function adds a document in the collection.

```
mydb> db.books.insertOne({id:1, title: "Decoupled Django",
author: "Gagliardi", price: 3874, publisher: "Apress"});
{
  acknowledged: true,
  insertedId: ObjectId('666ea2c7e1329c760790defe')
}
mydb>
```

Compass

MongoDB Compass is a free, GUI tool with which you can conveniently interact with MongoDB databases, instead of using the command-line MongoDB Shell.

The MongoDB server installer usually offers to install Compass while setting up the server, although it can be installed separately also.

Invoke the Compass app (ensure that either the local MongoDB server is running or you are connected with the Atlas cluster). Use the URL mongodb://localhost:27017 (as in the Figure 5-5) to connect with the locally deployed MongoDB server.

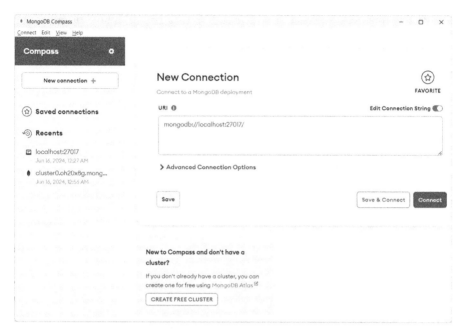

Figure 5-5. *Connect MongoDB Compass to the local MongoDB server*

Refer Figure 5-6 to open the required database and insert documents using the interface.

Figure 5-6. *Add a document*

You can also work with the Atlas cluster. Fetch the connection string (Figure 5-7) for Compass from the online interface.

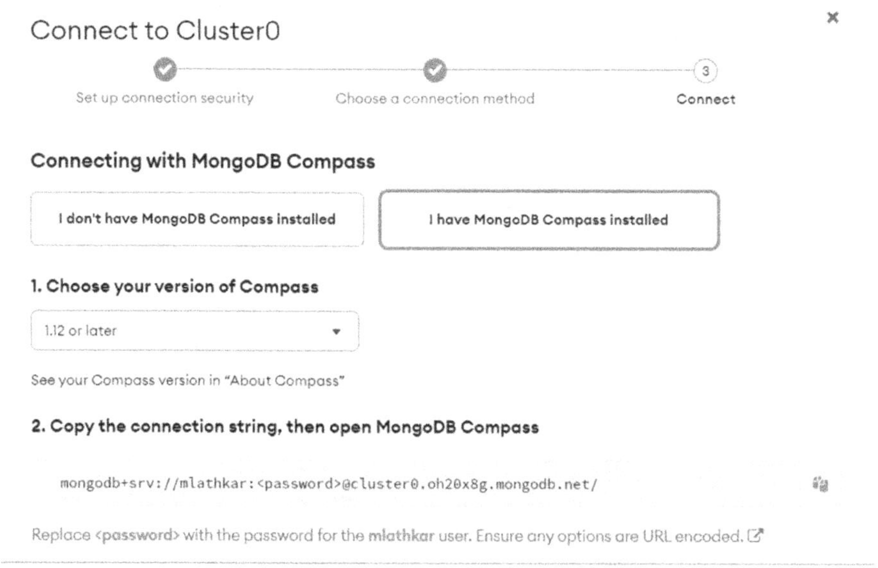

Connect to Cluster0

Set up connection security — Choose a connection method — Connect

Connecting with MongoDB Compass

| I don't have MongoDB Compass installed | I have MongoDB Compass installed |

1. Choose your version of Compass

1.12 or later ▾

See your Compass version in "About Compass"

2. Copy the connection string, then open MongoDB Compass

```
mongodb+srv://mlathkar:<password>@cluster0.oh20x8g.mongodb.net/
```

Replace <password> with the password for the **mlathkar** user. Ensure any options are URL encoded. ⧉

Figure 5-7. *Connection string of the Atlas cluster*

As shown in Figure 5-8, use the connection string for connection in the Compass app (replace the asterisks with your password).

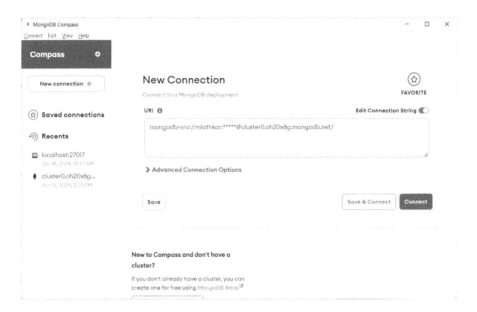

Figure 5-8. *Connect MongoDB Compass to Atlas*

However, we would rather work with the MongoDB database from within a Django app, instead of the MongoDB Shell or the Compass app.

You can use one of the following three approaches to use MongoDB as a database backend with Django:

> **PyMongo**: PyMongo is a Python package, developed by MongoDB as the official driver for interacting with Python in general and hence with Django.

> **MongoEngine**: MongoEngine is a Python library that acts as an Object-Document Mapper with MongoDB. It is similar to the Django ORM.

> **Djongo**: Djongo acts as a transpiler (layer of translation) between Django's ORM API and MongoDB's own queries.

PyMongo

Start by installing the PyMongo package from Python's standard package library. Certain additional libraries are also recommended to be installed alongside.

```
pip install pymongo[snappy,gssapi,srv,tls]
```

As mentioned, PyMongo itself is MongoDB's official Python driver. The Generic Security Service Application Program Interface (GSSAPI) is an application programming interface for programs to access security services. This also installs python-snappy, which is a Python binding for the snappy compression library from Google. python-libtls library provides a high-level interface for secure network communication.

It is also recommended to install dnspython, a DNS toolkit for Python, needed especially when working with MongoDB Atlas, where you need to use mongodb+srv:// URIs.

```
pip install dnspython
```

Set up a typical Django project with the startproject command, create a Django app (myapp) with the startapp command, and include it in the INSTALLED_APPS list, as we have done before. You should also register the URLs of myapp in the project's URLCONF as done earlier.

An object of MongoClient class in PyMongo provides the handle to your MongoDB instance. To set up the connection, you need the hostname, port number, and other optional parameters if needed.

```
from pymongo import MongoClient
client = MongoClient(host='localhost', port=27017)
```

To create a new MongoDB database on the server, use the newdb property:

```
db=client.newdb
```

We can now refer to this database with the db object. Create a Books collection in this database with the following statement:

```
col=db['books']
```

Put all this code in the models.py module in the app's package folder.

```
from pymongo import MongoClient
client = MongoClient()
db=client.newdb
col=db['books']
```

Insert Document

Let us write a simple view that uses the collection object and adds a book document with its insert_one() method. The document is a dict object, which PyMongo converts in a BSON document.

```
from django.shortcuts import render

# Create your views here.
from django.http import HttpResponse
from .models import col
def addbook(request):
    b1 = {"id":1, "title": "Decoupled Django",
    "author":"Gagliardi", "price":3874, "publisher":"Apress"}
    col.insert_one(b1)
    return HttpResponse("Document added")
```

To be more generic, and more user-friendly, render a template that presents a form for the user to fill. The form data is then used to insert a new document. Modify the addbook() function accordingly.

```
def addbook(request):
    if request.method=="POST":
        data = request.POST
        id = data["id"]
        ttl = data["title"]
        auth = data["author"]
        price = data["price"]
        pub = data["publisher"]
        book = {"id":id, "title": ttl, "author":auth,
        "price":price, "publisher":pub}
        col.insert_one(book)
        return HttpResponse("Document Added")
    else:
         return render(request, "book.html", {})
```

Retrieval

You can call the find_one() or find() method of the Collection object to retrieve one or all the documents satisfying the filter criteria:

> **col.find(filter)**: Retrieves all the documents from the database

> **col.find_one(filter)**: Retrieves a single document from the database

Here, filter is a dictionary specifying the query to be performed. PyMongo provides a number of filter operators to be used in these methods:

> **$eq**: Whether a field is equal to a specified value. Equivalent to ==

> **$gt**: Checks if a field's value is greater than a specified value. Equivalent to >

$gte: Corresponds to >= operator

$lt: Matches documents where a field's value is less than a specified value. Corresponds to < operator

$lte: Equivalent of the <= operator

$ne: PyMongo's equivalent of the != operator

$and: Combines multiple filter expressions using logical AND

$or: Combines multiple filter expressions using logical OR

$in: Emulates Python's IN operator

$exists: Checks if a field exists in a document (true) or not (false)

Let us implement some of these operators in the view functions. The books() view retrieves all the books with the price greater than a specified number in the books collection.

```
def books(request, price):
    books = col.find({"price": {"$gt": price}})
    lst=[]
    for book in books:
        lst+="<h2>Title: {} \t Author: {} \t Price: {}</h2>".
        format(book['title'], book['author'], book['price'])
    return HttpResponse(lst)
```

The find() method returns a list of dict objects, each corresponding to one document. Try using the URL http://localhost:8000/myapp/books/3500. You can use a suitable template in earlier chapters to render the list of books in an HTML table instead.

Similarly, the getbook() view function retrieves the document whose ID is passed as the path parameter.

```
def getbook(request, id):
    book = col.find_one({"id":id})
    return HttpResponse("<h2>Title: {} \t Author: {} \t
    Price: {}</h2>".format(book['title'], book['author'],
    book['price']))
```

PyMongo also supports update operation on the document, with the update_one() and update_many() methods. These methods need filter criteria and the dictionary of updated values of the required fields. For example, the statement

```
col.update_one({'id': 1}, {'$set': {'price': 3000}})
```

updates the price of the book whose ID is 1.

Similarly, the delete_one() method removes a document that satisfies the given filter criteria. This statement deletes a book authored by Alchin from the books collection.

```
col.delete_one({'$author': 'Alchin'})
```

You can add the appropriate view functions to perform the update and delete operations. Have a look at the code in this book's code repository if needed.

You need to ensure that the views are properly matched with the URL routes in the urlpatterns. For reference, the code for urls.py is listed here:

```
from django.urls import path, include

from . import views
```

```
urlpatterns = [
            path('',views.index,name='index'),
            path('addbook/', views.addbook,
            name='addbook'),
            path("getbook/<id>/", views.getbook,
            name="getbook"),
            path("books/<int:price>", views.books,
            name="books"),
            ]
```

This is, of course, a very brief account of the functionality of PyMongo. You can refer to its official documentation to enhance your Django application further.

MongoEngine

The Django ORM API that you learned earlier presents a layer of abstraction, mapping Python classes with the corresponding tables (relations) in Django-supported relational databases instead of writing raw SQL queries. SQLAlchemy does the same with all types of relational database – including those not officially supported by Django. MongoEngine is the equivalent of Python ORMs for MongoDB databases. Since a MongoDB database is a collection of documents (and not relations), it is appropriately known as an ODM (Object-Document Mapper).

MongoEngine is an open source Python package built on top of PyMongo driver. Obviously it is one of the dependencies for MongoEngine installation.

While in the current Django environment folder, install MongoEngine with

```
pip install mongoengine
```

The current version of MongoEngine is "0.28.2", compatible with the latest versions of Python.

Document Class

As mentioned earlier, a document in MongoDB is roughly equivalent to a row in a relational database. Though a row (stored in a table) follows a predefined schema very strictly, MongoDB doesn't enforce a schema on the documents in a collection.

Having said that, MongoEngine does allow you to define a schema for the documents. If needed, the document schema can be dynamically modified. You'll soon see how to do it.

The document schema is defined as a class that inherits the Document class in MongoEngine. You can think of the Document as an equivalent of Model in Django ORM, or DeclarativeBase in SQLAlchemy. MongoEngine provides different Field types (IntField, StringField, etc.) similar to the Field types in Django ORM and SQLAlchemy. Field objects are the attributes of the Document class.

Here is a declaration of Book class that is a subclass of Document:

```
from mongoengine import *

class Book(Document):
    title = StringField(max_length=50)
    author = StringField(max_length=50)
    price = IntField()
    publisher = StringField(max_length=50)
```

If you remember, MongoDB automatically allocates a unique _id, a field of the ObjectId type to each document that acts as a primary key. If you want, you can manage the primary key by yourself by specifying primary_key=True as a parameter to the required field.

```
class Book(Document):
    bookId = IntField(primary_key=True)
    title = StringField(max_length=50)
    author = StringField(max_length=50)
    price = IntField()
    publisher = StringField(max_length=50)
```

When the first document is saved, MongoDB creates the collection, whose name is the same as that of the Document class. However, you can change it. Add a meta attribute on your document, and set collection to the name of the collection that you want your document class to use.

```
class Book(Document):
    bookId = IntField(primary_key=True)
    title = StringField(max_length=50)
    author = StringField(max_length=50)
    price = IntField()
    publisher = StringField(max_length=50)
    meta = {'collection': 'Books'}
```

Connection

To interact with MongoDB, you need to establish a connection with it. To connect your application with a local MongoDB server running on the localhost, use the connect() function passing the name of the database as an argument.

```
from mongoengine import connect
connect('mydb')
```

MongoEngine assumes that the mongod instance is listening to port 27017 and running on localhost. To provide the arguments explicitly, use the following variation:

```
connect('mydb', host='127.0.0.1', port=27017)
```

A more general form of the connect() function is

```
connection = connect(db, username, password, host)
```

You can connect to the Atlas cluster also. Obtain the required connection string from the running cluster as done earlier.

```
connection = connect(db='mydb',
                     username='*****',
                     password='*****',       host='mongodb+srv://
                     username:password@cluster0.oh20x8g.mongodb.
                     net/?retryWrites=true&w=majority')
```

Once the connection is established, you can simply construct a Document object and call its save() method.

```
doc = Book(title="Decoupled Django", author=" Gagliardi ",
price=3874, publisher="Apress")
doc.save()
```

This results in the Books collection with a Book document in it, created inside the **mydb** database on the currently running MongoDB server (or the Atlas cluster if your connection points to it). You can verify it with the MongoDB Compass app.

Using MongoEngine in a Django application is fairly straightforward. Put the Document class (Book) in the models.py module.

```
from mongoengine import *

con = connect('mydb')

class Book(Document):
    title = StringField(max_length=50)
    author = StringField(max_length=50)
    price = IntField()
    publisher = StringField(max_length=50)
    meta = {'collection': 'Books'}
```

Define a view function that retrieves the data from an HTML form and uses it to populate the Book object. Call the save() method to cause the document to be persistently saved in the database.

```python
from django.shortcuts import render
def addbook(request):
    if request.method=="POST":
        data = request.POST
        title = data["title"]
        author = data["author"]
        price = data["price"]
        publisher = data["publisher"]
        doc = Book(title = title, author = author, price =
        price, publisher = publisher)

        doc.save()
        return HttpResponse("Document Successfully Added")
    else:
        return render(request, "book.html", {})
```

To fetch all the documents in the collection, use the objects property. It returns a QuerySet.

```python
documents = Book.objects
```

To refine the documents QuerySet, you can apply filtering criteria. Instead of the traditional comparison operators, MongoEngine defines its own query operators that are similar to what we used with PyMongo, with a slight change in the syntax. PyMongo operators have a $ prefix (e.g., $lte for less than or equal to). In MongoEngine, on the other hand, double underscores prefix the operator (e.g., __lte). To obtain the books with price greater than 3500, the statement would be

```python
documents = Book.objects(price__gt=3500)
```

To retrieve a single document that meets the given criteria, use the get() method. The following statement would return a Book document with the specified name of the author:

```
doc = Book.objects.get(author="Rubio")
```

Using these filter operations, you can modify the books() and get-book() views that we defined while working with PyMongo.

DynamicDocument

The single most important difference between the MongoDB database and the relational database, as was emphasized earlier, is the fact that the MongoDB document is schema-less. In fact, it is one of the benefits of MongoDB. However, the Document class is not different from the Model in Django ORM. MongoEngine does provide another type of Document class that allows storing documents with a variable number of fields in a collection.

Let us create a DynamicDocument class as follows (just change the base class in the previous definition):

```
class Book(DynamicDocument):
    title = StringField(max_length=50)
    author = StringField(max_length=50)
    price = IntField()
    publisher = StringField(max_length=50)
    meta = {'collection': 'Books'}
```

Ensure that your application is connected to the MongoDB server. Insert a book document as before:

```
doc = Book(title="Decoupled Django", author=" Gagliardi ",
price=3874, publisher="Apress")
doc.save()
```

The Books collection will have been created in the database.

Now, add another document with one extra attribute like year (for year of publication):

```
doc = Book(title="Beginning Django", author="Rubio ",
price=3053, publisher="Apress", year=2017)
doc.save()
```

The two documents, with an unequal number of fields, will be found in the Books collection.

```
[{
  "_id": {
    "$oid": "6677205a93b226b0ace10e21"
  },
  "title": "Decoupled Django",
  "author": " Gagliardi ",
  "price": 3874,
  "publisher": "Apress"
},
{
  "_id": {
    "$oid": "6677213b93b226b0ace10e22"
  },
  "title": "Beginning Django",
  "author": "Rubio ",
  "price": 3053,
  "publisher": "Apress",
  "year": 2017
}]
```

MongoEngine provides the update_one() method to modify the value of a certain field.

```
Book.objects(name="Rubio").update_one(set__price=4000)
```

Similarly, to remove a document from the collection, simply call the delete() method.

```
doc=MyBook.objects.get(author="Rubio")
doc.delete()
```

Use these inputs to provide suitable views in your Django application.

There's a lot more to MongoEngine than what has been described here. A number of useful Field types, signals, and a powerful search mechanism are some of its important features. The reader is encouraged to explore these and other features by referring to the official documentation of MongoEngine.

There is, however, one major drawback of using PyMongo or MongoEngine with your Django application. Neither of them works with Django's built-in apps such as admin and auth apps in the django.contrib module, which primarily rely on a relational database. When you run the database migration, the models required for these apps are propagated to the database for which your Django project is configured. Note that we haven't used the MongoDB database in the DATABASES settings of the project.

The Djongo package overcomes this problem. With Djongo, you can use the Django ORM terminology and still use the MongoDB database as a backend.

Djongo

As mentioned earlier, though you can connect your Django app with a MongoDB database with the PyMongo or MongoEngine libraries, Django's built-in apps (e.g., admin or auth app) are equipped to work with the

Django-supported relational databases only. If you need these apps in your project, you will have to adapt a hybrid model – relational database for built-in apps and MongoDB for the specific functionality of your project.

Djongo provides you the best of both worlds. You can continue to define the data models by following Django ORM and use the MongoDB database, but also for the built-in apps – that too with very little tinkering with your project's settings.

Technically speaking, Djongo is a SQL to mongodb query transpiler. It basically translates SQL queries to MQL (MongoDB Query Language). You will continue to define your models as per the Django ORM and call the same functionality for performing CRUD operations as with any relational database. With minimal changes to your project settings, you can ask your project to use MongoDB as the backend database.

Start by installing Djongo:

```
pip install djongo
```

Add djongo along with the name of your app in the INSTALLED_ APPS list.

```
INSTALLED_APPS = [
    'django.contrib.admin',
    'django.contrib.auth',
    'django.contrib.contenttypes',
    'django.contrib.sessions',
    'django.contrib.messages',
    'django.contrib.staticfiles',
    'djongo',
    'myapp',
]
```

Replace the default DATABASES section in the project's settings with

```
DATABASES = {
    'default': {
        'ENGINE': 'djongo',
        'NAME': 'djongodb',
        'CLIENT': {
            'host': 'mongodb://localhost:27017',
        }
    }
}
```

If you wish to host a database on a MongoDB Atlas cluster, use the following type of DATABASES configuration:

```
DATABASES = {
    'default': {
        'ENGINE': 'djongo',
        "CLIENT": {
            'name': 'djongodb',
            'host' :
'mongodb+srv://username:password@cluster0.oh20x8g.mongodb.net/?
retryWrites=true&w=majority ',
            'username': '<username>',
            'password' : '<password>'
        }
    }
}
```

And that's all. When you tell your Django project that you are using the Djongo driver for database handling, the Django ORM function calls are converted into MQL queries, directed toward the MongoDB database specified in the project. Run migrations as usual. All the models defined by you as well as those needed for the INSTALLED_APPS such as admin, auth, etc., will now be created in the MongoDB database referred to by the NAME field above.

One of the significant drawbacks of Djongo is that it simply converts SQL queries emitted by Django ORM API to MongoDB's own query language, without allowing you to use MongoDB's distinguishing features such as dynamic schema. The development of Djongo is also very much behind that of Django. Hence, Djongo may not work with your existing version of Django. You may have to downgrade it to version 4.x. Also, the latest version of PyMongo is not compliant – it needs version 3.7.2.

Summary

This chapter helps you to explore how you can use databases other than those officially supported by Django. SQLAlchemy is a powerful and popular Python ORM. On the other hand, more and more real-time modern applications need schema-less databases, one of the most popular being MongoDB. In this chapter, you learned how to connect a Django application with MongoDB with PyMongo, MongoEngine, and Djongo libraries.

CHAPTER 6

Advanced Django

In our journey thus far, we covered what can be called the core features of Django – the model, view, and template. However, Django packs a lot of other important features to make the application more robust, more secure, and more comprehensive.

This chapter introduces some of the advanced features of Django. The following topics are covered:

- Messages framework

- Authentication

- Security features

- Async support

- Reusable apps

- Django Debug Toolbar

Messages Framework

One of the important design considerations of a web app is to be able to give the user a seamless and engaging experience by providing useful feedback to their interactions. You often find the notifications such as "invalid username or password" or "the Country field cannot be empty" popping up on the screen, particularly after processing the user input such as an HTML form.

© Malhar Lathkar 2025
M. Lathkar, *Modern Django Web Development*,
https://doi.org/10.1007/979-8-8688-1472-3_6

Django's Messages framework is a handy mechanism to push certain temporary messages when it is processing a client request and consume them when a subsequent request is being processed. Django supports cookie-based and session-based messaging. When pushing a message in the queue, it is tagged on the basis of its priority level (DEBUG, INFO, SUCCESS, WARNING, and ERROR).

The standard Django project template (initialized with the startproject command) uses the session-based messaging by default. However, you can choose the other alternative of cookie-based messaging by modifying certain project settings.

Before we discuss the difference between the two, we need to understand what are cookies and what is a session.

Cookies

Most web applications employ the cookies to store and retrieve a stateful information regarding the client's usage. The HTTP protocol, which is the backbone of the World Wide Web, is a stateless protocol, which means the web server doesn't hold any information about the client when it processes the request. Cookie acts as a workaround, in a bid to provide an enhanced user experience. When the server sends its response to the client's request, it adds a small piece of text as a cookie along with the response body. This text is stored on the client's machine. When the same client sends another request, this cookie is sent to the server as a part of the request body.

The set_cookie() method of the HttpResponse object lets you add a cookie in the response body, before returning the response. Listing 6-1 shows how it is used.

Listing 6-1. setcookie() method

```
def setcookie(request):
    response = HttpResponse("Cookie Set!")
    response.set_cookie('username', 'admin')
    return response
```

On the subsequent request (as in Listing 6-2), this cookie becomes a part of the HttpRequest object, which can be retrieved as:

Listing 6-2. getcookie() method

```
def getcookie(request):
    user = request.COOKIES['username']
    return HttpResponse("Welcome back {}! ".format(user));
```

With certain additional arguments of the set_cookie() method, you can control how the cookie behaves. For example, max_age states for how long the cookie should stay in the client's machine. Similarly, the secure argument if set to True restricts the cookies to be passed only when a request is made with the https scheme.

Moreover, calling the delete_cookie() method on the response object will remove the cookie from the response.

Sessions

The time duration between logging in and logging out of a web application is called a session. The server stores one or more data values during the session and releases them when the session is terminated.

Django uses the sessions as another way to store the stateful information of the client. The session data is usually stored in the site database, although you can configure Django to store the session data in cache, or files.

The default Django project structure created by the startproject command already has the session handling capability enabled, by including django.contrib.sessions in the INSTALLED_APPS. If not, make sure the app is added.

```
INSTALLED_APPS = [
    # ...
    'django.contrib.sessions',
    # ...
]
```

Also, the MIDDLEWARE list in the project's settings.py file should contain the `SessionMiddleware`.

```
MIDDLEWARE = [
    # ...
    'django.contrib.sessions.middleware.SessionMiddleware',
    # ...
]
```

The session data is available as a dict-like attribute of the `HttpRequest` object. You can do all the normal dictionary operations such as adding or removing keys from the dictionary. Most of the time though, you'll need to set a session variable or retrieve its value inside the views.

Here is how you can add a key in the session attribute:

```
request.session['username'] = 'admin'
```

On the other hand, retrieve the value of a session key by using:

```
user = request.session['username']
```

Occasionally, you may want to remove a certain key from the session dictionary:

```
del request.session['username']
```

Note that this raises `KeyError` if the given key isn't already in the session.

Activating Messaging

As mentioned earlier, the messaging support is enabled in Django's default project template settings. To confirm, check if `django.contrib.messages` is included in the INSTALLED_APPS list.

```
INSTALLED_APPS = [
    #
    'django.contrib.messages',
    #
]
```

Another requirement already fulfilled by default is the inclusion of SessionMiddleware and MessageMiddleware in the MIDDLEWARE list of the project's settings.

```
MIDDLEWARE = [
    #
    'django.contrib.sessions.middleware.SessionMiddleware',
    #
    'django.contrib.messages.middleware.MessageMiddleware',
    #
]
```

The order of these two middleware classes is important. The SessionMiddleware must appear before MessageMiddleware.

Messages are pushed inside a view that Django executes in response to a certain request, and they are retrieved by the template that is rendered by the next client request. Hence, the context_processors attribute of the TEMPLATES setting should be properly configured by making sure that the context_processors.messages is included (shown in bold letters):

```
TEMPLATES = [
    {
        'BACKEND': 'django.template.backends.django.
        DjangoTemplates',
        #
        'OPTIONS': {
            'context_processors': [
```

```
        #,
        'django.contrib.messages.context_processors.
        messages',
      ],
    },
  },
]
```

Storage Backends

The handling of messages by your Django project depends on for which storage backend it is configured. The `django.contrib.messages` package defines three storage classes as follows.

The `storage.session.SessionStorage` class stores all messages inside of the request's session. To use this backend, your project needs to have `contrib.sessions` app in the INSTALLED_APPS.

The `storage.cookie.CookieStorage` class stores messages in a cookie to make them available across requests. However, the cookie data size cannot exceed 2048 bytes.

Django uses `storage.fallback.FallbackStorage` by default. It first uses `CookieStorage` but switches to the `SessionStorage` backend if the messages could not be fit in a single cookie. It also depends on the `contrib.sessions` app.

To override Django's default storage backend, you need to define MESSAGE_STORAGE in the project's settings. To set the `CookieStorage` class as the backend:

```
MESSAGE_STORAGE = "django.contrib.messages.storage.cookie.
CookieStorage"
```

Adding Messages

Once enabled, Django's messaging API is very easy to use. The messages class of django.contrib app (which has been included in the INSTALLED_ APPS) provides the add_message() method.

```
add_message(request, level, message, extra_tags='', fail_
silently=False)
```

The first argument is the HttpRequest object, which is provided by the view from inside which a message will be added. Django classifies the messages on the basis of priority levels (DEBUG, INFO, SUCCESS, WARNING, and ERROR); one of these is the second argument. The third one is the actual message string to be added. The other arguments are optional. If you set fail_silently to True, Django suppresses the MessageFailure error to be displayed.

For example, you may call the add_message() methods from a certain view as in Listing 6-3.

Listing 6-3. add_message() method

```
from django.contrib import messages

messages.add_message(request, messages.SUCCESS, "Record updated
successfully")
```

The messages class also defines a set of convenience methods, each matching with the predefined message levels as

```
messages.debug(request, "Counter: %s" % count)
messages.info(request, "Your free trial ends today")
messages.success(request, "Address updated.")
messages.warning(request, "Your password is weak")
messages.error(request, "File will be deleted.")
```

Fetching Messages

The messages pushed in the queue while processing one request are available for consumption in the view function that Django invokes when it receives the next request. If the view renders a template, the {% messages %} tag presents the collection of available messages. Mostly, the messages are flushed out with the help of the template syntax as shown in Listing 6-4.

Listing 6-4. Fetching messages

```
{% if messages %}
<ul>
    {% for message in messages %}
        <li>{{ message }}</li>
    {% endfor %}
</ul>
{% endif %}
```

This template code renders the messages in the form of an unordered list. However, you may format it as required. You can even use conditional template tags {% if %} and {% endif %} to filter a particular type of messages to be displayed (for instance, you may want only the error messages).

Let us test Django's messaging functionality with the help of a simple example. You need to add the above template code in the HTML page that renders a basic login form (index.html as in Listing 6-5), posting the form data to itself.

Listing 6-5. index.html

```
<form class="modal-content animate" action="" method="POST">
{% csrf_token %}
<div class="container">
<label for="username"><b>Username</b></label>
```

```
<input type="text" placeholder="Enter Username"
name="username">
<label for="password"><b>Password</b></label>
<input type="password" placeholder="Enter Password"
name="password">

<input type="submit" value="Login">
</div>
</form>
```

The index() view renders this form when the user visits its mapped URL. On submitting, the function pushes an error message if either the username or password (or both) is not entered, as also when the username is one of the reserved usernames and stays on the login page. Otherwise, Django pushes a success message to be consumed by a suitable template which the success() view renders. A warning message is also added to the message queue if the password is less than nine characters. Listing 6-6 shows the index view function.

Listing 6-6. index view

```python
from django.http import HttpResponse
from django.contrib import messages

def index(request):
    if request.method == 'POST':
        name = request.POST.get("username")
        password = request.POST.get("password")
        if name =="" or password =="":
            messages.error(request, "required")
        if len(request.POST.get('password'))<9:
            messages.warning(request, "Weak Password")
        if name in ['admin', 'manager', 'superuser']:
            messages.error(request, "Username Not Available")
```

```
    else:
        messages.success(request, "Login Successful.
        Welcome "+name)
        return HttpResponse("success")

return render(request, "index.html", {})
```

Ensure that the views are properly wired to the corresponding urlpatterns. The login form (refer Figure 6-1) opens in response to the URL: http://localhost:8000/myapp/. Try entering one of the reserved usernames with a shorter password.

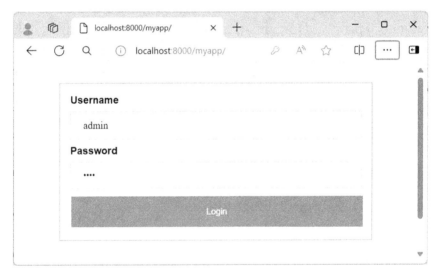

Figure 6-1. *Login screen*

Django responds with the error and warning messages, on top of the login form (Figure 6-2).

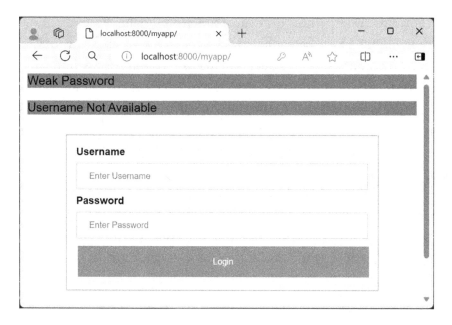

Figure 6-2. *Flashed message*

In other situations, you should see the success page rendered with a welcome message on top.

Authentication

As you learned earlier, Django's admin interface is one of its prominent tools. The Admin app is added to your Django project by default. With its convenient and user-friendly interface, you can perform managerial tasks such as creating users and assigning them roles.

The admin interface is built on top of the django.contrib.admin module, which you can import into your own Django app and incorporate the functionality in it. In most of the web applications, you find some of its resources are available for all. However, some of the features can be accessed by a registered user only. Hence, the application needs to let the visitor register and log in. You can then restrict the access to any view only to an authenticated user.

197

You already know how to create a superuser (using the command **python manage.py createsuperuser**), log into the admin site with it, and then create other users. The details of the users (name, password, groups and the roles assigned to them, etc.) are stored in the User model defined in the django.contrib.auth module. An elaborate API of this module lets you very conveniently handle the authentication of a user.

Login and Logout

There are three main steps involved in the authentication mechanism. First, call the authenticate() function by passing the username and password (possibly entered via a login form) that returns the authenticated User object.

```
from django.contrib.auth import authenticate
user = authenticate(username, password)
```

To log the authenticated user in, you need to add it to the current session by calling the login() function.

```
login(request, user)
```

To log the current user out, simply call the logout(request) function, which will pop out all the session data related to the logged-in user.

The registration of a new user is facilitated by a ModelForm named UserCreationForm in the auth app. When rendered, it shows a Username field (corresponding to the User model) and two password fields – password1 and password2. As the form is submitted, the validate_ password() function checks if both of them match and the password meets the stipulated criteria (such as it must not be less than eight characters, that it can't be entirely numeric, etc.). The mapped view then extracts the form data and saves it to the User model.

To demonstrate Django's authentication functionality, start by building a simple home page (as in Figure 6-3) that has links to let you log in and register a new user.

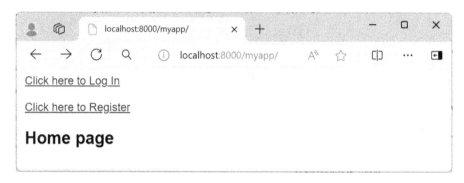

Figure 6-3. Home page

The login hyperlink invokes the login_user() view (the code in Listing 6-7) and renders a login form. When submitted, Django parses the name and password fields and calls the authenticate() function.

If the user is authenticated, the success message appears on the home page; otherwise, an error message is displayed.

Listing 6-7. login view

```
from django.shortcuts import render, redirect
from django.contrib.auth import authenticate, login, logout
from django.contrib import messages
def login_user(request):
    if request.method == "POST":
        username = request.POST['username']
        password = request.POST['password']
        user = authenticate(request, username=username,
        password=password)
```

```
    if user is not None:
        login(request, user)
        messages.success(request, "Login successful. Hello
        {}".format(user))
        return redirect('index')
    else:
        messages.error(request, ("There Was An Error
        Logging In, Try Again..."))
        return redirect('login')
else:
    return render(request, 'login.html', {})
```

It is assumed that a superuser for the admin site has already been created with admin as the username. Follow the login link from the home page, and use the admin credentials to be filled in the form. The home page after successful login appears as shown in Figure 6-4.

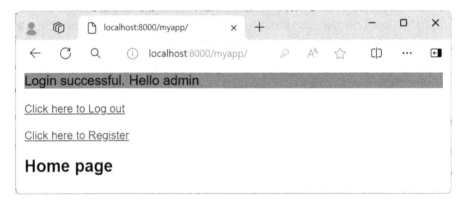

Figure 6-4. *Login message*

The Listing 6-8 shows the code for log_out() view, which when called when the logout link is accessed, simply removes the current user from the session and pushes the message, letting the user know that they have been logged out.

Listing 6-8. logout view

```
def logout_user(request):
    logout(request)
    messages.info(request, "You Were Logged Out!")
    return redirect('index')
```

The home page now appears as shown in Figure 6-5.

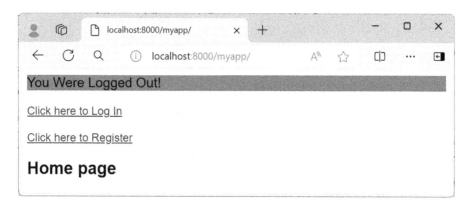

Figure 6-5. *Logout message*

You must have noted that link to the login changes to logout when a user logs in and back to login link when it logs out. This is effected by adding the template code shown in Listing 6-9 in the index.html page.

Listing 6-9. index.html

```
{% if messages %}
{% for message in messages %}
<p>{{ message }}</p>
{% if message.level == 25 %}
<a href={% url "logout" %}>Click here to Log out</a>
{% else %}
<a href={% url "login" %}>Click here to Log In</a>
```

```
        {% endif %}
        {% endfor %}
    {% else %}
    <a href={% url "login" %}>Click here to Log In</a>
{% endif %}
<br><br>
<a href={% url "register" %}>Click here to Register</a>
        <h2>Home page</h2>
```

New User

As mentioned earlier, we'll render the UserCreationForm to accept the username and password from the visitor to create a new User object, by saving the validated form. Add the register_user() view (as in Listing 6-10) in views.py code.

Listing 6-10. register view

```
def register_user(request):
    if request.method == "POST":
        form = UserCreationForm(request.POST)
        if form.is_valid():
            form.save()
            username = form.cleaned_data['username']
            password = form.cleaned_data['password1']
            user = authenticate(username=username,
            password=password)
            login(request, user)
            messages.success(request, ("Registration
            Successful!"))
            return redirect('index')
```

Note that the newly added user is authenticated and logged in as well, before returning to the home page. The /register route displays the form (Figure 6-6) for the visitor to fill.

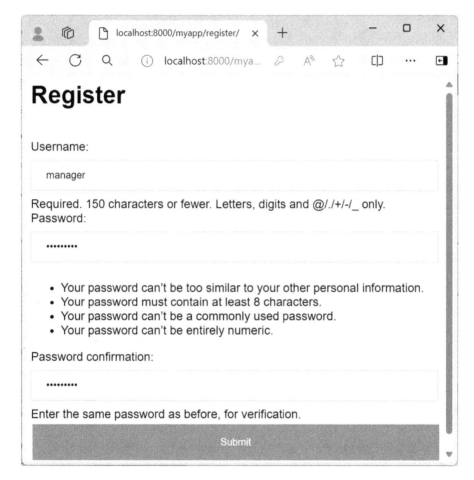

Figure 6-6. *UserCreationForm*

Log into the admin site and confirm that the newly registered user appears in the list of objects (shown in Figure 6-7) in the User model.

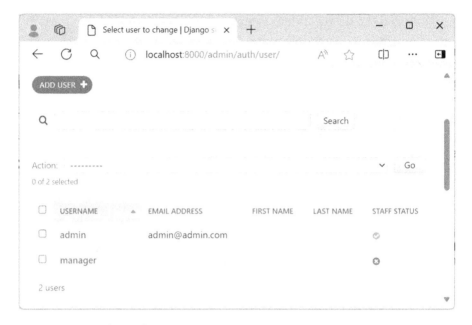

Figure 6-7. Admin home page

Note the cross mark against the new user. You can accord the manager a staff status by setting the is_staff property to True. Furthermore, you can also inherit the UserCreationForm and include the other fields first_name, last_name, and email, available to the User model in the auth app.

@login_required( )

Now that you have defined a view function that handles the user login and a route mapped to it, let us see how you can restrict access to any of the views only if an authenticated user has been logged in. Putting the login_required() decorator at the top of a view proves quite effective for this purpose. How does it work?

When a route mapped to such a protected view is visited, Django checks whether the session consists of the logged-in user's information. If yes, Django executes the view normally. If not, it redirects to the view designated as a login view while passing the current absolute path in the query string. You need to either have a LOGIN_URL variable set to the URL route corresponding to the login view or specify the login_url parameter to the login_required decorator itself.

To check how it works, add a new view (Listing 6-11) in the app's views. py code.

Listing 6-11. login_required decorator

```
from django.contrib.auth.decorators import login_required

@login_required(login_url="../login/")
def myview(request):
    return HttpResponse("This message will be displayed only if
    a user is logged in")
```

Remember, you should also add a URL pattern to wire up this view to a URL route, for example:

```
urlpatterns = [
    . . .
    path('myview/', views.myview, name="myview"),
]
```

If you visit the **myview/** URL route in the browser, two things happen. One, the browser is redirected to the login_url (which in this case is **login**/) and it appends a query string with next as the key and the current path as the value. The next field tells Django which view to execute after the user is authenticated and logged in.

So the URL http://localhost:8000/myapp/myview/ (with no user currently logged in) is entered, the browser goes to http://localhost:8000/?next=/myapp/myview/, and the login page opens up, as shown in Figure 6-8.

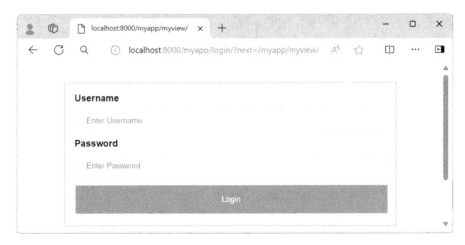

Figure 6-8. *Login page on redirect*

As you would expect, after the login credentials are verified, the myview() function gets called.

Another approach to restrict the view access only if a user has an active session is using the request.user.is_authenticated variable (refer Listing 6-12) – it will be True if a session is active.

Listing 6-12. is_authenticated

```
def myview(request):
    if request.user.is_authenticated:
        return HttpResponse("This message will be displayed
        only if a user is logged in")
    else:
        return redirect("login")
```

Security Features

While Django's authentication and authorization framework lets you control the access to the critical views in your application, it doesn't necessarily ensure that it is secured against various types of hacking attacks. Django API does have adequate provisions to counter some of the deadliest types of attacks that the hackers often indulge in. In this section, you will explore how Django tries to address certain security vulnerabilities.

CSRF

Earlier in this book (Chapter 4), you came across a template tag {% csrf_ token %} being used while building the form templates. This template tag is used inside an HTML form, especially having POST as its request method. You must have wondered what the role of this tag is. In this section, you'll get to know its purpose.

The term "CSRF" is an acronym for Cross-Site Request Forgery. One of the common types of attacks on the security of a web application, CSRF is known by various names – XSRF, one-click attack, etc.

Simply put, CSRF is an attack in which the perpetrator forces an already-authenticated user of the application to unknowingly submit a request that is intended to execute a potentially harmful instruction that will alter the state of a resource on the server. In other words, a malicious user executes certain harmful actions using the credentials of another user without the latter's knowledge.

The result of a CSRF attack may range from deleting one or more resources (such as objects in a model), resulting in change of user's password and thereby them losing the access, to even executing a financial transaction that siphons out the money from the user's bank account.

Fortunately, Django has a very easy-to-use provision to tackle the CSRF attacks very efficiently. First, you need to see that the CSRF middleware is enabled in the MIDDLEWARE setting (usually it is enabled by default, whenever a Django project is initialized with the startproject command).

```
MIDDLEWARE = [
    . . .,
    'django.middleware.csrf.CsrfViewMiddleware',
    . . .,
]
```

You also must see to it that the CSRF middleware appears before any view middleware. Secondly, whenever you are designing a form template with POST request, the csrf_token template tag is put inside the <form> and </form> tags.

```
<form method="post">
{% csrf_token %}
//other form elements
</form>
```

How does this anti-CSRF mechanism work?

The CsrfViewMiddleware causes the server to send a CSRF cookie with a random secret value this cookie within the response.

As a result of the csrf_token template tag, the HTML form is rendered with a hidden input field with its name as "csrfmiddlewaretoken" and value as the CSRF cookie.

```
<input type="hidden" name="csrfmiddlewaretoken" value="hYxmyDcC
3PqV30YJJawPmt3OAqlScfeZU9uTt4aANNtJe4Ufx3pssjUF1cxeQUIE">
```

When the form is submitted, Django checks if it contains the hidden field and its value matches with the cookie. If not, the user will get a 403 error, as the Figure 6-9 shows.

Figure 6-9. *CSRF failure*

XSS

Web applications often find themselves vulnerable against Cross-Site Scripting (XSS) attacks. Hence, you as a Django developer should be aware of how XSS attacks work and how to mitigate the threats.

The XSS attack involves luring the user to click a link that executes a harmful JavaScript code in the user's browser. The JavaScript code thus injected may be intended to fetch the personal data of the user, hijack the current session, or even a complete takeover of the system.

The use of Django templates does provide you a good enough protection against XSS attacks by escaping certain characters that are potentially dangerous to HTML. Imagine a form collecting certain input from (e.g., name) the user and passing it as the context to a template. The template code uses it to render a Hello message as

```
Hello {{ name }}
```

As a result, if the form input is Admin, the message would be Hello Admin. However, if the form input is something like

```
<script>alert('Admin')</script>
```

this will cause the HTML script to include the JavaScript, resulting in the alert message popping up on the browser. (In this case, the alert message may be harmless, but it could have been any JavaScript function capable of performing more damaging actions!) Thankfully Django doesn't let this happen, because of the automatic HTML escaping feature of Django Template Language. Since the `autoescape` tag is ON by default

- < is converted to <
- < is converted to >
- ' (single quote) is converted to '
- " (double quote) is converted to "

As a result, the above JavaScript code will become

```
&lt;script&gt;alert('Admin');&lt;/script&gt;
```

The XSS attack is thus averted.

There is, of course, a provision to turn the automatic escaping feature off. You can use the safe filter to disable escaping for a particular template variable, such as

```
Hello {{ name | safe }}
```

You can also turn `autoescape` off for a block of template code:

```
{% autoescape off %}
Hello {{ name }}
{% endautoescape %}
```

However, this paves the way for some harmful JavaScript to be inducted in your application. Hence, it is advised that you avoid turning `autoescape` mode off unless it is absolutely necessary. You should remember that storing HTML in the database should also be avoided as far as possible, especially if that HTML is retrieved through a query and rendered to the browser.

SQL Injection

If you use Django ORM for all your database handling requirements, you are more or less sufficiently protected against the SQL injection attacks. It is only if you need to execute SQL queries directly from inside your views that your application becomes vulnerable.

SQL injection is also one of the commonly employed techniques by the hackers to intrude into the system. The attacker uses the input fields in a form to inject malicious SQL commands, which affects the way your application behaves. The results may be disastrous, leading to information leaks and unauthorized access, or even it may result in erasing all the data.

Assume that a user is asked to enter their credentials, which in turn are used to form a SQL query to authenticate the user. The data in the form elements is stored in the two variables: username and password.

```
qry = "SELECT * FROM users WHERE username='"+username + "' AND
password='"+password+"';"
```

Assuming that the form inputs are 'test' and 'abcd1234' for username and password, respectively, the query string would become

```
SELECT * FROM users WHERE username='test' AND
password='abcd1234';
```

In this case, the query will return a row matching with the inputs. However, think of a case where the user inputs abcd1234 or 1=1 in the password field of the login form. The SQL query then becomes

```
SELECT * FROM users WHERE username='test' AND
password='abcd1234 or 1=1';
```

This string is a valid SQL query. However, the condition **or 1=1** causes it to evaluate as TRUE always irrespective of the inputs. As a result, the intruder gains access to the system, which can further cause potential damage.

So what are the measures to be taken to avert such attacks? Let us explore the available options.

First and foremost, use Django's built-in authentication mechanism to validate the user. Use the `authenticate()` function in the `django.contrib` package as explained earlier.

```
from django.contrib.auth import authenticate
username = request.POST['username']
password= request.POST['password']
user = authenticate(username=username , password=password)
```

Second, if you really need to use dynamically constructed SQL queries, always use parameterized queries. Instead of directly embedding user input into SQL queries (as done in the earlier example), create a query string with the ? symbol as the placeholders, such as

```
qry = "SELECT * FROM customers WHERE username = ? AND
password = ?"
```

The execute() method of a DBI-compliant module for any database will dynamically construct a query by inserting the values of the variables from the tuple parameter.

```
cursor = conn.cursor()
cursor.execute(qry, (username, password))
```

The ? placeholders in the string are replaced with the respective parameter values, and the safely constructed query is executed. Thus, SQL injection attempt is thwarted.

Last but not the least, you should use Django's ORM as much as possible. In fact, Django ORM internally uses SQL parameterization to provide built-in protection. Hence, Django's querysets are protected from SQL injection.

Let us also discuss some of the additional security considerations. One of the aspects is the SECRET_KEY in your project. While in the DEBUG stage, the secret key is stored in the SECRET_KEY variable in the settings.py file.

```
# SECURITY WARNING: keep the secret key used in production secret!
SECRET_KEY = 'django-insecure-n+7m3d+e_9wpe=n-+pz%3w-
g=3(0tws#gdi%6_9r^!v!yzbubp'
```

However, as the application is ready for launch on a public server, it should be stored using environment variables. Remove the KEY information from this module. Generate a strong, random SECRET_KEY using a secure method. Copy your secret key from your settings.py file and paste it into the **.env** or **.venv** file, and then make it available to the project's settings by including

```
SECRET_KEY = str(os.getenv('SECRET_KEY'))
```

Deploying your Django application behind HTTPS provides better security. To enable HTTPS support, set SECURE_PROXY_SSL_HEADER parameter to True, or else, your application may become vulnerable against CSRF attacks. You must also set SECURE_SSL_REDIRECT to True. Setting SESSION_COOKIE_SECURE and CSRF_COOKIE_SECURE settings to True is also highly recommended.

async Views

As you learned earlier (Chapter 1, section "Asynchronous Processing"), versions of Django from 3.1 onward support writing asynchronous views. Your Django application needs to be run on an ASGI server like Uvicorn or Daphne. The async views still work with the WSGI server, the one included in Django API itself. However, their efficiency is limited considerably.

Defining async views is not much different than defining a coroutine. You need to add async before the def keyword. If your application has class-based views, the HTTP methods, such as get() and post(), should be defined as async def.

Let us start by defining a simple async view that returns Hello World message.

```
from django.http import HttpResponse
async def index(request):
    return HttpResponse("<h2>Hello, World</h2>")
```

You can, of course, execute this view by visiting its mapped URL while the Django server is invoked with the runserver command. However, we would like to use an ASGI-enabled server. In Chapter 1, you used Daphne. Here we shall run this application with Uvicorn.

Install Uvicorn in the current Django environment:

```
pip3 install uvicorn
```

Use the command-line interface of Uvicorn to launch the server. Note that the command-line syntax is very similar to that of Daphne:

```
uvicorn asyncproject.asgi:application --reload
```

The terminal log shows that the server is up and running at port 8000 of the localhost.

```
INFO:     Will watch for changes in these directories:
          ['D:\\workspace\\asyncproject']
INFO:     Uvicorn running on http://127.0.0.1:8000
          (Press CTRL+C to quit)
INFO:     Started reloader process [19276] using StatReload
INFO:     Started server process [19296]
```

```
INFO:     Waiting for application startup.
INFO:     ASGI 'lifespan' protocol appears unsupported.
INFO:     Application startup complete.
```

You can visit the URL route mapped to the index view to get the Hello World message in the browser.

Let us add some really asynchronous activity in the views. First, install the HTTPX package in the current environment.

```
pip3 install httpx
```

The HTTPX library is an asynchronous HTTP client. It offers a fully asynchronous API for making HTTP requests and allows HTTP operations to be performed asynchronously. However, you can also make synchronous calls also with it.

Use the AsyncClient class in HTTPX for asynchronous requests.

```
import httpx
    async with httpx.AsyncClient() as client:
        response = await client.get("https://httpbin.org/")
```

httpbin.org is an open source HTTP request and response service that is helpful to test and debug HTTP requests and responses.

This async call is made from inside an async helper function that calls a sleep() function asynchronously and also makes a GET call on httpbin. org. When the function is called by some async view, Uvicorn goes ahead with the GET call to httpbin.org while the awaitable sleep() function is run. Listing 6-13 shows the async_call() function.

Listing 6-13. async view

```
async def async_call():
    await asyncio.sleep(10)
    async with httpx.AsyncClient() as client:
```

```
        response = await client.get("https://httpbin.org/")
        print("Response From httpbin: ", response)

    print ("async call completed..")
```

Let us call this function from an async view:

```
async def async_view(request):
    loop = asyncio.get_event_loop()
    loop.create_task(async_call())
    return HttpResponse("Non-blocking HTTP Response")
```

When you visit the URL that is mapped to this view ("async/" in this case), Django immediately renders its HTTP response to the browser (Non-blocking HTTP Response) while the async_call() function executes asynchronously.

On the terminal, you should get the output as

```
INFO:      127.0.0.1:52590 - "GET /myapp/async/ HTTP/1.1" 200 OK
Response From httpbin:   <Response [200 OK]>
async call completed..
```

It can be seen that the view's response is rendered first, followed, after the sleep time, by the response from httpbin.org service.

To compare this with the synchronous behavior, define another helper function (refer Listing 6-14):

Listing 6-14. sync view with helper function

```
def sync_call():
    time.sleep(10)
    response = httpx.get("https://httpbin.org/")
    print("Response From httpbin: ",response)
    print ("sync call completed..")
```

Invoke this from inside a normal view:

```
def sync_view(request):
    sync_call()
    return HttpResponse("Blocking HTTP Response")
```

The "sync/" URL route that takes the server to this view first performs the GET call to httpbin.org. After its response is obtained, the view response is then rendered.

```
Response From httpbin:   <Response [200 OK]>
sync call completed..
INFO:     127.0.0.1:52591 - "GET /myapp/sync/ HTTP/1.1" 200 OK
```

Adapter Functions

Django API provides a couple of adapter functions in the `asgiref.sync` module. These functions act as a bridge between the synchronous and asynchronous context.

async_to_sync(): Give an asynchronous callable (coroutine) as an argument to this function. It returns a synchronous wrapper around it. You can then call synchronous code within an asynchronous context.

To use any of Django's synchronous functions, such as render(), from an async view, you can wrap them using async_to_sync.

sync_to_async(): A synchronous function goes as an argument to this function and returns an asynchronous wrapper around it so that you can call asynchronous code within a synchronous context. Use it especially when you have an existing synchronous function and you want it to be used within an async context or when you need to call async functions from synchronous Django code.

async QuerySets

Django has extended the async capability to run ORM queries also. All QuerySet methods that you used earlier have an a-prefixed asynchronous counterpart. For example, the get() method now becomes aget() and delete() needs to be replaced by adelete() in async context. For example:

```
book = await Book.objects.filter(author='Alchin').afirst()
```

returns the first occurrence of the object satisfying the given condition.

Instead of using for statement for iterating over a queryset, use async for

```
async for entry in Book.objects.filter(name__startswith="A"):
  ...
```

Some queryset methods like get() and first() are blocking in nature. Hence, they have sync counterparts with names starting with "a" – such as aget() and afirst(). Others, like filter() and exclude(), are safe to be run from asynchronous code.

Reusable Apps

So far, you have learned to create a Django app inside a project, with the help of the startapp command. You can also have more than one app in a project. But how about making your app reusable to other users? In Django, a reusable app is a self-contained package that can be easily plugged into different projects.

When you build a Django project, a number of Django apps are installed by default. The admin app is an example, which is distributed with the Django software itself. In addition, you can add other third-party apps in your project. For that, you need to install it first and then include it in the list of INSTALLED_APPS.

You are familiar with installing a Python package from the PyPI repository with the PIP utility and then using its functionality. A Django application is also a package folder having models, tests, urls, and views submodules in addition to static and template folders. How would you distribute your app for others to download, install, and use?

Let us find out what are the steps involved. Assume that you have an app called myapp in your Django project, which you have already put in the INSTALLED_APPS list.

```
INSTALLED_APPS = [
    . . .
    'myapp',
]
```

Before proceeding, ensure that your Python environment has setuptools installed. It is a Python module with which you can compile, distribute, and install Python packages. If not already available, install the same with the PIP command:

```
pip3 install setuptools
```

Coming back to your app, note that it is recommended to use a django- prefix for package name, to make your package as specific to Django, and a corresponding django_ prefix for your module name. So move the myapp app folder from your project to the django-myapp folder and rename the myapp folder itself to django_myapp.

Open the django_myapp/apps.py file and set the name attribute of MyappConfig class to django_myapp as shown here:

```
from django.apps import AppConfig
class MyappConfig(AppConfig):
    default_auto_field = 'django.db.models.BigAutoField'
    name = 'django_myapp'
    label = 'myapp'
```

Now you need to create some new files in the package folder, i.e., django-myapp folder.

Create a README.rst file, which essentially contains the technical documentation of how to install and use your app.

Also put in a LICENSE file, a text illustrating the terms of use. Most Django apps are distributed under BSD license; however, you are free to choose any.

The setup.cfg is a configuration file used by the `setuptools` packaging library. It specifies the metadata of the app including the version, the license type, author's details, etc. It also defines the desired versions of Python and Django, also certain dependencies if any. Here is an example of setup.cfg:

```
[metadata]
name = django-myapp
version = 0.1
description = An example Django app
long_description = file: README.rst
url = https://www.example.com/
author = Your Name
author_email = yourname@example.com
license = BSD-3-Clause
classifiers =
    Environment :: Web Environment
    Framework :: Django
    Framework :: Django :: 5.0
    Intended Audience :: Developers
    License :: OSI Approved :: BSD License
    Operating System :: OS Independent
    Programming Language :: Python :: 3 :: Only
    Topic :: Internet :: WWW/HTTP
    Topic :: Internet :: WWW/HTTP :: Dynamic Content
```

```
[options]
include_package_data = true
packages = find:
python_requires = >=3.10
install_requires =
    Django >= 4.2
```

Finally, create a setup.py file. It simply invokes the setup() function from the setuptools module. The setup() function makes use of the configuration details in the setup.cfg file.

```
from setuptools import setup
setup()
```

While building the package, the setup() function copies only the Python modules and subpackages. If you need to include any other assets, such as the templates and static files, you should also provide a MANIFEST.in file.

```
include LICENSE
include README.rst
recursive-include django_myapp/static *
```

With all the prerequisites in place, you are now in a position to build the package, with the following command:

```
python setup.py sdist
```

Make sure that this command is run while in the django-myapp folder. This will create a dist folder that holds the django_myapp-0.1.tar.gz file.

The activity log in the terminal goes something like this:

```
running sdist
running egg_info
creating django_myapp.egg-info
```

```
. . .
. . .
adding license file 'LICENSE'
writing manifest file 'django_myapp.egg-info\SOURCES.txt'
running check
creating django_myapp-0.1
creating django_myapp-0.1\django_myapp
creating django_myapp-0.1\django_myapp.egg-info
creating django_myapp-0.1\django_myapp\migrations
creating django_myapp-0.1\django_myapp\static
copying files . ..
Writing django_myapp-0.1\setup.cfg
creating dist
Creating tar archive
```

To be able to use this app, install it with the PIP command:

```
pip3 install dist/django-myapp-0.1.tar.gz
```

Go back to your project now. Since you have removed the myapp app folder, it won't function properly now. Let us add the newly installed app in the INSTALLED_APPS list:

```
INSTALLED_APPS = [

    . . .
    'django_myapp.apps.MyappConfig',
]
```

You must also update the URLCONF of your project by including the urls of the django_myapp app:

```
from django.contrib import admin
from django.urls import path, include
```

```
urlpatterns = [
    . . .
    path('myapp/', include('django_myapp.urls')),
]
```

Incorporate carefully all the above steps, and launch the Django development server and check if it works fine, which it should if everything has been done accordingly.

Finally, you may want to make your package available for public consumption by uploading it to https://pypi.org/ – the Python package index repository. PyPI recommends using Twine, a utility for publishing Python packages. So you need to install it first.

```
pip3 install twine
```

To publish your package, register with https://pypi.org/account/register/ and log in with your credentials. From your package directory, run the following command:

```
twine upload dist/*
```

Enter your username and password when prompted. After the upload is finished, your package is now available on PyPI.

Django Debug Toolbar

One of the defining features of Django is its rich ecosystem of reusable apps for different use cases. Most of them are available in an open source domain; a comprehensive repository of Django apps is maintained at https://djangopackages.org/. Incorporating such apps in your core project helps you extend it with additional functionality without reinventing the wheel.

You will learn about working with a couple of such third-party apps during the course of this book. This section introduces one of the must-have apps – Django Debug Toolbar.

As the name suggests, the objective of the Django Debug Toolbar is to provide useful debugging information about Django web applications. With the help of this app, you can easily identify and debug any problems in your application. The debugging information is available in a collapsible and customizable set of panels. For instance, the SQL panel shows details of SQL queries, and the Setting panel lists of the parameters and their value of various settings variables without looking at the source code of the settings.py module.

Like any reusable app, you need to install it in the current Django environment with the PIP utility.

```
pip3 install django-debug-toolbar
```

You can now add this app in the list of INSTALLED_APPS.

```
INSTALLED_APPS = [
    . . .
    'debug_toolbar',
    'myapp',
]
```

To update the project's URLCONF accordingly, add debug toolbar's URL:

```
from django.contrib import admin
from django.urls import path, include
import debug_toolbar.toolbar

urlpatterns = [
    . . .
    path("__debug__/", include(debug_toolbar.urls)),
]
```

You also need to update the MIDDLEWARE list:

```
MIDDLEWARE = [
    "debug_toolbar.middleware.DebugToolbarMiddleware",
    . . .,
]
```

Note that this app is intended for use in DEBUG mode, i.e., when Debug parameter is set to True. In the development stage, the INTERNAL_ IPS setting must include the IP address of the localhost – 127.0.0.1.

```
INTERNAL_IPS = [
    "127.0.0.1",
]
```

If properly installed, you should get to see a DjDT handle appearing on the right-hand side of the browser (as in Figure 6-10) when you visit any of the application routes, including the Admin page.

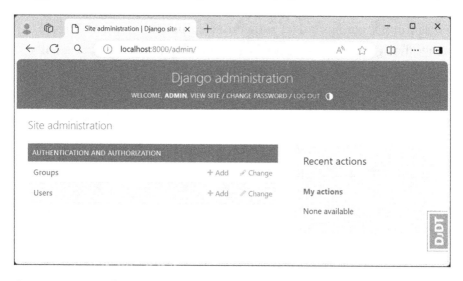

Figure 6-10. *Admin home page with a DjDT handle*

The toolbar will be expanded when you click on the handle. A list of debug panels will appear (Figure 6-11).

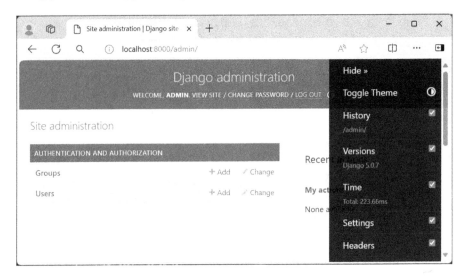

Figure 6-11. *Debug toolbar panels*

The app is configured for showing some panels by default. Figure 6-12 shows the SQL panel that lists SQL queries along with the time taken to execute and the link to explain the queries.

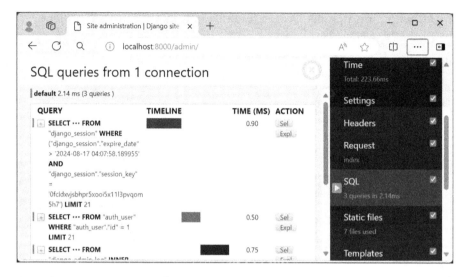

Figure 6-12. *SQL panel*

Click the Expl button and the browser "explains" the query, as the Figure 6-13 shows.

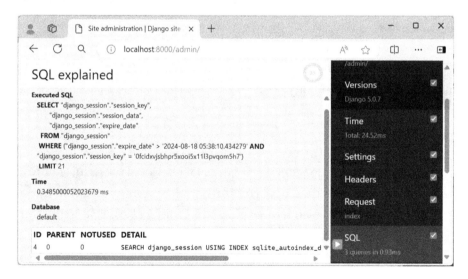

Figure 6-13. *SQL explained*

227

Other panels that display useful information are Settings (project settings parameters and their values) and Request panels (Figure 6-14), displaying the view executed, cookies, session data, etc.

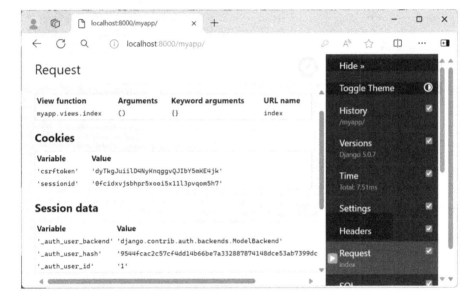

Figure 6-14. *Request panel*

You can work with this app extensively and explore how best you can make use of its functionality.

Summary

Django is a full-stack web framework, packed with a lot of powerful features. In this chapter, you learned how you can enhance your application by including messaging and authentication. This chapter also discussed various security provisions and how you can enable async support for Django application. In the end, you explored the Django Debug Toolbar and how it proves to be effective in debugging an application.

In the next chapter, we shall discuss one of the most popular Django apps: the Django Rest Framework.

CHAPTER 7

REST API with Django

Django is a popular choice for building robust data-driven web applications. In recent years, there is a growing trend of adding a web API component to the application so that various frontend apps can interact with the resources of the main applications. Django's large ecosystem of reusable apps offers tools, such as Django REST Framework and others, that help you add the API functionality to a Django project.

In this chapter, you will acquaint yourself with the basics of REST. You will also explore the important features such as serialization and authentication offered by the Django REST Framework app. Toward the end, this chapter introduces Django Ninja, a modern API building tool that provides async support.

Here are the main topics to be covered in this chapter:

- What is API?
- REST architecture
- Serialization
- Django REST Framework
- Django Ninja

© Malhar Lathkar 2025
M. Lathkar, *Modern Django Web Development*,
https://doi.org/10.1007/979-8-8688-1472-3_7

What Is API?

The term "API" (which stands for Application Programming Interface) is a popular buzzword these days among the developer community. In general, an interface is an entity where two different environments meet and interact. A seaport, for example, can be considered as an interface between a sea and the land. A receptionist that sits at the front desk of an office is also an interface between the visitors and the office internals such as employees, procedures, and information. A computer's main unit interacts with the peripheral devices such as keyboard, mouse, and printer through different interfaces (serial, parallel, and USB interfaces).

The API is a software interface between two software applications. It acts as a contract between the two, defining how one of them requests the other for a certain information and how the other responds. In the IT-enabled world around us, we routinely work with so many APIs. Different payment apps act as an interface between the customers, banks, and merchants. When we come across numerous websites letting you to log in with the IDs of social media apps like Facebook, LinkedIn, etc., the APIs exposed by them are at work (Figure 7-1).

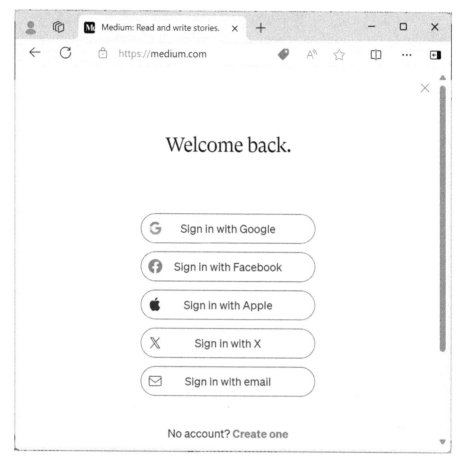

Figure 7-1. *Social login API*

Different weather data aggregators collect data from various sources such as satellites. Their APIs are consumed by weather apps and websites that provide weather forecast over a certain period.

Over the years, various different protocols and specifications for building API solutions have been employed by the developers. Let us have a brief introduction of some of them:

> **SOAP:** Simple Object Access Protocol is one of the earliest protocols used for the development of APIs. This protocol primarily uses XML to transmit data over an HTTP or HTTPS connection. The requests are composed with a fairly rigid set of rules of WSDL – Web Services Description Language.

> **RPC:** The Remote Procedure Call allows a program to execute a procedure (function) residing on another computer or server. RPC is used in a client-server environment, where the client initiates a request to the server, and the server executes the request and sends the results back to the client. The XDR (eXternal Data Representation) protocol, on top of which the RPC is built, standardizes the representation of data in remote communications.

> **gRPC:** The Google Remote Procedure Call is a specific implementation of RPC with a focus on efficiency. Developed by Google, this open source framework is designed for establishing efficient distributed systems and makes it easier to build microservices that enable communication between applications.

> **REST:** A de facto standard in today's world of API-first approach of web application development, **RElational State Transfer** is more of a collection of principles or guidelines rather than a protocol. REST is an architectural style and a set of constraints that

define how the web services should interact with each other. In this chapter, we shall be discussing how to build a REST API with Django, specifically with the Django REST Framework app. In the next section, we shall discuss the REST architecture in more details.

REST Architecture

As mentioned above, REST is the preferred approach to create stateless, reliable web-based applications throughout the software industry. The term "REST" was first coined by Roy Fielding in the year 2000, when he was working on the creation of formal descriptions of HTTP standards. He recommended an architectural style that entails certain constraints, which, when implemented, provides advantages such as simplicity of a uniform interface, scalability and portability of components, and more.

Given below is a brief overview of the six guiding constraints defined in Fielding's PhD thesis, "Architectural Styles and the Design of Network-based Software Architectures."

Uniform Interface

Unlike SOAP and RPC, which are action-based protocols, REST is a resource-based architecture. A file, an image, or a row in a table of a database, everything is considered as a resource on the server. A resource on the server is identified by a Uniform Resource Identifier (URI). When a client sends the request for a resource, it should contain all the information required for retrieving and processing it.

This constraint requires that the client request should contain everything that is required for it to be processed. The request must include the URI of the resource and the action to be taken on it, along with some additional data if required, especially if the request involves creating a new resource. HTTP verbs (also known as HTTP methods) represent the action to be performed. The HTTP methods POST, GET, PUT, and DELETE are defined in the HTTP protocol specification and correspond to CREATE, READ, UPDATE, and DELETE operations on the server's resource.

Statelessness

The REST architecture requires that each request should be treated as separate and independent transaction. Neither the details of a client's request nor the server's response to it is stored on the server. While this constraint makes it possible for the API to be scalable, it also results in increased network traffic as a client may need to send the same information again and again for subsequent transactions. As a workaround, techniques such as cookies and session data are often employed in designing RESTful APIs.

Client-Server

Due to the fact that the HTTP protocol that drives the REST principle is also based on the client-server architecture, imposition of this constraint on REST is obvious. As the main advantage of this, the client and server can be scaled independently as required. This along with increased flexibility and reliability are the other advantages.

Cacheability

REST allows the client to store server responses in a cache. By setting appropriate response headers such as Cache-Control, Expires, and ETag, the responses can be stored and reused. This feature reduces the network traffic and improves the performance. For large-scale applications, implementing caching can be complex. One also needs to ensure data consistency by ensuring that stale data is not served.

Layered System

The client-server constraint takes care of the separation of client and server-side functionality. You can further compose the server component in more than one layer that are independent of each other. To ensure improved scalability, the layers are configured to interact only with the immediate ones and not any other.

Code on Demand

In any RESTful API, most of the time the server's response is in serializable data format such as XML or JSON. However, as per this constraint, the response can be a certain script, which the client can download and execute. However, REST applications very seldom gave this feature, since it can be a potential security threat. The REST architecture specification stipulates this constraint as optional.

Serialization

As mentioned earlier, modern web application development adopts the API-first approach, in which the concept and implementation of serialization (and deserialization) are of crucial importance. In response to the client request, the server in a RESTful application needs to send complex data structures (not just the plain text).

Serialization refers to the conversion of these objects (e.g., the model objects in a Django app) into a byte stream in a format that can be easily transferred from the server to the client via HTTP and may be stored in a disk file or database. On the client end, the byte stream needs to be converted back into the original state of the object for further consumption – this process is called deserialization. The Figure 7-2 is a schematic representation of this process. JSON (JavaScript Object Notation) is the most preferred data exchange format in API design, although XML (Extensible Markup Language) is also frequently used.

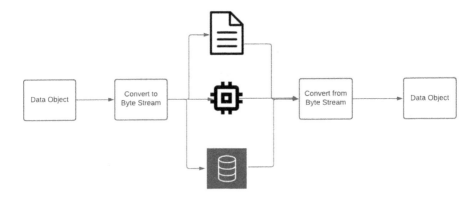

Figure 7-2. Object serialization

Django provides a serialization framework with which you can translate Django models into JSON, XML, as well as YAML (YAML Ain't Markup Language) format. The serializers module in the django.core package is a collection of several built-in serializer classes that handle different data formats. The serialize() method serializes a queryset of Django model objects in the desired format.

JSON serializer serializes the given object to JSON format, the one most commonly used in Web APIs.

```
json = serializers.serialize("json", some_queryset)
```

Conversely, the deserialize() function obtains the original Python object. Since the queryset is a list of model objects, you should cast it to list type.

```
objects = list(serializers.deserialize("json", json))
```

The first argument to the serialize() function is one of the data formats supported by Django. For example, the following statement returns the XML representation:

```
xml = serializers.serialize("xml", some_queryset)
```

You can even create a Custom Serializer class by subclassing the Serializer class and implement the functionality for serialization and deserialization.

```
from django.core.serializers import Serializer

class MySerializer(Serializer):
        def serialize(self, queryset, **options):
                #serialization logic

        def deserialize(self, queryset, **options):
                #deserialization logic
```

Once the custom serializer is created, you register it within Django's serializer framework so you can use it with the serialize() and deserialize() functions.

To add your own serializers, use the SERIALIZATION_MODULES setting:

```
SERIALIZATION_MODULES = {
    "myformat": "MySerializer",
}
```

The serializers module is primarily designed for exporting models to the JSON or XML format. However, it's not suitable for building REST APIs. First of all, performing serialization and deserialization manually for every request is error-prone and introduces vulnerabilities. Furthermore, features such as field validation are not provided by Django's core serializers. Hence, Django developers use a third-party app for this purpose such as Django REST Framework (DRF), which is what you will learn about in the next sections of this chapter.

Django REST Framework

Django REST Framework is easily one of the most popular reusable apps in the Django ecosystem. You can add a robust RESTful API to your Django project with the help of this package. DRF takes you beyond the limitations of core Django as far as the serialization support is concerned. Django REST Framework comes with several additional enhancements.

One of the standout features of DRF is the browsable API. Instead of using other tools and apps (such as cURL, Postman, and others), the browsable API allows you to test the API endpoints directly in the browser.

DRF supports various authentication schemes and authorization support such as OAuth2, TokenAuthentication, and JSON Web Token to secure your API.

Like most open source products, DRF too has a great supportive community and is used extensively by some of the well-known companies like Mozilla, Red Hat, and Heroku.

DRF – Get Started

The Django REST Framework package was first released in 2011. Its latest version – 3.15.2 – is compatible with the latest versions of Python as well as Django. Along with this package, you may want to use Markdown and Pygments to add Markdown support for the browsable API and the syntax highlighting of Markdown – a popular text-to-HTML conversion tool.

As always, PIP installer is the most convenient tool for Python package installation:

```
pip3 install djangorestframework markdown pygments
```

You need to include the 'rest_framework' app in the list of INSTALLED_APPS of your Django project, along with the Django app in which you will define your API endpoints. Assuming that you have already created a new Django app named myapi in your project, the INSTALLED_APPS setting should look like

```
INSTALLED_APPS = [
    . . .
    'rest_framework',
    'myapi',
]
```

The views in Django REST Framework are primarily class-based views. It does support defining the function-based views in the classical manner, but the view function is decorated by the @api_view decorator. This decorator converts the view function into a subclass of APIView class. Note that the request parameter of the function is an object of Request class in DRF and not the HttpRequest object. Also, it returns a Response object – it's an object of the Response class in the rest_framework.response module, not the HttpResponse object.

Listing 7-1 defines a simple view function sayHello() that returns a Hello World JSON response.

Listing 7-1. hello.py

```
from rest_framework.decorators import api_view
from rest_framework.response import Response

@api_view()
def sayHello(request):
    return Response({"message": "Hello, world!"})
```

The api_view() decorator has one argument in the form of http_method_names list. Here, the sayHello() view is invoked in response to a GET request. For others, the corresponding HTTP verbs should be included in the list.

```
@api_view(http_method_names=['GET'])
```

Associate this function with a suitable URL route in the app's urls module, as in Listing 7-2.

Listing 7-2. urls.py in app

```
from django.urls import path
from . import views

urlpatterns = [
    path('hello/',views.sayHello),
]
```

As a final step, update the project's URLCONF by including the myapi. urls module (Listing 7-3).

Listing 7-3. urls.py in project

```
from django.contrib import admin
from django.urls import include, path

urlpatterns = [
    path('admin/', admin.site.urls),
    path('myapi/', include('myapi.urls')),
]
```

The browsable API will show up in the browser in response to the URL http://localhost:8000/myapi/hello/ (refer Figure 7-3) when Django's built-in server is launched.

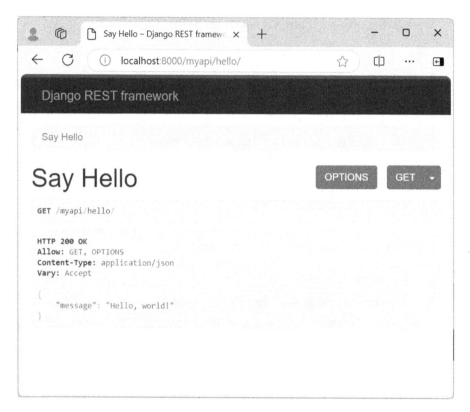

Figure 7-3. *Browsable API*

As mentioned earlier, the browsable API is a unique offering of DRF. It is an interactive web interface automatically generated for your API endpoints. The browsable API allows you to perform not only the GET but POST, PUT, and DELETE requests as well directly from the browser. Hence, you don't need tools such as Postman to test and debug your API.

Let us add another view function to this API.

```
@api_view()
def drfRoute(request):
    return Response({'message': 'REST API designed by Django
    REST Framework'})
```

241

Update the app's urlpatterns list by including its path:

```
urlpatterns  += [path('drf/', views.drfRoute, name='drf')]
```

It is always a good practice to define a root endpoint that shows the links to the other endpoints in your API.

```
from rest_framework.reverse import reverse
@api_view()
def api_root(request):
    return Response({
        'hello': reverse('hello', request=request),
        'drf': reverse('drf', request=request),
    })
```

The reverse() function in the rest_framework.reverse module is a handy shortcut function that returns a fully qualified URL associated with a view function.

Again, update the urlpatterns list to include the path to the api_root() function:

```
urlpatterns += [path('', views.api_root, name='api-root')]
```

As a result (Figure 7-4), the http://localhost:8000/myapi/ URL in the browser displays the links to the /**hello** and /**drf** endpoints, so your API is truly browsable.

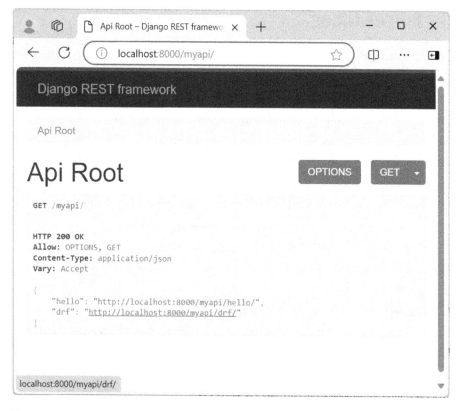

Figure 7-4. *Api root*

This provides you the glimpse of how an API is built with Django REST Framework. Obviously, you would like to develop an API that exposes endpoints for performing the CRUD operations on database models. For that, you should know how the model objects are serialized in the JSON format. The Django REST Framework comes with the `serializers` module, having different serializer classes, serializer fields, etc.

243

Serializer Class

Serialization, as you have learned in the previous section, is a process that transforms data into a format that can be stored or transmitted and then reconstructed. The built-in serializers in core Django are mainly used for things like database dumps, importing/exporting data, or integrating with external systems. On the other hand, the serializers in Django REST Framework are much more powerful and flexible, designed specifically for building REST APIs. Some of the key features of serializers in DRF are the field customization and robust validation capabilities. The views and routers in DRF are integrated with the serializers.

The `rest_framework.serializers` module includes various classes and utilities, such as serialization classes, field classes, and validation utilities.

The Serializer class defined in this module helps you to covert a Python object – more specifically an object of Django model into native Python data type, which then can be rendered in serializable data formats such as JSON or XML.

Let us start by adding a Django model in our app, as the Listing 7-4 shows.

Listing 7-4. Ticket model

```
from django.db import models

class Ticket(models.Model):
    flight_number = models.CharField(max_length=10)
    passenger_name = models.CharField(max_length=100)
    departure_time = models.DateTimeField()
    seat_number = models.CharField(max_length=5)
```

Yes, you guessed it right, we shall use this model to build a Ticketing API during the course of this chapter.

Next up, define a TicketSerializer class (refer Listing 7-5) with `rest_framework.serializers.Serializer` as its base. This class will be placed inside the *serializers.py* module. The attributes in the Serializer class are the objects of serializer field classes, very similar to the model fields. Ensure that the attributes match with those used in the model class.

Listing 7-5. serializers.py

```python
from rest_framework import serializers

class TicketSerializer(serializers.Serializer):
    flight_number = serializers.CharField(max_length=10)
    passenger_name = serializers.CharField(max_length=100)
    departure_time = serializers.DateTimeField()
    seat_number = serializers.CharField(max_length=5)
```

Both these classes are placed in the *models.py* module.
Launch the Django shell and import these two classes.

```python
python manage.py shell
>>> from myapi.models import Ticket
>>> from myapi.serializers import TicketSerializer
```

Declare a Ticket object:

```python
>>> ticket = Ticket(    flight_number='AI123',    passenger_
name='John Doe',    departure_time='2024-10-05
14:30:00',    seat_number='12A')
```

To serialize the Ticket object, pass it to the TicketSerializer constructor:

```python
>>> serialized_ticket = TicketSerializer(ticket)
```

The Serializer class is characterized by some useful attributes and methods.

> **data**: This property holds the serialized data of the Python object.
>
> **validated_data**: The cleaned and validated data after calling is_valid() is stored in this property. This is used to create or update objects during the deserialization process.

```
>>> serialized_ticket.data
{'flight_number': 'AI123', 'passenger_name': 'John Doe',
'departure_time': '2024-10-05 14:30:00', 'seat_number': '12A'}
```

The rest_framework package defines a JSONRenderer for rendering the serialized data to JSON format.

```
>>> from rest_framework.renderers import JSONRenderer
>>> json_ticket = JSONRenderer().render(serialized_ticket.data)
>>> print (json_ticket)
b'{"flight_number":"AI123","passenger_name":"John
Doe","departure_time":"2024-10-05 14:30:00","seat_
number":"12A"}'
```

On the other hand, we can parse the serialized stream to deserialize this object to Python's native data types. You will get the dictionary representation of the original Ticket object.

```
>>> from rest_framework.parsers import JSONParser
>>> import io
>>> stream = io.BytesIO(json_ticket)
>>> data = JSONParser().parse(stream)
>>> serialized_data=TicketSerializer(data=data)
>>> serialized_data.is_valid()
```

```
True
>>> print (serialized_data.validated_data)
{'flight_number': 'AI123', 'passenger_name': 'John Doe',
'departure_time': datetime.datetime(2024, 10, 5, 14, 30,
tzinfo=zoneinfo.ZoneInfo(key='UTC')), 'seat_number': '12A'}
```

Obviously, we would like the serialization to be performed inside the views. Before we actually write the views to handle the CRUD operations, we need to carefully design and develop the endpoints of our API. An API endpoint is actually a specific URL route that will be exposed to the API clients. They send their requests to the endpoints in order to access the resources made available by the API server.

As mentioned earlier, we shall be developing a Ticketing API, where all the CRUD operations will be done on the Ticket model. Since myapi is the name of our Django app, it will be the preceding part of the endpoint, followed by an identifier referring to either a collection of resources or a specific instance of the resource. The HTTP method used to invoke the endpoint indicates the type of operation to be performed.

In the case of this Ticketing API, the /**myapi/tickets** endpoint called with the GET method conventionally retrieves all the instances of Ticket model, and the same endpoint called with the POST method is linked to the creation of a new Ticket instance. On the other hand, the /**myapi/ tickets/id** endpoint called with PUT and DELETE methods is assumed to perform the UPDATE and DELETE operations.

Endpoint	Method	Operation
/myapi/tickets	GET	List of tickets
/myapi/tickets	POST	Create a new ticket
/myapi/ticket/id	GET	Retrieve a ticket
/myapi/ticket/id	PUT	Update a ticket
/myapi/ticket/id	DELETE	Delete a ticket

Django REST Framework has a unique `Router` class that provides an automatically generated root view. You shall learn about this in one of the subsequent sections.

Serializer Fields

The attributes of a Serializer class are the objects of Field classes. Much like the Form fields, the serializer fields handle the conversion between model attributes and serializable objects, as well as the validation part.

The field types in Django REST Framework are more or less the same as Django's Form fields; some of them are

- BooleanField

- CharField

- IntegerField

- FloatField

- DateTimeField

- EmailField

Each of these field types has its own validation mechanism. For example, the `UniqueValidator` enforces the `unique=True` constraint on model fields. The arguments used in the construction of fields, such as `max_length, min_value, max_value,` etc., act as validation constraints.

Serializer Methods

is_valid(): This method checks if the data provided is valid as per the validation rules of the serializer.

validate(): This is the object-level validation method, used to perform validation on the entire object. You may override this method in your serializer class to add custom validation logic.

save(): This method saves the validated data, usually by creating or updating an instance. If your serializer needs a custom logic for saving the data, this method may be overridden accordingly.

create(): This is a method used to create a new instance when calling save() with deserialized data. Normally you would override this method when handling object creation for custom serializers.

update(): An existing instance is updated when calling save() with deserialized data.

ModelSerializer

More often than not, the serializer fields correspond to the model fields. So here is a shortcut approach. The ModelSerializer class automatically maps its field attributes to the model attributes of its inner Meta class. Moreover, the ModelSerializer also generates the required validators. In other words, the ModelSerializer class is a specialized Serializer class that automatically generates the fields for you, based on the model. It also includes simple default implementations of create() and update() methods.

We have already declared the Ticket model; let us migrate it to a corresponding database table. Create the object as in the previous section, and save it to the database.

```
>>> from myapi.models import Ticket
>>> ticket = Ticket(    flight_number='AI123',    passenger_
name='John Doe',    departure_time='2024-10-05
14:30:00',    seat_number='12A')
>>> ticket.save()
```

Similarly, go ahead and add a few more instances of the Ticket model.

Let us change the TicketSerializer class to make it a subclass of ModelSerializer. As the Listing 7-6 shows, we need not define the individual field attributes. Instead, tell Django to map the fields of Django models to corresponding serializer fields.

Listing 7-6. ModelSerializer

```
from rest_framework import serializers
from .models import Ticket

class TicketSerializer(serializers.ModelSerializer):
    class Meta:
        model = Ticket
        fields = "__all__"
```

Here, Meta is an inner class that provides metadata about the serializer. Two essential attributes to define in the Meta class are model and fields. The model attribute is actually the Django model to be mapped to the serializer (in this case, the Ticket model). The fields attribute is the list of model fields to be included in the serialized representation.

You can either give the list of fields explicitly such as

```
fields = ['passenger_name', 'passenger_name', 'seat_number']
```

or set the property to all fields:

```
fields = "__all__"
```

You can also ask certain fields to be excluded.

```
exclude = ['field1', 'field2']
```

We shall now define a `tickets()` view that renders a serialized representation of the objects from the Ticket model (Listing 7-7). In other words, this will be the implementation of GET request in our Ticketing API.

Listing 7-7. Using serializer in DRF view

```
from .models import Ticket
from .serializers import TicketSerializer

@api_view()
def tickets(request):
    tickets = Ticket.objects.all()
    serialized_tickets = TicketSerializer(tickets, many=True)
    return Response(serialized_tickets.data)
```

Update the app's urlpatterns list by including the URL mapping for the tickets() view.

```
urlpatterns += [path('tickets/', views.tickets,
name='tickets')]
```

Visit the URL http://localhost:8000/myapi/tickets/ in your browser to get the JSON response containing the list of tickets, as in the Figure 7-5.

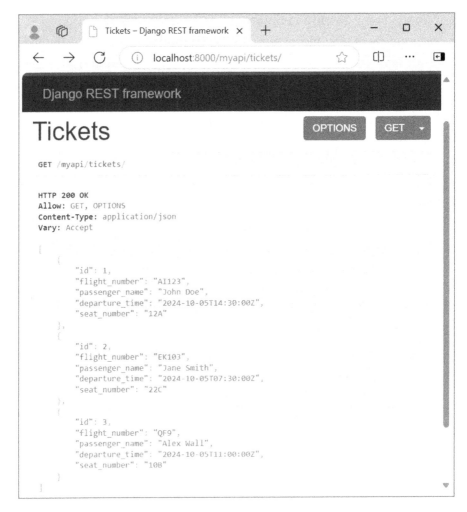

Figure 7-5. JSON response

Since the **'tickets/'** endpoint is used for both the GET and POST methods, the mapped `tickets()` view function should process both the request types. The `@api_view` decorator on the top should be instructed to allow both the methods.

```
@api_view(['GET', 'POST'])
```

When the same view is called with the POST request, it comes with the body parameters passed by the client. The browsable API of Django REST Framework lets you pass the data in a JSON format when the POST request is used to visit the **'tickets/'** endpoint.

To create a new Ticket instance, you need to construct the TicketSerializer object using the request data. After verifying its validity, the save() method is called to persist the Ticket instance in the database. This logic is implemented by adding the conditional block inside the tickets() function in the Listing 7-8.

Listing 7-8. GET and POST with serialized view

```
from rest_framework import status
@api_view(['GET', 'POST'])
def tickets(request):
    if request.method=='GET':
        tickets = Ticket.objects.all()
        serialized_tickets = TicketSerializer(tickets,
        many=True)
        return Response(serialized_tickets.data)

    elif request.method=='POST':
            serialized_ticket = TicketSerializer
            (data=request.data)
            serialized_ticket.is_valid(raise_
            exception=True)
            serialized_ticket.save()
            return Response(serialized_ticket.validated_
            data,status.HTTP_201_CREATED)
```

The browsable API page (Figure 7-6) displays the list of all instances as before. However, when you scroll down the page, a POST section is present. Enter the JSON representation of a new Ticket object to be created in the Content box, and press the POST button at the bottom.

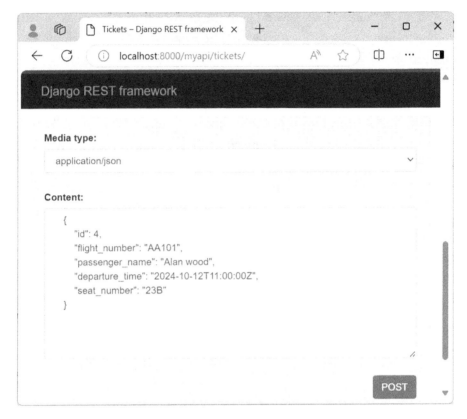

Figure 7-6. *POST form in the browsable API*

Note that both the GET and POST methods are allowed for the **tickets/**
endpoint. The POST request is processed with 201 response, as in
Figure 7-7, indicating that a new resource has been successfully created.

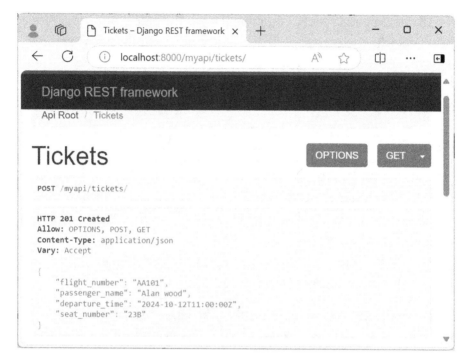

Figure 7-7. *POST endpoint returning 201 response*

The other API endpoint that we have planned earlier is **/myapi/ticket/id**, where id is the primary key for the Ticket object to be retrieved, updated, or deleted. We need to map this URL route to the ticket() view function that has an int path parameter. Accordingly, let us update the urlpatterns list by adding a path:

```
urlpatterns  += [path('ticket/<int:id>', views.ticket,
name='ticket')]
```

Note that the URL pattern ticket/id is the same for GET (a single Ticket resource), PUT (update a Ticket), and DELETE (delete a Ticket); the @api_view() decorator must be configured to allow these methods.

```
@api_view(['GET','PUT', 'DELETE'])
```

The decorated `ticket()` function fetches the path parameter, retrieves the object with the corresponding primary key, and processes the three HTTP requests with three conditional blocks inside it.

The GET request handling is straightforward (Listing 7-9); return the serialized object to the client.

Listing 7-9. GET, PUT, and DELETE in serialized view

```
@api_view(['GET','PUT', 'DELETE'])
def ticket(request, id):
    ticket = Ticket.objects.get(pk=id)
    if request.method=='GET':
        serialized_ticket = TicketSerializer(ticket)
        return Response(serialized_ticket.data)
```

To handle the PUT request, the request data is used to update one or more attributes of the Ticket object. In this case, we update the flight number of an existing booking.

```
elif request.method=='PUT':
    ticket.flight_number = request.data['flight_number']
    ticket.save()
    serialized_ticket=TicketSerializer(ticket)
    return Response(serialized_ticket.data, status=400)
```

The DELETE handler block simply calls the `delete()` method on the ticket object.

```
elif request.method=='DELETE':
    ticket.delete()
    return Response(status=status.HTTP_204_NO_CONTENT)
```

In response to the URL http://localhost:8000/myapi/ticket/1, the browsable API returns the Ticket instance with the corresponding primary key (GET operation), which you can delete – the DELETE button appears in the response, as in Figure 7-8.

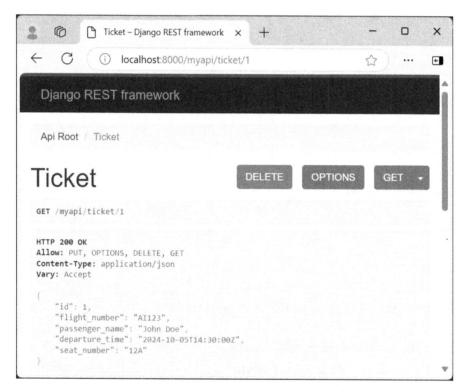

Figure 7-8. *Browsable API with the DELETE button*

Scroll down the page to locate the PUT section (Figure 7-9), enter the value for the flight number to be updated, and click the PUT button.

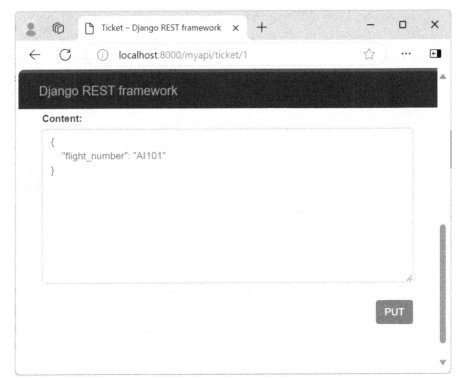

Figure 7-9. *PUT form in the browsable API*

So here is a complete API, capable of serving the GET, POST, PUT, and DELETE requests from any HTTP client. DRF's built-in Browsable API feature is extremely useful to test the API endpoints. However, you may use any other tool, such as Postman, HTTPie, or even the cURL command-line tool.

Figure 7-10 shows the GET request being tested in the HTTPie app.

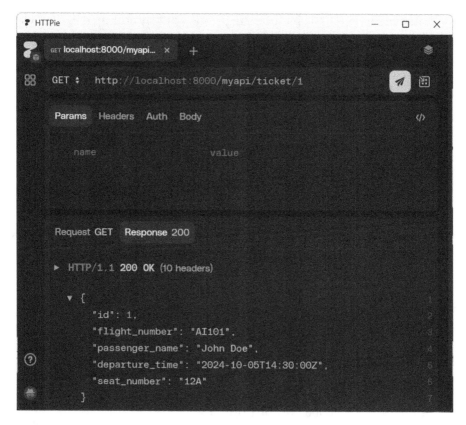

Figure 7-10. Testing API endpoints with HTTPie

HyperlinkedModelSerializer

A specialized variant of ModelSerializer, the HyperlinkedModelSerializer – as the name implies – uses hyperlinks instead of the primary keys to represent the relationships between objects.

This is particularly useful for APIs where you want to expose related objects via their URLs, making the API more intuitive and navigable.

This serializer uses a url field instead of a primary key field. The url field is a serializer field of the type HyperlinkedIdentityField. Any relationships on the model will be represented in this field.

You need to explicitly include the primary key by adding it to the fields option. The Meta subclass in this serializer for the Ticket model should include a fields attribute as

```
fields = ['url', 'flight_number', 'passenger_name', 'departure_
time', 'seat_number']
```

You should also include the extra_kwargs attribute that determines how the URL is formed, by specifying the view_name and the lookup_fields properties.

By default, the view_name property should be set to the style '{model_name}-detail', and lookup_field takes pk as its values. You can, of course, override both by setting appropriate values. We shall stick to the defaults, although it is better to set them explicitly.

```
extra_kwargs = {'url': {'view_name': 'ticket-detail', 'lookup_
field': 'pk'}
```

As a result, each resource in the Ticket model will be represented as a hyperlink in this form:

http://localhost:8000/myapi/ticket/1

Hence, the TicketSerializer class will now be derived from HyperlinkedModelSerializer, and its definition is shown in Listing 7-10.

Listing 7-10. HyperlinkedModelSerializer class

```
from rest_framework import serializers
from .models import Ticket
class TicketSerializer(serializers.HyperlinkedModelSerializer):
    class Meta:
        model = Ticket
        fields = ['url', 'flight_number', 'passenger_name',
        'departure_time', 'seat_number']
```

```
extra_kwargs = {
    'url': {'view_name': 'ticket-detail', 'lookup_
    field': 'pk'}
}
```

We also need to ensure that the view function that handles the GET and POST requests should be in the form `model_list` and the function that handles GET, PUT, and DELETE requests for a single model instance as `model_detail`. Also, the name of the view in the URL mapping should be in the form `model-list` and `model-detail` So we need to change the function names to `ticket_list()` and `ticket_detail()`.

So let us update the urlpattern of the API as

```
urlpatterns = [
    path('tickets/', views.ticket_list, name='ticket-list'),
    path('ticket/<int:pk>/', views.ticket_detail, name='ticket-
    detail'),
]
```

Another crucial requirement for the `HyperlinkedSerializer` is that we pass the request object to the serializer's context. This is required to correctly generate the full URL for the serialized object.

Accordingly the earlier `tickets()` view function is renamed as `ticket_all()`, and while handling the GET request, the `TicketSerializer` object is obtained as

```
serializer = TicketSerializer(tickets, many=True,
context={'request': request})
```

Similarly, inside the conditional block that handles the POST request, the context data must be passed to the TicketSerializer constructor.

```
serializer = TicketSerializer(data=request.data,
context={'request': request})
```

No other changes are needed in the function that processes the GET and POST requests.

On similar lines, you should rename the earlier ticket() view function to ticket_detail() and pass Request object as the context while instantiating the TicketSerializer object.

For GET request:

```
serializer = TicketSerializer(ticket, context={'request':
request})
```

and for PUT request:

```
serializer = TicketSerializer(ticket, data=request.data,
context={'request': request})
```

The complete code for the API with HyperlinkedModelSerializer can be accessed from the book's GitHub repository.

How does the browsable API show the effect of these changes? Well, incorporate all the above changes, fire the Django development server, and point your browser to http://localhost:8000/tickets/.

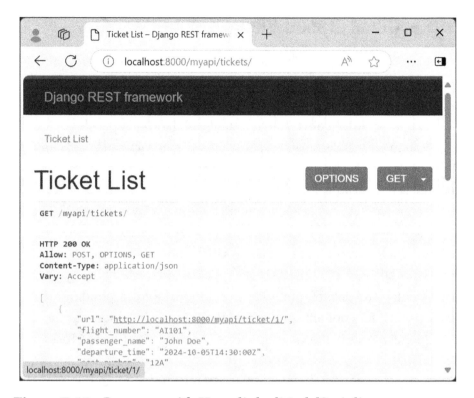

Figure 7-11. *Response with HyperlinkedModelSerializer*

As can be seen in Figure 7-11, the JSON representation of each ticket instance has a url attribute with a hyperlink to its detailed representation – such as http://localhost:8000/ticket/1, which, when clicked, shows up in the browser with the provision to perform GET, PUT, and DELETE operations.

DRF – Class-Based Views

As mentioned earlier, the views in DRF are primarily class based. Even though you used the classical function-based views in the previous section, you must have noticed that the view functions are annotated by `@api_view()`, which converts it as a subclass of the `APIView` class.

Remember you also learned about class-based views in core Django? A class in a core Django app with the View class from the `django.views` module was used as its base. In the Django REST Framework, we have the `rest_framework.views` module that includes the `APIView` class. The DRF class-based view is a class that inherits the `APIView` class. Note that the `APIView` class is also based on Django's `View` class.

Just as Django's CBV, the `APIView` subclass also includes the get(), post(), put(), and delete() methods that handle the corresponding HTTP requests. The functionality of these methods is much the same as the conditional blocks in the view functions – `ticket_list()` and `ticket_detail()`.

In the beginning of our discussion on DRF and serialization, we had identified two API endpoints:

> **/myapi/tickets/:** To process the GET method (retrieve all tickets) and POST method (create a new ticket)

> **/myapi/ticket/id:** To process the GET method (retrieve a given ticket), PUT method (update a ticket) and DELETE method (delete a ticket)

Hence, we need to design two subclasses of the APIView class: `TicketListView` having get() and post() methods and `TicketDetailView` having get(), put(), and delete() methods. Recollect the fact that you need to use the `as_view()` method of these classes to map the URL with the `path()` function to build the urlpatterns list.

```
urlpatterns = [
    path('tickets/', views.TicketListView.as_view(),
    name='ticket-list'),
    path('ticket/<int:pk>/', views.TicketDetailView.as_view(),
    name='ticket-detail'), exists
]
```

As mentioned above, the TicketListView (the APIView subclass) defined the get() and post() methods. The get() method returns the serialized data of all the Ticket instances. The post() method serializes the data in the request body and saves it as a new Ticket instance.

Listing 7-11. TicketListView

```
from rest_framework.views import APIView
from rest_framework import status
from rest_framework.response import Response
from .models import Ticket
from .serializers import TicketSerializer

class TicketListView(APIView):
    def get(self, request):
        tickets = Ticket.objects.all()
        serialized_tickets = TicketSerializer(tickets,
        many=True)
        return Response(serialized_tickets.data)
    def post(self, request):
        serialized_ticket = TicketSerializer(data=request.data)
        serialized_ticket.is_valid(raise_exception=True)
        serialized_ticket.save()
        return Response(serialized_ticket.validated_
        data,status.HTTP_201_CREATED)
```

Note that the get() and post() methods (in the Listing 7-11) each perform exactly the same steps as you find in the conditional code blocks in the `ticket_all()` view function.

Keeping this fact in mind, you can easily design the `TicketDetailView` class. All you need to do is put the conditional blocks from the `ticket_detail()` view functions in the corresponding methods – get(), put(), and delete() methods.

When the development server is launched, your API works exactly as before. Figure 7-12 shows a screenshot of the request to display the details of the ticket instance with 1 as its primary key.

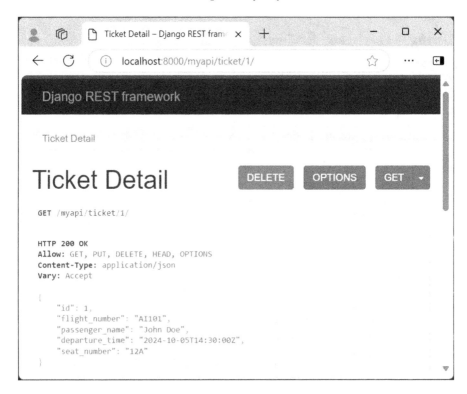

Figure 7-12. *Using APIView*

DRF – Generic Views

Again, you might recollect that you learned about the generic views in core Django as well. They (like `ListView, DetailView, CreateView`, etc.) are designed to be used in a classical web application that serves HTML templates. These views help you write concise code to perform the CURD operations (CRUD) on models and work well with Django's form system.

The generic views in Django REST Framework, on the other hand, are specifically designed to handle API requests and render serialized responses. While the function-based and class-based views are more verbose, the generic views in DRF simplify the creation of RESTful APIs that map closely to the database models by automating common actions while handling different HTTP methods.

The `rest_framework.generics` module defines the `GenericAPIView` class (which in fact extends the APIView class) that acts as the parent class for other concrete generic class-based views. As in the case of the core Django generic classes, in the case of DRF also, you need to design a custom class with one of the generic classes as the parent.

Different generic view classes in the generics module can be clubbed in two categories. In the first category, there is a separate view class that handles each of the HTTP methods.

> **ListAPIView:** A subclass of this view class handles the GET method that is to be mapped to a read-only API endpoint and fetches a collection of resources of a certain type (all the tickets in the Ticket model in this case).

> **CreateAPIView:** This view corresponds to the POST request, responsible for creating a new instance of the given model.

RetrieveAPIView: This view is responsible for handling a GET request that retrieves a single instance of the given model.

UpdateAPIView: As you would imagine, a subclass of this view class is mapped to the endpoint that will perform the UPDATE operation on a single model instance, in response to the PUT request.

DestroyAPIView: Finally, this view handles a DELETE method, causing a single model instance to be removed.

The subclasses of these views follow a similar syntax pattern:

```
from rest_framework import generics
class Class_name(generics.XXXAPIView):
    queryset = Ticket.objects.all()
    serializer_class = TicketSerializer
```

Here, XXX will be List, Create, Retrieve, Update, or Destroy. Let us assume the names of respective classes would be TicketList, NewTicket, TicketDetail, TicketUpdate, and TicketDelete.

As you must have noted, each of these views handles a different request. Hence, you need to form a different API endpoint to map with each.

Hence, the urlpatterns list has the following structure:

```
urlpatterns = [
    path('tickets/list/', views.TicketList.as_view()),
    path('tickets/new/', views.TicketNew.as_view()),
    path('tickets/detail/<int:pk>/', views.TicketDetail.as_
    view()),
```

```
path('tickets/update/<int:pk>/', views.TicketUpdate.as_
view()),
path('tickets/delete/<int:pk>/', views.TicketDelete.as_
view()),
]
```

The second category of classes in the generics module combines handling of more than one HTTP method.

Recall that we had two function-based views. The `tickets()` view function to process a GET method to fetch all the model instances and to create a new instance. The `ticket()` view function deals with the request that retrieves, updates, and deletes a single model instance. We had also registered two URL endpoints mapped to them: **'tickets/'** and **'ticket/<int:pk>/'**.

On similar lines, we have four different concrete generic view classes that combine more than one request handler.

> **ListCreateAPIView:** Subclass this view to fetch all the model instances in response to a GET request and as a POST handler to create a new instance.
>
> **RetrieveUpdateAPIView:** If you need to define a single endpoint for retrieval and update of a single instance, define a subclass of this view.
>
> **RetrieveDestroyAPIView:** Similarly, define a class with this generic class as the parent if you need to have an endpoint that sends requests for retrieval and deletion of a single resource.
>
> **RetrieveUpdateDestroyAPIView:** This is a generic class that works as a handler for requests of the type retrieval, update, and deletion of a single instance.

Generally, an API has two URL endpoints for performing the CRUD operations: one for fetching all instances and creating a new instance and the other to handle READ, UPDATE, and DELTE requests on a single instance.

Hence, the usual practice is to define a subclass of ListCreateAPIView (for the first endpoint) and another subclass of RetrieveUpdateDestroyAPIView (to be mapped with the second endpoint).

```
class TicketListCreateView(generics.ListCreateAPIView):
    queryset = Ticket.objects.all()
    serializer_class = TicketSerializer

class TicketRetrieveUpdateDeleteView(generics.
RetrieveUpdateDestroyAPIView):
    queryset = Ticket.objects.all()
    serializer_class = TicketSerializer
```

Accordingly, the urlpatterns list defines the URL mapping with these views:

```
urlpatterns = [
    path('tickets/', views.TicketListCreateView.as_view(),
    name='ticket-list'),
    path('tickets/<int:pk>/', views.TicketRetrieve
    UpdateDeleteView.as_view(), name='ticket-
    detail'),
]
```

Look how compact the API design has become with the use of these compound generic views. Another noteworthy feature of these generic views is that while testing the endpoints with the browsable API – especially those handling the POST and PUT requests – you get a nice HTML form (refer Figure 7-13) to send the request body data (the option to send it in JSON format is always there).

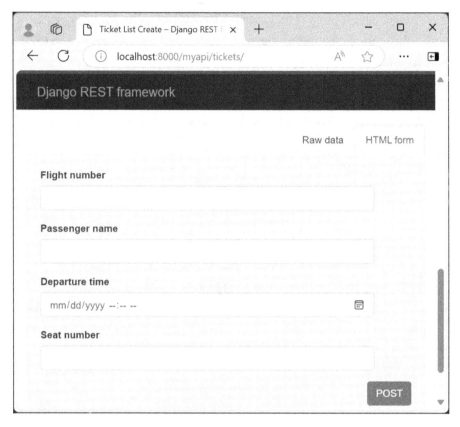

Figure 7-13. *Generic views provide an HTML form for the POST method*

ViewSets

The Django REST Framework offers another feature of ViewSet classes with which writing the CRUD operations becomes even more concise. In the previous section, you used two compound generic view classes – one to handle the list and create operations and the other to process the retrieve, update, and delete operations. With the ViewSet, a single class holds the handler methods for all the operations. The ViewSet class is defined in the `rest_framework.viewsets` module. Although the ViewSet is a type of class-based view, it doesn't include HTTP handler methods - like get() or post() - Instead, the names of the methods are indicative of the action to be performed – such as list(), create(), retrieve(), update(), and destroy() methods. These methods are bound to the HTTP methods when you map a URL endpoint to the as_view() method of the ViewSet. We shall shortly find out how the binding of the viewset actions with HTTP methods works.

ModelViewSet

In most use cases, we define a subclass of ModelViewSet class (instead of the ViewSet class); it includes the default implementations of actions (list(), retrieve(), create(), update(), and destroy()). As you would expect, the ModelViewSet class extends the GenericAPIView class. Hence, you need to set the queryset and serializer_class attributes.

Let us define a ModelViewSet class to handle the serialization of Ticket models, as in Listing 7-12.

Listing 7-12. Using ModelViewSet

```
from rest_framework import viewsets
from .models import Ticket
from .serializers import TicketSerializer

class TicketViewSet(viewsets.ModelViewSet):
    queryset = Ticket.objects.all()
    serializer_class = TicketSerializer
```

As mentioned earlier, the ViewSet actions are bound with the required HTTP methods to let Django know which type of HTTP requests you want to be processed when a particular endpoint is accessed. To maintain the consistency with the previous examples, when the client hits the **'tickets/'** URL with the GET request, it should perform the list() action; for POST request, the create() action should be invoked. This association is spelled out as a dict argument to the as_view() method of the ViewSet class.

```
urlpatterns = [
    path(
        'tickets/', views.TicketViewSet.as_view(
        {'get': 'list', 'post': 'create'}
        ), name='ticket-list'),
    path(
        'ticket/<int:pk>/', views.TicketViewSet.as_view(
        {'get': 'retrieve', 'put': 'update', 'delete':
        'destroy'}
        ), name='ticket-detail')
]
```

Note that the **'ticket/<int:pk>/'** URL invokes the retrieve(), update(), and destroy() actions, respectively, in the case of HTTP requests of the type GET, PUT, and DELETE.

Routers

Normally, you don't explicitly register the views in a viewset in the URLCONF as done here; instead, you'll register the viewset with a router class, which automatically creates the associations between the URLs and views.

The rest_framework.routers module includes the definitions of router classes. With the routers, you can quickly wire up your view logic to a set of URLs.

So far our approach to establish URL routing has been to construct the urlpatterns of a Django app and then include it in the URLCONF of the Django project. When using the routers, the urlpatterns of the app are no longer needed. All you need to do is to call the register() method of a Router class, which will automatically generate the urlpatterns for a given viewset. You can then include the urls property of the Router in the URLCONF of the project. Effectively, the need of the urlpatterns list of the Django app is eliminated.

The routers module includes two classes: `SimpleRouter` and `DefaultRouter`. While the behavior is more or less the same, the `DefualtRouter` generates an additional root view that returns a response containing hyperlinks to all the list views.

To let DRF generate the urlpatterns, obtain an object of `DefaultRouter` class and call its `register()` method, as the Listing 7-13 does.

Listing 7-13. Registering router

```
from rest_framework.routers import DefaultRouter
from myapi.views import TicketViewSet

router = DefaultRouter()
router.register('tickets', TicketViewSet)
```

The `register()` method needs two arguments:

> **prefix:** A string that serves as the URL prefix for the viewset. In the above example, the value of prefix is **'tickets'**, which means that the URLs for listing, creating, retrieving, updating, and deleting tickets will be prefixed with /**tickets**/.

> **viewset:** The viewset class you want to associate with this prefix. This should be a subclass of ViewSet or ModelViewSet that defines the actions (list, create, retrieve, update, destroy) you want.

The various HTTP methods, the ViewSet actions bound to them, and the corresponding auto-generated URL routes are summarized in Table 7-1.

Table 7-1. *URL routes of ViewSet*

URL Route	HTTP Method	Action	URL Name
myapi/	GET	Automatically generated root view	api-root
myapi/tickets/	GET	list( )	ticket-list
	POST	create( )	
myapi/tickets/pk	GET	retrieve( )	ticket-detail
	PUT	update( )	
	DELETE	destroy( )	

Once this is done, the auto-generated urlpatterns are added to the urlpatterns list of the Django project (not the Django app).

```
urlpatterns = [
    path('admin/', admin.site.urls),
    path('myapi/', include(router.urls)),
]
```

The URL http://localhost:8000/myapi/ is the Api root of your REST server. Check if the browser output is as shown in Figure 7-14.

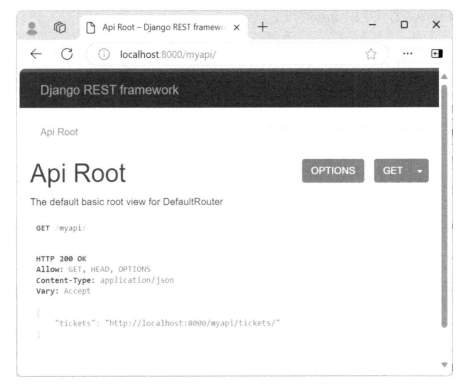

Figure 7-14. *Auto-generated Api root*

DRF – Authentication

How does the authentication work? The user authentication is performed before the execution of a view mapped to a certain URL route. It is only after the user is authenticated that the view code is processed.

You have already learned how the authentication system works in the core Django, wherein once the user is logged in, multiple requests may be handled till they log out – that is till the session lasts. The Django REST Framework expands on it specifically for the API scenario. As you know, the API interactions are REST compliant, which means that they are stateless.

Another important point of difference in how the authentication works in Django and DRF is that in the case of the former, it relies on session authentication, whereas there are multiple authentication schemes available for the latter.

Apart from Django's default session authentication, Django REST Framework provides out-of-the-box support for the following authentication schemes:

> **BasicAuthentication:** Under this type of authentication, the client includes the username and password of the user with each request. It is recommended for testing purpose and not suitable for the production environment as including the user credentials in the request poses a security threat.

> **TokenAuthentication:** This is a much more robust option for authentication of client requests where a unique token is generated for each user and that is sent with each request as the Authorization header.

With the Ticketing API that we now have, any user can perform any ticketing operations. Ideally, you would like to restrict the access to only those users who have been authenticated, and the user is authorized to perform the operation.

As you install Django REST Framework, you need to include the REST_ FRAMEWORK section in the *settings.py* module of your project. Here, you specify the global authentication schemes to be used. Let us include BasicAuthentication and SessionAuthentication as the DEFAULT_ AUTHENTICATION_CLASSES:

```
REST_FRAMEWORK = {
    'DEFAULT_AUTHENTICATION_CLASSES': (
        'rest_framework.authentication.BasicAuthentication',
```

```
        'rest_framework.authentication.SessionAuthentication',
    )
}
```

Also, the DEFAULT_PERMISSION_CLASSES variable sets the permission types globally.

```
REST_FRAMEWORK = {
    'DEFAULT_PERMISSION_CLASSES': [
        'rest_framework.permissions.IsAuthenticated',
    ]
}
```

To enforce the permission on the view, include the permission_classes attribute in our TicketViewSet class (Listing 7-14).

Listing 7-14. permission_classes attribute

```
from rest_framework.permissions import IsAuthenticated

class TicketViewSet(viewsets.ModelViewSet):
    queryset = Ticket.objects.all()
    serializer_class = TicketSerializer
    permission_classes = [IsAuthenticated]
```

As a result, the **'tickets/'** endpoint responds with a 403 Forbidden message. Obviously, this means that the client needs to log in as one of the users in the User model in the contrib.auth package.

You can first visit the admin site URL, log in, and then fire a request to the **'tickets/'** endpoint to get past the IsAuthenticated permission and obtain the list of tickets as the response. Instead, you can add the login view to the browsable API itself. Include rest_framework.urls in the URLCONF of your project.

```
urlpatterns += [
    path('', include('rest_framework.urls')),
]
```

The browsable API shows a Login link toward the top right of the browser, as the Figure 7-15 shows.

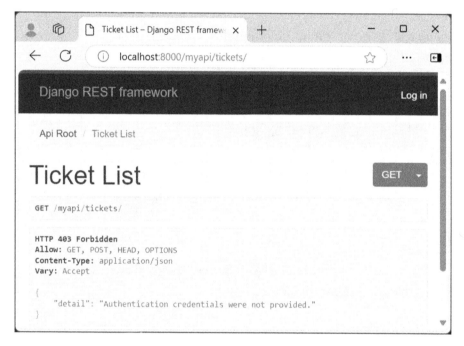

Figure 7-15. *Unauthenticated request*

This link takes the browser to the login page of the admin site. After successfully logging in, the browser returns to the view protected with the IsAuthenticated permission.

TokenAuthentication

Using BasicAuthentication is simple but poses a considerable security risk as the user credentials are included with each request. Apart from testing purpose, it is not advisable to be used in the production environment.

The other authentication scheme that DRF supports is TokenAuthentication. It can be effectively implemented in situations where client-server setups are required.

To enable this scheme globally, it should be added to the list of DEFAULT_AUTHENTICATION_CLASSES:

```
REST_FRAMEWORK = {
    'DEFAULT_AUTHENTICATION_CLASSES': [
        'rest_framework.authentication.BasicAuthentication',
        'rest_framework.authentication.SessionAuthentication',
        'rest_framework.authentication.TokenAuthentication',
    ]
}
```

Additionally, the list of INSTALLED_APPS should have the rest_framework.authtoken app added in it.

```
INSTALLED_APPS = [
    . . .
    'rest_framework.authtoken',
    . . .,
]
```

This app needs the authtoken model to be added to the current database. Hence, you need to run the migrations:

```
python manage.py migrate
Operations to perform:
```

```
Apply all migrations: admin, auth, authtoken, contenttypes,
myapi, sessions
Running migrations:
  Applying authtoken.0001_initial... OK
  Applying authtoken.0002_auto_20160226_1747... OK
  Applying authtoken.0003_tokenproxy... OK
  Applying authtoken.0004_alter_tokenproxy_options... OK
```

To understand how the token authentication works, let us define a function-based view in the *views.py* module. Unlike in the viewset, in a function-based view, the authentication is enforced by the @permission_ classes annotation.

```
from rest_framework.decorators import api_view,
permission_classes

@api_view()
@permission_classes([IsAuthenticated])
def authenticated_view(request):
    return Response({"message":"Hello, This is a
    protected view"})
```

Obviously, you need to add a path that maps an endpoint (**'secured/'**) with this function. When visited, the authentication naturally fails, and you get the HTTP 401 Unauthorized response with an appropriate WWW-Authenticate header.

```
WWW-Authenticate: Basic realm="api"
```

Token authentication mechanism involves generating a token and then including it as a Header in the request. A token is a long alphanumeric string that is a unique identity of the user.

The TokenAuthentication class defines the obtain_auth_token view, which, when invoked with POST request, returns the token string. Let us add a URL route that invokes this view in the URLCONF of the Django project.

```
from rest_framework.authtoken.views import obtain_auth_token
from myapi import views
urlpatterns += [
    path('secured/', views.authenticated_view),
    path('api-token/', obtain_auth_token),
]
```

To generate the Auth token, log in to the admin site of your Django application. You will find the AUTH TOKEN section in the site administration page. Refer to the Figure 7-16.

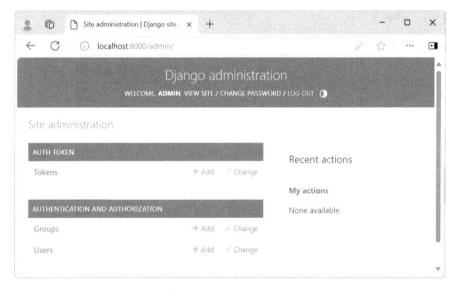

Figure 7-16. *Tokens model*

Choose the admin user and save the Auth token generated for it (Figure 7-17).

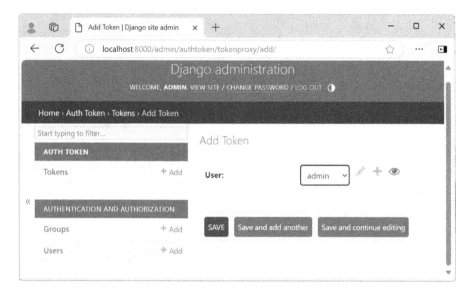

Figure 7-17. *Adding a token*

As you can see in Figure 7-18, under the list of generated tokens, you'll now find the token key corresponding to admin user.

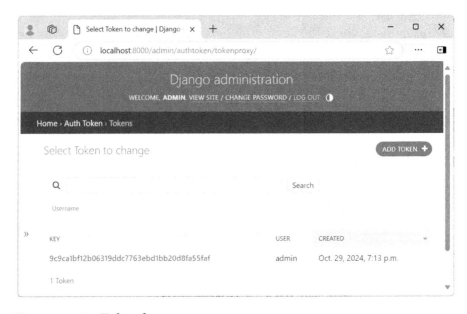

Figure 7-18. *Token key*

Now that the token is generated, go back and visit the endpoint
(Figure 7-19) that runs the protected view in your API; the browser displays
its response after it passes the authentication.

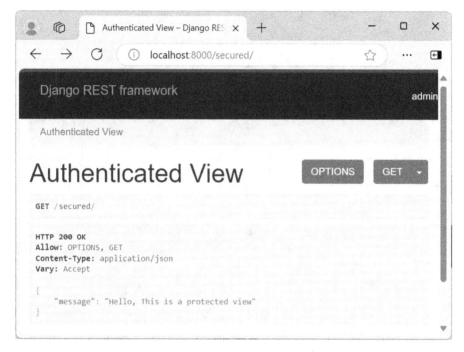

Figure 7-19. *Authenticated view*

You also have the option to use any third-party HTTP client. Here, we use HTTPie to obtain the token, as the Figure 7-20 shows.

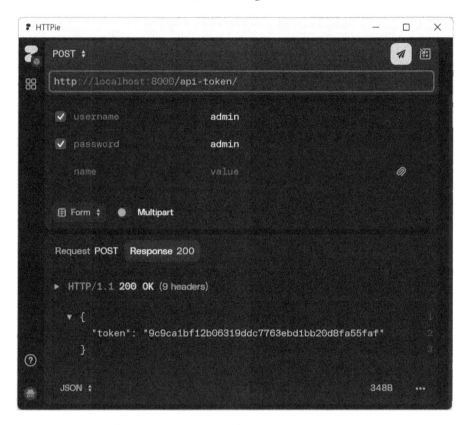

Figure 7-20. *Token generation with HTTPie*

Then, include the generated token in the Authorization header when visiting the URL to your protected view to obtain its response (Figure 7-21).

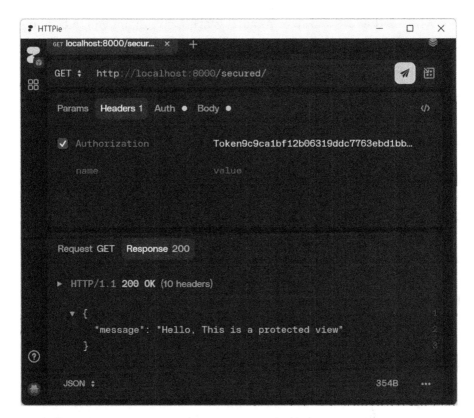

Figure 7-21. *Authenticated response in HTTPie*

You can generate the token Django's drf_create_token management command made available by the 'rest_framework.authtoken' app you had included in the project's settings. Execute the following statement in the command terminal of your operating system. You need to specify the user for which the token is to be created.

```
python manage.py drf_create_token admin
Generated token 9c9ca1bf12b06319ddc7763ebd1bb20d8fa55faf for
user admin
```

While in the command terminal, this cURL command will fetch you the response of the protected view in your API.

```
curl -H "Authorization: Token
9c9ca1bf12b06319ddc7763ebd1bb20d8fa55faf" http://
localhost:8000/secured/
{"message":"Hello, This is a protected view"}
```

In addition to these built-in authentication schemes, many third-party Django apps are also available. For example, the `djangorestframework-simplejwt` package is a JWT plug-in for Django REST Framework. It implements the JSON Web Token (JWT) authentication. Then there is also the `django-oauth2` package that adds the OAuth2Authentication to your DRF app. However, the discussion of these types of authentication has been excluded from the scope of this book.

Alternatives to DRF

Django REST Framework is by far the most powerful Django app when it comes to building REST APIs. It comes with all the necessary features (such as authentication, permission handling, pagination, etc.). Having said that, there are a few other Django packages for API creation, each with its own distinct features.

Django Ninja is one such reusable app in the Django ecosystem. It leverages the features of modern Python such as async support and type hints to build high-performance and lightweight APIs. We shall explore this app in the next section.

Tastypie has been in use as a tool for API development. However, it hasn't been able to match with DRF in offering a number of advanced features.

The **Graphene-Django** package lets you develop GraphQL APIs rather than REST APIs. Its ability to integrate with Django models is one of its important features. We shall discuss Graphene-Django in a later chapter.

Django Channels is an ideal choice if you intend to have Python applications having WebSocket support along with the regular REST API endpoints. You will know more about Channels later in the book.

Django Ninja

This is one app that has been making rapid strides in the popularity rankings of Django packages. Django Ninja, with its ability to leverage Python features like async support and type hints, lets you build lightweight yet high-performance APIs. Django Ninja is highly inspired by FastAPI, another popular asynchronous web framework.

Like FastAPI, Django Ninja also uses **Pydantic** for request and response data validation. Django Ninja also provides the auto-generated API documentation with Swagger UI.

Let us go ahead and build a ticketing API with Django Ninja. To start with, install it with the PIP utility.

```
pip install django-ninja
```

This installs the required dependencies – annotated-types, pydantic, and typing-extensions.

Just like any other reusable app, add ninja to the INSTALLED_APPS list (along with your testing API app named as api).

```
INSTALLED_APPS = [
    . . . ,
    'ninja',
    'api',
]
```

An object of NinjaAPI class in the ninja package is the main application object. It is responsible for managing the API endpoints, automatic documentation, Pydantic integration, etc. Apart from the others, its decorator methods – @api.get(), @api.post(), @api.put(), and @api.delete() – help in defining the API endpoints.

These decorator methods map a given endpoint to a view function defined just below it. Let's define a /**hello** endpoint (refer Listing 7-15) that, when visited with a GET request, calls the test() view function and renders a Hello World response.

Listing 7-15. NinjaAPI object

```
from ninja import NinjaAPI

api = NinjaAPI()

@api.get("/hello")
def test(request):
    return {'message': 'Hello World!'}
```

As usual, you need to update the URLCONF of the Django project by including the api/ as the base URL to the endpoints in your app.

```
from django.contrib import admin
from django.urls import path
from api.views import api

urlpatterns = [
    path('admin/', admin.site.urls),
    path('api/', api.urls)
]
```

As usual, you obtain the Hello World response with the http://localhost:8000/api/hello route. One of the important features of Django Ninja – the auto-generated API documentation will be available http://localhost:8000/api/docs URL in the browser.

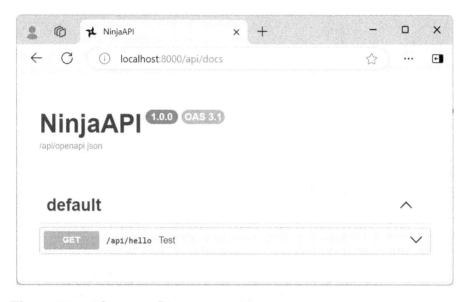

Figure 7-22. *Swagger Docs*

Test the GET response by executing the mapped method. The OpenAPI
(known as Swagger UI) documentation reveals the cURL equivalent
of the request, the response body along with the status code, etc.
The Figure 7-23 shows a typical Swagger UI result.

Figure 7-23. *Testing with Swagger UI*

However, you would like the API to send the HTTP requests to perform CRUD operations on the Ticket model used earlier. To validate the data returned by the server in response to GET requests, as well as the data sent to the server as a part of the request body as a part of the POST request, you need to define a subclass of Schema class, as in Listing 7-16. The Schema class in Django Ninja is inherited from the BaseModel class in the Pydantic library.

Listing 7-16. Ninja Schema

```
from datetime import datetime
from ninja import Schema

class TicketSchema(Schema):
    flight_number : str
    passenger_name : str
```

```
departure_time : datetime
seat_number : str
```

The **tickets/** endpoint invokes the tickets() view when requested with the GET method. The server response is the list of Ticket instances cast as a list of TicketSchema objects.

```
from typing import List
from .models import TicketSchema, Ticket
@api.get("/tickets", response=List[TicketSchema])
def tickets(request):
    return Ticket.objects.all()
```

The Swagger UI (refer Figure 7-24) shows that the tickets() view has been mapped to the tickets/ URL.

Figure 7-24. *TicketSchema in Swagger UI*

You can test this endpoint to find its response body to be the list of tickets with a 200OK as the status code, as displayed in Figure 7-25.

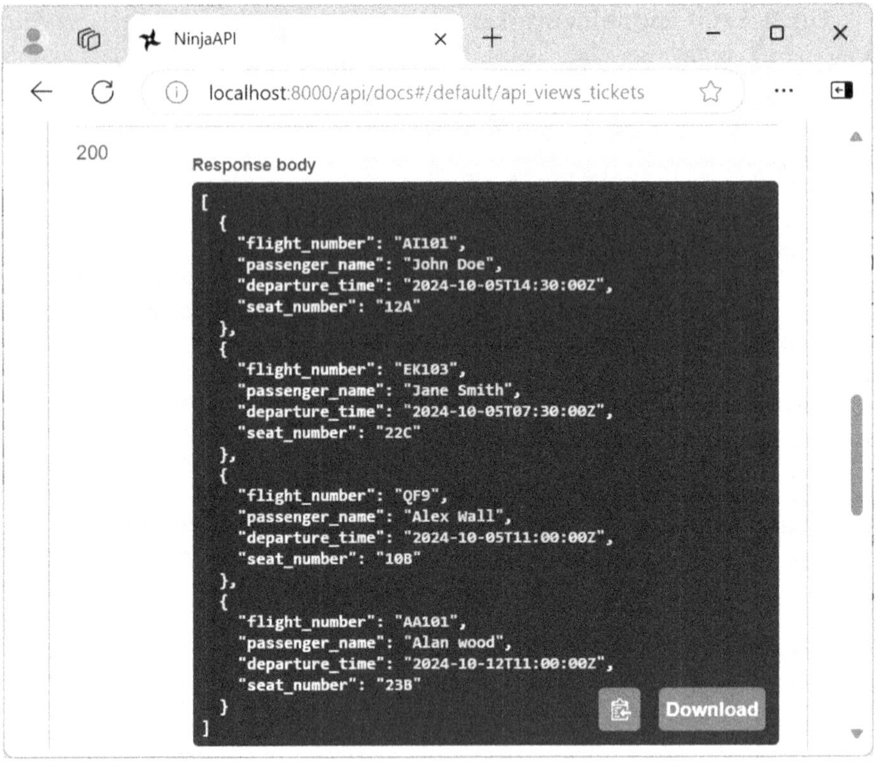

Figure 7-25. *JSON response*

Similarly, the create_ticket() view function handles the POST request. The response argument to the api.post() decorator specifies that the server response has to be a newly created Ticket instance.

```
@api.post("/tickets", response={201: TicketSchema})
def create_ticket(request, ticket: TicketSchema):
    Ticket.objects.create(**ticket.dict())
    return ticket
```

Figure 7-26 shows how it reflects in the Swagger UI documentation.

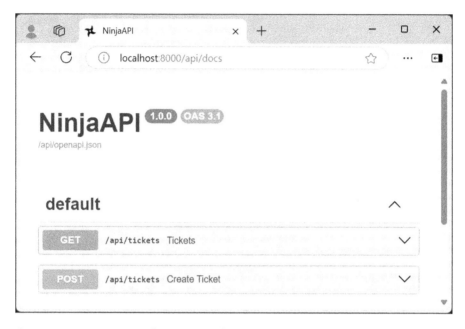

Figure 7-26. *GET and POST endpoints in Swagger UI*

Go ahead and test the POST endpoint (Figure 7-27). You need to populate the request body as the data for a new Ticket object in JSON form.

Figure 7-27. *Request body in Swagger UI*

The Figure 7-28 shows that the Swagger UI generates 201 as the status code with the newly added ticket in the response body.

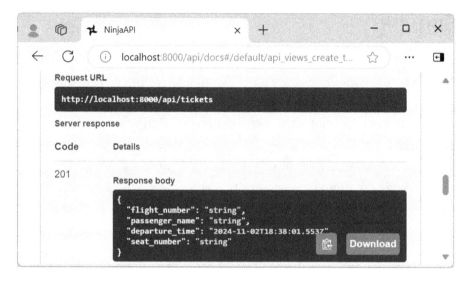

Figure 7-28. *Response showing the creation of new resource*

You can easily expand the code to add the other API endpoint tickets/ pk to process the remaining HTTP methods – GET, PUT, and DELETE.

Thus, Django Ninja offers a simple and lightweight alternative to the DRF-based API. It also supports Python's async capabilities. So you can also write async views in your API. Django Ninja also provides the features such as authentication, pagination, and throttling. Since this section is intended to provide just an overview of Django Ninja, the more advanced features are not discussed here.

Summary

This chapter covers an important aspect of modern web development – the REST API. With the Django REST Framework as the API creation tool, you learned how to add essential features such as authentication to your API. You also had a brief introduction to Django Ninja – a new kid on the block.

Next, we move on to another powerful API protocol – GraphQL – and learn how to build Django apps that serve GraphQL queries with Strawberry and Graphene.

CHAPTER 8

GraphQL with Django

For long, REST has been the go-to choice of developers for handling efficient data exchange between the clients and the servers. However, owing to the complex requirements of client-side applications that need flexibility and efficiency in fetching the data, GraphQL has emerged as an alternative API technology.

In this chapter, you are going to be introduced to the concepts of GraphQL and how you can build powerful GraphQL-based API solutions with the help of Django apps.

Some of the topics to be discussed in this chapter are

- GraphQL vs. REST

- GraphQL features

- GraphQL architecture

- Schema Definition Language

- GraphQL and Python

- Strawberry

- Strawberry-Django

- Graphene

- Graphene-Django

© Malhar Lathkar 2025
M. Lathkar, *Modern Django Web Development*,
https://doi.org/10.1007/979-8-8688-1472-3_8

GraphQL vs. REST

Ever since Roy Fielding proposed the concept in the year 2000, REST has been the de facto standard for developing API solutions. However, over a period, developers started finding certain limitations and shortcomings in the concept of REST. In certain situations, REST proves to be rather inefficient. One must first understand these limitations and then find out how GraphQL tries to address them.

While REST is an architectural style that defines how the web services should interact with each other, GraphQL is a query language for APIs with which a client can specify what data it needs.

In the case of a REST API, when the client sends a request to an endpoint, it fetches the data that is either more or less than it requires. This over-fetching or under-fetching introduces inefficiency. The GraphQL API, on the other hand, is capable of fetching the information exactly as required.

As you have seen throughout, the REST application consists of multiple endpoints and responds to different HTTP methods. In contrast, the GraphQL API has only one endpoint for all types of operations on a resource. REST relies on HTTP verbs (GET, POST, PUT, and DELETE) to indicate the type of operation, whereas GraphQL requests use queries for fetching data and mutations for creating new resources/modifying an existing resource.

Having said that, REST and GraphQL APIs can be used interchangeably. But as a thumb rule, GraphQL may be a better choice in case of a limited bandwidth, as it minimizes the number of requests and responses. It may also be helpful in situations where the client requests vary significantly and you expect very different responses.

All in all, the differences between the two can be summarized as in Table 8-1.

Table 8-1. REST vs. GraphQL

REST	GraphQL
REST is a set of constraints that defines structured data exchange between a client and a server.	GraphQL is a query language, for APIs with which a client can specify what data it needs.
REST has multiple endpoints for various operations on the resource.	GraphQL has a single URL endpoint.
REST returns data in a fixed structure defined by the server.	Data returned by a GraphQL query in a flexible structure defined by the client.
With REST, the client must check if the returned data is valid.	With GraphQL, invalid requests are typically rejected by schema structure.
REST is good for simple data sources where resources are well defined.	GraphQL is good for large, complex, and interrelated data sources.

Facebook (now Meta) started the development of GraphQL in 2012. It has since been open-sourced and moved to GraphQL Foundation. GraphQL is now being extensively used in many popular public APIs of Facebook, GitHub, etc.

GraphQL Architecture

GraphQL specifications describe how a GraphQL server functions. In most of the use cases, a GraphQL server interacts with a connected database. The clients (web or mobile clients) communicate with the server through the GraphQL API. The server fetches the resources from the database in response to the GraphQL queries. Sometimes the server acts as a layer in front of multiple systems and integrates them with the GraphQL API. GraphQL is transport-agnostic, meaning it can operate over various protocols (such as HTTP, WebSocket, gRPC, etc.) depending on the application's requirements. Figure 8-1 schematically represents the architecture of the GraphQL system.

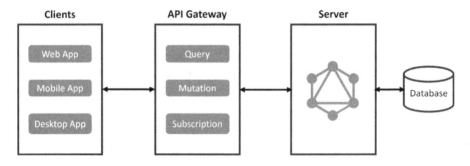

Figure 8-1. *GraphQL architecture*

Schema Definition Language

In GraphQL, the structure of the API is written using the Schema Definition Language (SDL). The GraphQL API itself comprises important building blocks such as types, queries, mutations, subscriptions, and schema.

Types

Types are equivalent of data types in any programming language. The data objects to be queried are described in the form of types. There are two data types in GraphQL; scalar types are the primitive types, and object types are the user-defined data types.

Scalar types are the predefined primitive types.

Int: A signed 32-bit integer

Float: A signed double-precision floating-point number

String: A sequence of UTF-8 encoded characters

Boolean: True or false

ID: A unique identifier

Object types are similar to Python classes, representing complex objects with one or more fields of either scalar types or other object types.

Listing 8-1 is an example of an object defined in GraphQL.

Listing 8-1. GraphQL type

```
type Book {
  id: ID!
  title: String!
  author: String
  price: Int
}
```

Book is a GraphQL Object type, meaning it's a type with some fields. To indicate that a field is of Not-Null type, SDL needs it to be post-fixed by an exclamation mark (!).

The GraphQL Schema defines what different operations can be performed on the given Object type. The Query operation defines the ready-only fetch operations, and the Mutation operation defines the write and update operations.

Queries

Every GraphQL schema must support the query operation. The composition of query lets the client decide exactly which fields are expected to be retrieved from the server. This is precisely how a GraphQL API avoids over-fetching and under-fetching issues faced with REST API.

A GraphQL query that fetches title and price of a Book type could be written as shown in Listing 8-2.

Listing 8-2. GraphQL query

```
query {
  book {
    title
    price
  }
}
```

The query keyword indicates the retrieve operation, book being the object type queried. The book query in the schema resolves to the Book object. The inner pair of braces is the payload of the query, specifying the fields to be fetched (title and price).

If the server had an instance of Book type (title="Numerical Python", author="Johansan", and price=4000), the server response might look like that shown in Listing 8-3.

Listing 8-3. Query result

```
{
  "data": {
    "book": {
      "title": "Numerical Python",
       author: "Johansan",
      "price": 4000
```

```
    }
  }
}
```

A query can include arguments if you want specific objects to be fetched. For example, to fetch the book with a given id (provided you have defined the Book type with id as one of its fields), the query would be as shown in Listing 8-4.

Listing 8-4. Query with arguments

```
query {
  book(id: "1") {
    title
    price
  }
}
```

In this case, the server would resolve the query for the book with id = 1.

Mutations

Mutations are equivalent of the POST, PUT, and DELETE in the REST API. It clearly means that mutations are used to create, modify, or delete data on the server.

Mutation fields are one of the root operation types that provide an entry point to the API. The mutation keyword is used to define operations for creating, modifying, as well as deleting the data.

Taking the example of Book type further, a mutation type to add a new book is defined as that shown in Listing 8-5.

Listing 8-5. GraphQL mutation

```
mutation {
  createBook(title: "Numerical Python", author="Johansan",
  price: 750) {
    title
    author
    price
  }
}
```

You can similarly define mutation types for updating and deleting a book.

Subscriptions

Subscription allows a GraphQL server to push notifications of real-time updates to the clients that subscribe to a specified event. Subscription is a way to establish a long-lived connection between the client and the server. Unlike in the case of the REST, where the client polls the server at intervals, the server pushes updates to the client when specific events occur.

An example of GraphQL Subscription type is shown in Listing 8-6.

Listing 8-6. GraphQL subscription

```
subscription {
  newBookAdded {
    title
    author
    price
  }
}
```

Schema

A GraphQL schema is the blueprint that defines the structure, types, and capabilities of a GraphQL API. The three root types – queries, mutations, and subscriptions – are part of the schema definition. These root types act as entry points for interacting with the GraphQL API.

The query type defines the structure for read operations in the API, mutation defines the structure for write operations, while the subscription type defines the structure for real-time updates.

For the Book type example, the GraphQL schema can be expressed as shown in Listing 8-7.

Listing 8-7. GraphQL schema

```
type Query {
  books: [Book]
  book(id: ID!): Book
}
type Mutation {
  addBook(title: String!, author: String, price: Int): Book
}

type Subscription {
  bookAdded: Book
}

schema {
  query: Query
  mutation: Mutation
  subscription: Subscription
}
```

GraphQL and Python

It is possible to construct a GraphQL API service in any language, and the core components of SDL (Schema Definition Language) can be built with many different approaches.

Python, because of its clean syntax and ease of use, is found to be extremely suitable. Python ecosystem has many excellent libraries like Graphene, Strawberry, and Ariadne for implementing GraphQL APIs and can be seamlessly integrated with the Django framework.

In this chapter, you'll explore how to use Strawberry and Graphene libraries, especially their Django-specific apps Strawberry-Django and Graphene-Django.

Graphene is a framework-agnostic Python library. It allows you to define your schema and integrate queries, mutations, and subscriptions. Graphene-Django is a popular Django reusable app, providing easy integration with Django ORM models. It has adequate tools for connecting Django's authentication and permissions to GraphQL resolvers.

In comparison, Strawberry is a more recent library with which you can leverage features of modern Python, such as type hints and async support. Strawberry-Django is built on top of Strawberry.

Both these libraries take different approach toward GraphQL implementation. Each one has its own design philosophy and features.

As far as the definition of GraphQL schema is concerned, in Graphene, a schema is defined using Python classes. Strawberry, on the other hand, makes use of Python's @dataclass decorator for defining types. This lets you leverage the feature of type hints, making it more intuitive.

Graphene has its own field types (graphene.String, graphene.Int, etc.), while Strawberry uses Python's native type hints for field definitions, making it more natural and readable. This, as a result, enhances the type safety and integrates well with Python's type-checking tools.

Graphene has been around for a while. The `graphene-django` package is a popular choice among developers to integrate GraphQL in a Django app. `Strawberry` is comparatively recent, but making rapid strides in the popularity charts owing to its ability to support powerful features of modern Python such as `dataclass`, type hints, and asynchronous processing.

Programming languages and their libraries adapt either a code-first approach or a schema-first approach for defining the GraphQL schema. In the code-first approach, the schema is defined programmatically in classes or functions representing types, queries, mutations, and resolvers. The schema is automatically generated from the code. On the other hand, the schema is written using the GraphQL Schema Definition Language (**SDL**). The resolvers are implemented in the corresponding language, followed by connecting the schema and the resolvers. `Strawberry` uses the code-first approach, whereas a hybrid approach is adopted by Graphene.

Strawberry

As mentioned earlier, `Strawberry` is a library for GraphQL API development, based on modern Python (Python 3.8 onward). It supports all the latest features of Python including type hints, async support, dataclasses, generics, etc. These features help you in building high-performance, nonblocking GraphQL APIs.

Naturally, one has to start by getting `Strawberry` installed in the current working environment. Use PIP installer to install `strawberry-graphql` package from PyPI repository. One of the unique features of Strawberry is that it also provides a development server (similar to Django development server) to test the GraphQL API in an interactive playground. So install Strawberry along with the development server with the following command:

```
pip install "strawberry-graphql[debug-server]"
```

It has also been mentioned earlier that Strawberry uses the code-first approach for defining GraphQL schema. The `@strawberry.type` decorator is the cornerstone of Strawberry's code-first approach. Put this decorator on top of a Python class and it will be transformed into a GraphQL object type.

You can, therefore, define a Book type with the code in Listing 8-8.

Listing 8-8. Strawberry type

```
import strawberry

@strawberry.type
class Book:
    title: str
    author: str
    price: int
```

Strawberry coverts the Book class into the corresponding GraphQL object type with fields: `title`, `author`, and `price`.

The type annotation feature of Python lets you indicate the expected data type when you define an attribute. The Python types (`str` and `int`) are mapped to their corresponding GraphQL types (String and Int).

The generated GraphQL schema would be

```
type Book {
  title: String!
  author: String!
  price: Int!
}
```

The Query type is similarly defined by decorating the Query class with the `@strawberry.type` decorator. To fetch a Book object, you need to define a resolver function. It must be decorated by the `@strawberry.field` decorator, as in Listing 8-9.

Listing 8-9. Strawberry Query

```
@strawberry.type
class Query:
    @strawberry.field
    def book(self) -> Book:
        return Book(title="Numerical Python",
        author="Johansan", price = 750)
```

The schema object is obtained by calling the `strawberry.Schema()` constructor and passing the Query type to it as an argument.

```
schema = strawberry.Schema(query=Query)
```

Strawberry package comes with an embedded development server with which you can test and debug your API in the GraphQL playground.

Put the above code for Book type and Query type in a Python script (Listing 8-10) *app.py.*

Listing 8-10. app.py (Strawberry schema)

```
import strawberry

@strawberry.type
class Book:
    title: str
    author: str
    price: int

@strawberry.type
class Query:
    @strawberry.field
    def book(self) -> Book:
        return Book(title="Numerical Python",
        author="Johansan", price: 750)

schema = strawberry.Schema(query=Query)
```

311

Start the Strawberry server with the following command:

```
>strawberry server app
Running strawberry on http://0.0.0.0:8000/graphql
```

Open your browser and point it to the URL http://localhost:8000/
graphql to start **GraphiQL** – a browser-based user interface with which you
can interactively execute queries against a GraphQL API.

Display the explorer bar of the interface, and add a new Query by the
name NewQuery. Select the required fields to be fetched. (Select all the
fields for now.) It will generate the following GraphQL query code:

```
query NewQuery {
  book {
    author
    price
    title
  }
}
```

Click the ▶ button to run the query. The result will be displayed in the
output pane on the right (as in Figure 8-2).

Figure 8-2. *GraphiQL interface*

Let us add a mutation type to the API, as in Listing 8-11. Strawberry provides the @strawberry.mutation decorator to be put on top of the function inside the Mutation class.

Listing 8-11. app.py (Strawberry mutation)

```
@strawberry.type
class Mutation:
    @strawberry.mutation
    def add_book(self, title: str, author: str, price: int)
    -> Book:
        print(f"Adding new book: {title}")

        return Book(title=title, author=author, price=price)
```

Start the server again and run the GraphQL mutation in the GraphiQL interface.

```
mutation NewMutaton {
  addBook(author: "Johansan",
    price: 750,
    title: "Numerical Python")
  {
    author
    price
    title
  }
}
```

Update the declaration of the Schema object by including the mutation argument in its constructor.

```
schema = strawberry.Schema(query=Query, mutation=Mutation)
```

The browser displays the result as shown in Figure 8-3.

Figure 8-3. *GraphiQL showing mutation*

You can make the definition of query and mutation more flexible by defining resolver functions with arguments and passing their values while executing the schema. To define a variable, Strawberry requires it to be prefixed by the $ symbol.

The NewMutation type (in Listing 8-12) accepts three variables: $title, $author, and $price (first two of String! and the third of Int! type). The addbook() resolver then uses them to initialize the fields.

Listing 8-12. Mutation with variables

```
mutation NewMutaton(
  $title:String!,$author:String!,  $price: Int!
) {
  addBook(title: $title,
    author: $author,
    price: $price)
  {
```

```
      author
      price
      title
    }
}
```

The values for these variables are assigned in the variables editor section at the bottom of the **GraphiQL** interface.

```
{
  "title": "Numerical Python",
  "author": "Johansan",
  "price": 750
}
```

On running the schema, the output is displayed as shown in Figure 8-4.

Figure 8-4. *GraphiQL interface with Variable editor*

A GraphQL schema can have more than one query and mutation – especially for update and delete operations. The resolver functions usually consist of business logic that adds, updates, or deletes records in a connected database table.

Strawberry-Django is an ideal Django package to build a data-driven GraphQL API. Strawberry has various ports for seamlessly integrating with various other Python web frameworks such as Flask and FastAPI. In the next section, you will explore how to add Strawberry to a Django application.

Strawberry-Django

The integration of GraphQL with Django is facilitated by the Python package Strawberry-GraphQL-Django. This package makes it very easy to generate GraphQL types, queries, mutations, and resolvers from the Django's ORM.

Start by installing this package with the PIP utility.

```
pip install strawberry-graphql-django
```

As usual, start a new Django project and an app. Add the 'strawberry.django' app along with your app in the INSTALLED_APPS list.

```
INSTALLED_APPS = [
    . . .,
    'strawberry.django',
    'myapi',
]
```

Strawberry-Django provides a built-in view called AsyncGraphQLView. It is defined in the strawberry.django.views module and is specifically designed to handle asynchronous GraphQL requests in Django applications. A standard synchronous counterpart of this view – GraphQLView – is also available in the same module.

To serve the Schema object (as defined in the app.py script above), you need to add AsyncGraphQLView in the URLCONF of your Django project. Modify your project's urls.py as per the code in Listing 8-13.

Listing 8-13. URLCONF with AsyncGraphQLView

```
from django.contrib import admin
from django.urls import path
from strawberry.django.views import AsyncGraphQLView
from myapi.app import schema

urlpatterns = [
    path('admin/', admin.site.urls),
    path('graphql', AsyncGraphQLView.as_view(schema=schema)),
]
```

Make sure that the app.py script is present in the myapi package folder. If you start the Django development server, the URL http://localhost:8000/graphql/ now serves the GraphQL API, and you can test the query and mutation as done earlier.

The Strawberry-Django app brings much more functionality than just the ability to serve the core Strawberry at the URL mapped to the GraphQLView. The @strawberry_django.type decorator defined in this package is extremely powerful. It extends the functionality of the core Strawberry's @strawberry.type decorator by integrating with Django models, allowing automatic mapping of model fields to GraphQL fields when you need to define GraphQL types based on Django models.

Let us use the same book model in for a new Django project that uses the Strawberry-Django app to build a GraphQL API and add a functionality to perform CRUD operations on the mapped SQLite database table.

Instead of @strawberry.type, use the @strawberry_django.type decorator to map a BookType class to a GraphQL type. Pass the book model as an argument.

317

Listing 8-14 shows the code for *models.py* in the app.

Listing 8-14. models.py

```python
from django.db import models
import strawberry_django
import strawberry

# Create your models here.
class Book(models.Model):
    id = models.IntegerField(primary_key=True)
    title = models.CharField(max_length=50)
    author = models.CharField(max_length=50)
    price = models.IntegerField()
    publisher = models.CharField(max_length=50)

    class Meta:
        db_table = "books"

@strawberry_django.type(Book)
class BookType:
    id: strawberry.ID
    title: str
    author: str
    price: int
    publisher: str
```

In the earlier case, you had defined a query class (decorated by
@strawberry.type which you will now replace by @strawberry_django.
type) and defined a resolver function in it to return Book objects. In the
strawberry-Django package, the @strawberry_django.field decorator
automatically handles fetching data for the specified model fields. The
Django model fields are mapped directly to GraphQL fields. As such, you
don't need to write resolvers for basic fetch operations.

Listing 8-15 shows how a query is defined for the Django app implementing a GraphQL API.

Listing 8-15. Query with strawberry_django.field()

```
import strawberry
@strawberry.type
class Query:
    all_books: list[BookType] = strawberry_django.field()
```

That's it. The all_books field effectively acts as the resolver function decorated by @strawberry.field in the core strawberry example. Obtain the Schema object, using the above Query class as an argument.

```
schema = strawberry.Schema(query=Query)
```

Start the Django server, and enter the following code in the query designer of the GraphiQL interface:

```
query MyQuery{
allBooks {
  id
  title
  author
  publisher
  price
}
}
```

The selected fields from all the records in the books table in your database will be fetched, as shown in Figure 8-5.

Figure 8-5. *Query fetching books from the database*

You can also apply filter criteria on the retrieved data. You need to first define input types by using the `@strawberry.input` decorator (refer Listing 8-16) and use it as the filter criteria in the query field.

Listing 8-16. Filtered query

```
@strawberry.input
class BookFilterInput:
    id: strawberry.ID

@strawberry.type
class Query:
    all_books: list[BookType] = strawberry_django.field()
    book_by_id: BookType | None = strawberry_django.field
    (filters=BookFilterInput)
```

The above query type defines two query fields: one to retrieve all books and the other a book with the given id. To test this filtered query, enter the following in the query designer. Check the query code and the output in Figure 8-6.

Figure 8-6. *Result of the filtered query*

You can make it dynamic by using Strawberry variables in the query and inserting the values from the variables section at the bottom.

Adding mutation to the schema is similar. Just like the Query type, define a `Mutation` class decorated by the `@strawberry.type` decorator. Inside the class, define a `createBook()` function, which is again decorated by `@strawberry_django.mutation`. Pass the values of the model fields as the arguments, and call the `create()` method of the Django ORM API. The Listing 8-17 defines the Mutation class.

Listing 8-17. Mutation to add book

```
@strawberry.type
class Mutation:
    @strawberry_django.mutation
    def create_book(self, title: str, author: str, price: int,
    publisher: str) -> BookType:
        return Book.objects.create(title=title, author=author,
        price=price, publisher=publisher)
```

In the GraphiQL interface, form a `createBook` mutation and pass values. The output pane shows (in Figure 8-7) the JSON version of the new book.

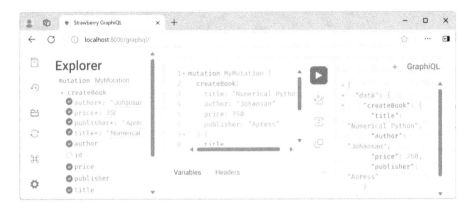

Figure 8-7. *GraphIQL output of createBook mutation*

To confirm, go back to the SQLite viewer; a new book will have been added. You can also add an `update_book()` function with relevant code for updating the data of a book record of a specified id and `delete_book()` to delete a book from the database.

Graphene

Graphene is another popular Python library for GraphQL implementation. It is a little opinionated as compared to Strawberry, in the sense that it adapts a schema-first approach rather than Strawberry's type-first approach. Also, Graphene doesn't fully support modern features such as type hints, dataclasses, async, etc. Having said that, Graphene is a mature and robust package. It can be easily integrated with Python's Django framework and **Relay**, a React-based client library for GraphQL.

Before you start exploring the features of Graphene, you need to install it in the current Python environment.

```
pip install graphene
```

Graphene's type system is a little different from that of Strawberry. Graphene has its own built-in scalar types that map to the corresponding GraphQL scalar types.

graphene.String corresponds to String type in GraphQL.

graphene.Int maps with GraphQL's Int type.

graphene.Float is equivalent to Float in GraphQL.

graphene.Boolean indicates Boolean type in GraphQL.

graphene.ID is used to represent ID type in GraphQL.

graphene.List is also a scalar type. It is a collection of objects of other scalar types or even other object types, for example, graphene.List(Book), where Book is a Graphene object type.

A Graphene ObjectType defines the relationship between the fields in your Schema. It acts as the building block of the GraphQL API.

To define an object type, you need to have a Python class with its attributes of any of the above scalar types and extend Graphene's ObjectType class. Each attribute represents a Field.

Listing 8-18 defines a Graphene object type named Book.

Listing 8-18. Graphene ObjectType

```
import graphene

class Book(graphene.ObjectType):
    title = graphene.String()
    author = graphene.String()
    price = graphene.Int()
    publisher = graphene.String()
```

Let us use an in-memory database of books in the form of a Python list for testing the API.

```
books = [
    {"title": "Beginning Django", "author": "Rubio",
    "price":3053, "publisher":"Apress"},
    {"title": "Pro Django", "author": "Alchin", "price":4284,
    "publisher":"Apress"},
]
```

A Query type is also a Python class that extends ObjectType. Each field in the query type should have a corresponding resolver method to fetch data. This resolver method should match the field name. When a client queries a field, Graphene looks for the corresponding resolver method and returns the value.

Here is the Query class (Listing 8-19) with a field all_books, which is a list of all the objects of book type.

Listing 8-19. Graphene query

```
class Query(graphene.ObjectType):
    all_books = graphene.List(Book)
```

Inside this class, you need to define a resolver method – resolve_all_ books(). The two mandatory arguments each resolver method should have are

> **root**: The parent object, useful for resolving fields of nested types

> **info**: An info object that contains context about the execution state, including the request, user, and schema

Additionally, you can have a resolver with a variable number of arguments (**kwargs).

Accordingly, a resolve_all_books() resolver should be defined inside the Query class, as in Listing 8-20. It returns the books list.

Listing 8-20. Graphene resolver function

```
# Resolver to fetch all books
def resolve_all_books(root, info) -> List[Book]:
    return books
```

As in the case of Strawberry code, get a Schema object, this time by passing the Query type as the argument to the graphene.Schema() constructor:

```
schema = graphene.Schema(query=Query)
```

Unlike Strawberry, Graphene doesn't come bundled with its own development server. So to test the query, you will have to create a /graphql endpoint for a Python web app based on Flask or Django and serve the schema on that endpoint. While you will be accessing the Graphene schema with the Django server in the next session, for now, let us use the schema.execute() function.

The execute() function needs one mandatory string argument that represents a query (or mutation or subscription). It returns the ExecutionResult containing any data and errors for the operation.

The query to be executed may be constructed as

```
query_string = '''
    query {
        allBooks {
            title
            author
```

```
            price
            publisher
        }
    }
'''
```

Pass this query_string to the execute() function:

```
result = schema.execute(query_string)
```

Here is the result, based on the books list defined earlier:

```
{
    "allBooks":[
        {
            "title":"Beginning Django",
            "author":"Rubio",
            "price":3053,
            "publisher":"Apress"
        },
        {
            "title":"Pro Django",
            "author":"Alchin",
            "price":4284,
            "publisher":"Apress"
        }
    ]
}
```

Let us add one more field to the query, to fetch books by a specific author as

```
books_by_author = graphene.List(Book, author=graphene.
String(required=True))
```

The corresponding resolver function returns the corresponding book object with matching value for the author field.

```
# Resolver to fetch books by a specific author
def resolve_books_by_author(root, info, author: str) ->
List[Book]:
    return [Book(**book) for book in books if
    book["author"] == author]
```

The required string to test this query is

```
query_string = '''
    query {
        booksByAuthor(author: "Alchin") {
            title
            author
        }
    }
'''

result = schema.execute(query_string)
```

You should get the result as

```
{
    "booksByAuthor":[
        {
            "title":"Pro Django",
            "author":"Alchin"
        }
    ]
}
```

Let us now add mutations in the schema. In Graphene, a mutation type is a class that extends graphene.Mutation. The CreateBook mutation (as in Listing 8-21) adds a new book in the books list. Inside this class, include an inner Arguments class with its attributes needed for resolving the Book type fields. The mutate() method is a resolver, invoked once the mutation is called. It takes the same arguments as the query Resolver. In this case, the mutate() method adds a new book to the list.

Listing 8-21. Graphene mutation

```
class CreateBook(graphene.Mutation):
    class Arguments:
        title = graphene.String(required=True)
        author = graphene.String(required=True)
        price = graphene.Int(required=True)
        publisher = graphene.String(required=True)

    book = graphene.Field(Book)

    def mutate(self, root, info, title: str, author:str,
    price:int, publisher:str) -> "CreateBook":
        new_book = {"title": title, "author": author,
        "price":price, "publisher":publisher}
        books.append(new_book)
        return CreateBook(book=Book(**new_book))
```

An object type Mutation with create_book as a field whose value is obtained with the Field() attribute of the CreateBook mutation.

```
class Mutation(graphene.ObjectType):
    create_book = CreateBook.Field()
```

Update the schema by adding the mutation parameter.

```
schema = graphene.Schema(query=Query, mutation=Mutation)
```

328

As before, the schema.execute() returns the result of this mutation when the appropriate query string is passed, like the one in Listing 8-22.

Listing 8-22. Mutation string

```
mutation_string = '''
    mutation {
        createBook(title: "Numerical Python", author:
        "Johansan", price: 4000, publisher:"Springer") {
            book {
                title
                author
                price
                publisher
            }
        }
    }
'''

result = schema.execute(mutation_string)
```

You can expect a result to be

```
{
    "createBook":{
        "book":{
            "title":"Numerical Python",
            "author":"Johansan",
            "price":4000,
            "publisher":"Springer"
        }
    }
}
```

Following the similar approach, you may define the mutations for updating and deleting a book (CreateBook and DeleteBook classes extending graphene.Mutation) and add them as fields in the Mutation type. You may refer to the code for this part available on the code repository of this book.

In this exercise, a Python list of books has been used as an in-memory database. In reality, a more persistent database such as a SQLite database will be used. Graphene-Django integrates Graphene with Django, which helps to build robust Django-based data-driven GraphQL APIs.

Graphene-Django

Graphene has been integrated with different Python frameworks including Django (others being Flask, FastAPI, etc.). Its additional abstractions are extremely useful for building a Django app that implements the GraphQL protocol.

Start building a Django-based GraphQL API by installing Graphene-Django package.

```
pip install graphene-django
```

As you would expect, you have to add 'graphene_django' along with the django app ('myapi') to the INSTALLED_APPS setting of the Django project.

```
INSTALLED_APPS = [
    . . .,
    'graphene_django',
    'myapi',
]
```

There is one more configuration to be made to the project's setting. You have to specify the location of your schema.

```
GRAPHENE = {
    'SCHEMA': 'myapi.schema.schema'
}
```

This SCHEMA key lets Django know where to find the root schema object (Schema) for your GraphQL API. Note that such setting is not necessary in Strawberry-Django. From the above, it is clear that the *schema.py* script in the myapi app package folder will have the declaration of schema object.

Since we intend to build the GraphQL API around a database, there should be a model defined in the Django application. The by now familiar Book model will be used in this discussion.

Like you did in the case of the strawberry-django example, you have to define an object type. Instead of the graphene.ObjectType, the GraphQL type will be obtained by extending the graphene_django. DjangoObjectType class.

The DjangoObjectType class makes it easy to expose Django models in your GraphQL API. As such, the type fields will be directly picked from the attributes of the Django model. Enter the script shown in Listing 8-23 in the *schema.py* file (in the myapi folder).

Listing 8-23. DjangoObjectType

```
from graphene_django import DjangoObjectType
from .models import Book

# Define a GraphQL type for the Book model
class BookType(DjangoObjectType):
    class Meta:
        model = Book
        fields = ("id", "title", "author", "publisher", "price")
```

Defining the queries is more or less similar to what was done in the core Graphene example, except the resolver `resolve_all_books()` calls the `objects.all()` method on the model to return a list of books in the table (Listing 8-24). Similarly, the `resolve_book()` resolver retrieves a book of the specified primary key.

Listing 8-24. Query for graphene_django

```
class Query(graphene.ObjectType):
    all_books = graphene.List(BookType)
    book = graphene.Field(BookType, id=graphene.Int())

    def resolve_all_books(self, info):
        return Book.objects.all()

    def resolve_book(self, info, id):
        try:
            return Book.objects.get(pk=id)
        except Book.DoesNotExist:
            return None
```

All you have to do now is to define an endpoint /graphql in the URLCONF of the Django project so that it presents the GraphiQL interface in the browser. Just as `strawberry-django`, the graphene-django app also provides an inbuilt view called GraphQLView and maps it with the /graphql endpoint inside the urls.py module (refer Listing 8-25).

Listing 8-25. URLCONF for graphene_django

```
from django.contrib import admin
from django.urls import path

from graphene_django.views import GraphQLView
```

```
urlpatterns = [
    path('admin/', admin.site.urls),
    path('graphql/', GraphQLView.as_view(graphiql=True)),
    # Enable GraphiQL interface
]
```

You are now ready to test the GraphQL queries that fetch the list of books and retrieve a single book. Fire the Django development server and visit the graphql endpoint.

To add a mutation to this API, follow the same logic implemented in the core Graphene example. Define the CreateBook class, and extend graphene.Mutation.

Inside the inner `Arguments` class, define the same attributes as in the Book model.

Define the `mutate()` method which takes values to match with the arguments, and uses them in the `create()` method of the Django model to actually add a new Book object in the corresponding books table in the database.

Define a Mutation type with `create_book` as a field, as in Listing 8-26.

Listing 8-26. Mutation for graphene_django

```
# Define Mutations
class CreateBook(graphene.Mutation):
    class Arguments:
        title = graphene.String(required=True)
        author = graphene.String(required=True)
        publisher = graphene.String(required=True)
        price = graphene.Int(required=True)

    book = graphene.Field(BookType)
```

```
def mutate(self, info, title, author, publisher, price):
    book = Book.objects.create(
        title=title,
        author=author,
        publisher=publisher,
        price=price
    )
    return CreateBook(book=book)

class Mutation(graphene.ObjectType):
    create_book = CreateBook.Field()
```

Make sure you update the Schema object by adding the mutation parameter.

```
schema = graphene.Schema(query=Query, mutation=Mutation)
```

You are now ready to test the mutation as well. As an exercise, add the update as well as delete mutations to the schema. You can refer to the code available in the repository of this book in case of any doubt.

Summary

This chapter has been a journey of exploring the world of GraphQL and its implementation in Python and Django. You learned how the GraphQL protocol is implemented with two widely popular Python libraries, Strawberry and Graphene, and their Django extensions. Subscriptions and other features such as authorization have not been discussed here. Interested readers are encouraged to explore the official documentation and other resources to learn about these aspects.

CHAPTER 9

WebSockets with Django

One of the major limitations of the HTTP protocol is that it is a strictly unidirectional protocol, in the sense that the client has to first send a request in response to which any data is sent from the server. Also, the fact that HTTP is a stateless protocol necessitates the connection to be re-established for each subsequent request. The **WebSocket protocol** overcomes these limitations and enables a simultaneous two-way communication channel over a single Transmission Control Protocol (TCP) connection. In this chapter, you will be introduced to handling the WebSocket protocol in Python in general and Django in particular with the help of its Channels app.

This chapter covers the following topics:

- WebSocket protocol
- WebSocket in Python
- Django Channels
- Consumers
- Routing

© Malhar Lathkar 2025
M. Lathkar, *Modern Django Web Development*,
https://doi.org/10.1007/979-8-8688-1472-3_9

- Channel layers
- WebSocket client template
- Login/logout

WebSocket Protocol

The term "WebSocket" was first used by Ian Hickson and Michael Carter in 2008. WebSocket uses HTTP as the initial transport mechanism, but because the TCP connection is kept alive after the HTTP response is received, WebSocket makes it possible to send message-based data, similar to UDP, at the same time ensuring the reliability of TCP. Figure 9-1 illustrates how the Websocket protocol works.

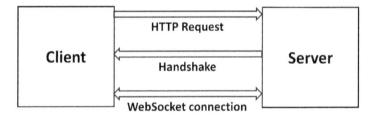

Figure 9-1. *WebSocket protocol*

The WebSocket URIs use a new scheme **ws://** (or **wss://** for a secure WebSocket). A WebSocket communication actually starts on an HTTP connection. If the client wants to upgrade the normal HTTP connection, it should include a connection header to upgrade, the Upgrade header itself set to WebSocket to indicate its intent to establish a WebSocket connection. The Sec-WebSocket-Key header is a base-64 encoded 16-bit value.

A typical GET request from an HTTP client to a **ws://** URI might look like this:

```
GET ws://example.com:8765/ HTTP/1.1
Host: localhost: 8765
Connection: Upgrade
Pragma: no-cache
Cache-Control: no-cache
Upgrade: websocket
Sec-WebSocket-Version: 13
Sec-WebSocket-Key: q4xkcO32u266gldTuKaSOw==
```

If and when the server accepts this handshake extended by the client, its response code is HTTP 101 Switching Protocols, implying that the server is switching to the WebSocket protocol as requested by the client.

```
HTTP/1.1 101 Switching Protocols
Upgrade: websocket
Connection: Upgrade
Sec-WebSocket-Accept: fA9dggdnMPU79lJgAE3W4TRnyDM=
```

This provides a two-way full-duplex communication channel between the two that doesn't get disconnected after every transaction and is suitable for real-time applications. One of the major departures from HTTP is that either the client or the server can choose to send a message at any time.

Any server-side application written in a programming language (such as Python) that is capable of Berkeley sockets can act as a WebSocket server. The server waits for incoming socket connections using a standard TCP socket.

Note that the client still has to start the WebSocket handshake process by contacting the server and requesting a WebSocket connection.

To initiate WebSocket communication, you need to create a WebSocket object.

Listing 9-1. WebSocket object

```
const ws = new WebSocket('ws://localhost:8765');
```

This sends a handshake request to the server. Once accepted, the `readyState` property of the WebSocket object will become OPEN, and the connection is ready to transfer data. You can now begin transmitting data to the server.

To do this, call the WebSocket object's `send()` method once a connection is established by defining an `onopen` event handler, as in Listing 9-2.

Listing 9-2. Sending message

```
ws.onopen = (event) => {
  ws.send("some message");
};
```

When the client receives messages, a `onmessage` event handler is sent to the WebSocket object to begin listening for incoming data (Listing 9-3).

Listing 9-3. Receiving message

```
ws.onmessage = (event) => {
  console.log(event.data);
};
```

WebSocket and Python

While you can use JavaScript inside a web page that works as a WebSocket client, you need to write the server in a language that supports BSD sockets. A Python library called `websockets` helps in building a WebSocket server as client application. It provides a coroutine-based API; hence, it allows the WebSocket server to handle multiple clients asynchronously.

The websockets library depends on asyncio and requires Python version 3.9 or newer. Use PIP to install it in the current environment.

```
pip install websockets
```

The serve() method of the server class in the websockets.asyncio module starts the WebSocket server (refer Listing 9-4). It needs a handler coroutine, the host, and a port number on which it starts listening to the incoming requests.

Listing 9-4. Starting the WebSocket server

```
from websockets.asyncio import server
server.serve(handler, host, port)
```

Whenever a new client sends a connection request, the server creates a WebSocket connection object, which is passed to the handler.

To keep the server in an event loop that runs forever, use the create_future() function (Listing 9-5).

Listing 9-5. WebSocket server loop

```
async with serve(handler, "localhost", 8765):
    await asyncio.get_running_loop().create_future()
```

The websocket object (actually it is an instance of WebSocketServerProtocol) is passed to the asynchronous handler coroutine. The send() and recv() methods let you to send and receive messages to and from the WebSocket client.

To handle continuous communication between the server and the client, an async for loop is used.

```
async for message in websocket:
```

The receive and send actions are often enclosed inside a try - except block. Listing 9-6 shows the code for the handler coroutine.

Listing 9-6. WebSocket Handler

```
async def handler(websocket):
    try:
        async for message in websocket:
            print(f"Received: {message}")
            msg=input("enter server message: ")
            await websocket.send(f"Server says: {msg}")
    except Exception as e:
        print(f"Connection closed: {e}")
```

Listing 9-7 shows the complete code for setting up a WebSocket server capable of receiving messages from a client and sending back its own message.

Listing 9-7. WebSocket server code

```
import asyncio
from websockets.asyncio.server import serve

async def wshandler(websocket):
    print("Client connected")
    try:
        async for message in websocket:
            print(f"Received: {message}")
            msg=input("enter server message: ")
            await websocket.send(f"Server says: {msg}")
    except Exception as e:
        print(f"Connection closed: {e}")

async def main():
    async with serve(wshandler, "localhost", 8765):
        await asyncio.get_running_loop().create_future()
        # Run forever
```

```
if __name__ == "__main__":
    asyncio.run(main())
```

Python's WebSocket client calls the connect() method of the client class defined in the websockets.asyncio module. To enable the client to send and receive messages in a loop, you can use a while loop (as in Listing 9-8) within the async with block of the WebSocket client.

Listing 9-8. WebSocket client code

```
import asyncio
from websockets.asyncio.client import connect

async def client_logic():
    uri = "ws://localhost:8765"
    async with connect(uri) as websocket:
        print("Connected to the server. Type 'exit' to quit.")
        while True:
            # Get user input
            message = input("Enter a message: ")

            # Exit condition
            if message.lower() == "exit":
                print("Closing connection.")
                break

            # Send message to the server
            await websocket.send(message)
            print(f"Sent: {message}")

            # Wait for response from the server
            response = await websocket.recv()
            print(f"Received: {response}")
```

```
if __name__ == "__main__":
    asyncio.run(client_logic())
```

To test the interaction, run the server and client codes in two separate terminals (start the server first). As the client's request is accepted, the two-way communication begins.

Server terminal:

```
python ws_server.py
Client connected
Received: Hello Server
enter server message: Hi client
```

Client terminal:

```
python ws_client.py
Connected to the server. Type 'exit' to quit.
Enter a message: Hello Server
Sent: Hello Server
Received: Server says: Hi client
```

To establish WebSocket connection from a browser, you can open a web page in which a JavaScript function logs messages from the server in response to the onmessage event and sends the contents of a text field as a message when an HTML button is clicked.

Save the HTML script shown in Listing 9-9 as ws_client.html.

Listing 9-9. ws_client.html

```
<body>
    <h1>WebSocket Client</h1>
    <input type="text" id="messageInput" placeholder="Type your
    message here">
    <button id="sendMessage">Send Message</button>
    <div id="messages"></div>
```

```
<script>
    const ws = new WebSocket('ws://localhost:8765');

    // Log when the connection is open
    ws.onopen = () => {
        console.log('Connected to WebSocket server');
    };

    // Log messages from the server
    ws.onmessage = (event) => {
        const messageDiv = document.getElementById
        ('messages');
        const newMessage = document.createElement('p');
        newMessage.textContent = `${event.data}`;
        messageDiv.appendChild(newMessage);
    };

    // Send a message when the button is clicked
    document.getElementById('sendMessage').
    addEventListener('click', () => {
        const messageInput = document.getElementById
        ('messageInput');
        const message = messageInput.value.trim();
        // Get the input value

        if (message) {
            if (ws.readyState === WebSocket.OPEN) {
                console.log(`Sending: ${message}`);
                ws.send(message); // Send the message to
                                  the server
                messageInput.value = ''; // Clear the
                                         input field
```

```
            } else {
                console.log('WebSocket is not open.');
            }
        } else {
            console.log('Please enter a message before
            sending.');
        }
    });
    </script>
</body>
```

When opened in the browser (Figure 9-2 shows the screenshot), the connection is established, and you can start sending and receiving messages.

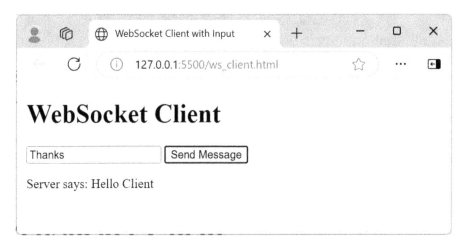

Figure 9-2. *WebSocket client*

Django Channels

To integrate the WebSocket server with a Django application, it is recommended that you use the Channels app. Channels is a reusable Django app that adds an asynchronous layer to your Django application so that it can implement the WebSocket protocol. By default, Django follows a request-response model. Including the Channels app extends Django for long-lived communications facilitating real-time applications like live notifications or chats.

To install the Channels app in your Python and Django environment, use the PIP utility. You can install Daphne as well if you haven't done so earlier.

```
pip install -U 'channels[daphne]'
```

Once installed, add Channels and Daphne to the list of installed apps in the project's settings. To avoid any conflicts, add them to the top of the installed apps list. Assuming that you already have a Django project in place and an app chatApp in it, update the *settings.py* file as

```
INSTALLED_APPS = [
    'daphne',
    'channels',
    . . . ,
    'chatApp',
]
```

As you know, Django is bundled with a WSGI-compliant development server. However, here you want to use Daphne to server your app asynchronously. When a project is set up (with the startproject command), Django creates a *wsgi.py* script (Listing 9-10), which provides the application object.

Listing 9-10. wsgi.py

```
import os
from django.core.wsgi import get_wsgi_application
os.environ.setdefault('DJANGO_SETTINGS_MODULE',
'channelproject.settings')
application = get_wsgi_application()
```

To force Django to use the ASGI application, you need to integrate Channels and Daphne with the Django project by creating the routing configuration. It is similar to a Django URLCONF that tells Channels what code to run when an HTTP request is received by a channel server.

Modify your project's *asgi.py* file as in Listing 9-11.

Listing 9-11. asgi.py

```python
import os
from django.core.asgi import get_asgi_application
from channels.routing import ProtocolTypeRouter
os.environ.setdefault('DJANGO_SETTINGS_MODULE',
'channelproject.settings')
application = ProtocolTypeRouter({
    'http': get_asgi_application()
})
```

ProtocolTypeRouter acts as the entry point for ASGI applications. It routes incoming connections to appropriate handlers based on the protocol type. For now, the http protocol is included. Later on, we shall add the WebSocket protocol.

To let your Django project know, add ASGI_APPLICATION variable in the settings and set it to the application object provided by the *asgi. py* module.

```python
ASGI_APPLICATION = 'channelproject.asgi.application'
```

If you start the server with the runserver command, you should now find that channel's development server has taken over our Django development server.

```
python manage.py migrate
December 29, 2024 - 20:03:05
Django version 5.0.7, using settings 'channelproject.settings'
```

346

```
Starting ASGI/Daphne version 4.1.2 development server at
http://127.0.0.1:8000/
Quit the server with CTRL-BREAK.
```

To serve a WebSocket connection, you need to incorporate a few new features in your Django project. You know that in a synchronous Django app, any HTTP request is mapped to the corresponding view. However, in the case of a WebSocket connection, Django looks for consumers rather than views. The Channels app also needs routing rules to be defined for individual protocol types. Channel layers is another useful feature of Django Channels that allows you to broadcast messages to all consumers simultaneously.

A Django app that serves WebSocket is a combination of traditional Django views that are mapped to the URL routes and consumers controlled by channel routers. Figure 9-3 illustrates the Django Channels architecture.

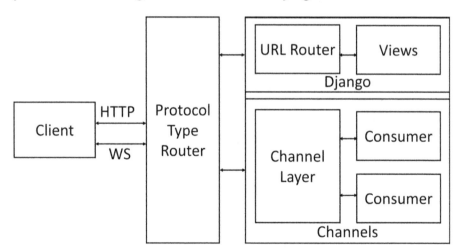

Figure 9-3. *Channels architecture*

Consumers

Consumers are the channel's version of Django views. A consumer defines the logic for handling events such as connection establishment, message receipt, and connection closure.

There are two types of consumers – a synchronous consumer handles events in a blocking manner, whereas an asynchronous consumer handles the events using Python's `asyncio`. In your project, you can declare a subclass of either `AsyncConsumer` or `SyncConsumer` both available in the `channels.consumer` module.

A consumer class includes the following methods:

- `connect()` method is called when a WebSocket connection is opened.

- `disconnect()` method is called when the connection is closed.

- `receive()` handles incoming messages.

Similar to Django's generic views, Channels package also consists of generic consumers that wrap common functionality for HTTP and WebSocket handling.

`WebsocketConsumer` wraps the ASGI message sending and receiving into handling that just deals with text and binary frames. `AsyncWebsocketConsumer` is same, just that its methods are coroutines.

Let us provide `ChatConsumer` as a consumer class in the Django project. To start with, define the `connect()` method, as in Listing 9-12. It accepts the incoming connection request and sends back a JSON data to the client to let it know that the connection has been established.

Listing 9-12. Consumer class

```
import json
from channels.generic.websocket import WebsocketConsumer

class ChatConsumer(WebsocketConsumer):
    def connect(self):
        self.accept()
        self.send(text_data=json.dumps({
            'type': 'chat.message',
            'message': 'Connection established!'
        }))
```

Routing

Routing in Channels is what URL routing is in the classical Django app. It determines how different WebSocket connections are handled by associating them with specific consumers. The routing classes in Channels allow you to combine and stack your consumers to dispatch based on what the connection is.

The channels.routing module contains utilities for routing protocols to specific consumers. The main class provided by this module is ProtocolTypeRouter. It allows you to define protocol-specific handling within your ASGI application. Each protocol (e.g., http, WebSocket) can be mapped to its respective handler.

Routing is provided by defining the websockets_urlpatterns list (note the similarity of the urlpatterns list in the case of Django views) in the *routing.py* file in the app folder.

Listing 9-13. WebSocket router

```
from django.urls import re_path
from chatApp.consumers import ChatConsumer

websocket_urlpatterns = [
re_path(r'ws/socket-server/', ChatConsumer.as_asgi()),
]
```

Note the use of re_path() function instead of path() in the Listing 9-13. The re_path() function allows for more complex urlpatterns using regular expressions. The **ws/chat/** URL is mapped to the ASGI callable object returned by the as_asgi() method. It has a similar purpose to Django's as_view().

The AuthMiddleware in Channels supports standard Django authentication, where the user details are stored in the session. It allows read-only access to a user object in the scope.

For convenience, these are also provided as a combined callable called AuthMiddlewareStack that includes all three.

The channels.auth module provides authentication and session handling for WebSocket connections. AuthMiddlewareStack is a convenient middleware stack as a combined callable comprising AuthMiddleware, SessionMiddleware, and CookieMiddleware. It adds Django's authentication and session middleware to WebSocket connections. It allows WebSocket consumers to access the scope["user"] attribute, enabling user authentication.

Go back to the asgi.py code and import the AuthMiddlewareStack middleware, and update the list of protocols in the ASGI application object (Listing 9-14).

Listing 9-14. Protocol router

```
import os
from django.core.asgi import get_asgi_application
from channels.routing import ProtocolTypeRouter, URLRouter
from channels.auth import AuthMiddlewareStack
from chatApp.routing import websocket_urlpatterns

os.environ.setdefault('DJANGO_SETTINGS_MODULE',
'channelproject.settings')

application = ProtocolTypeRouter({
    'http': get_asgi_application(),
    'websocket': AuthMiddlewareStack(
        URLRouter(
            websocket_urlpatterns
        )
    ),
})
```

As mentioned earlier, the client first has to send an HTTP request and subsequently establish the WebSocket connection. Hence, define a view function (as in Listing 9-15) that serves an index template.

Listing 9-15. index view

```
from django.shortcuts import render

# Create your views here.
def index(request):
    return render(request, 'channelApp/index.html')
```

As always, register this view with a URL route, as Listing 9-16 shows.

Listing 9-16. urls.py (chatApp)

```python
from django.urls import path
from . import views

urlpatterns = [
    path('', views.index, name='index'),
]
```

Finally, refer the Listing 9-17 to update the URLCONF of the project.

Listing 9-17. URLCONF

```python
from django.contrib import admin
from django.urls import path, include

urlpatterns = [
    path('admin/', admin.site.urls),
    path('', include('channelApp.urls')),
]
```

Put a JavaScript code inside the index template (Listing 9-18), which sends the connection request at the URL with the **ws**:// protocol.

Listing 9-18. index.html as WS client

```html
<html>
<head>
    <title>Index Page</title>

        <h1>Let's chat</h1>
        <script>
            let url = 'ws://' + window.location.host + '/
            ws/chat/';
            const chatSocket = new WebSocket(url);
```

```
        chatSocket.onmessage = function(e) {
            const data = JSON.parse(e.data);
            console.log("Data: ", data);
        };
    </script>
  </body>
</html>
```

Note that the onmessage event is sending the data passed by the consumer's connect() method to the browser's JavaScript console.

Start the Django server (Channels and Daphne take over the default development server). The index page opens at the URL http://localhost:8000/. The JavaScript console in the developer tools of your browser reveals that the WebSocket connection has been established. Refer to the browser screenshot in the Figure 9-4.

Figure 9-4. *JS console*

Go ahead and add a simple chat interface to the index template. As in the Listing 9-19, add an HTML form that has a <div> element to display the log of chat messages exchanged and a text field for entering a message.

Listing 9-19. Client interface

```
<body onload="myFunction()">
    <p id="Log"></p>
    <h1>Let Us Chat!</h1>

    <form id="form">
        <input type="text" name="message"/>

    <p><b>Messages</b></p>

    <div id="messages" style="border: thin solid black">
    </div>
    </form>
```

Channel Layers

The Django Channels app has a feature of Channel layers, which is especially useful for making a distributed real-time application. It allows you to talk between different instances of an application. Channel layers allow the consumers to send and receive messages, and it makes it possible to broadcast messages to multiple consumers in a group.

Note that if you are using any SyncConsumer, you should wrap the Channel Layer functionality in async_to_sync adapter function.

Channel layers are configured by defining the CHANEL_LAYERS in the project's *settings.py* module. The default channel layer is obtained from a project with channels.layers.get_channel_layer(), but if you are using consumers, then self.channel_layer automatically provides a copy for you on the consumer.

Django Channels provides two backends for Channel layers:

> **Redis Channel Layer**: RedisChannelLayer is a
> Django-maintained channel that uses Redis as
> its backing store. A single-server and sharded
> configurations are supported. This layer is
> recommended for production use.

> **In-Memory Channel Layer**: Channels also comes
> packaged with an InMemoryChannelLayer. This
> should be used in testing environment or for local-
> development purpose.

To configure a Django project for Redis, use the following setting:

```
CHANNEL_LAYERS = {
    'default': {
        'BACKEND': 'channels_redis.core.RedisChannelLayer',
        'CONFIG': {
            'hosts': [('127.0.0.1', 6379)],
        },
    },
}
```

The setting may be modified as below for the in-memory layer:

```
CHANNEL_LAYERS = {
    'default':{
        'BACKEND':'channels.layers.InMemoryChannelLayer'
    }
}
```

As mentioned above, if your consumer class is derived from
AsyncConsumer, its send(), receive(), and other functions are async
coroutines, so you need to await them. However, if it is a SyncConsumer,
you will need to use the async_to_sync wrapper.

Single Channel

When the channel layer is enabled, an open WebSocket in your application has a single Consumer instance, and it has a unique channel name: `self.channel_name`.

Listing 9-20. Single channel

```
from asgiref.sync import async_to_sync
from .models import Clients
class ChatConsumer(WebsocketConsumer):
    def connect(self):
        # Make a database row with our channel name
        Clients.objects.create(channel_name=self.channel_name)
```

To send to a single channel, just find its channel name (Listing 9-21) and use `channel_layer.send`.

Listing 9-21. Sending message to a channel

```
from channels.layers import get_channel_layer

channel_layer = get_channel_layer()
async_to_sync (channel_layer.send("channel_name", {
    "type": "chat.message",
    "text": "Hello there!",
}))
```

Groups

Instead of sending the messages to individual channels, you'll ideally want to broadcast them to multiple consumers simultaneously. For this purpose, Channels provides the Groups. Groups is a broadcast system that allows you to add and remove channel names from named groups and send messages to those named groups.

The group_add() method is used to add a channel (or a consumer) to a given group. In Listing 9-22, it is called from inside the connect() method of the consumer.

Listing 9-22. Channel group

```
def connect(self):
    self.room_group_name = 'test'

    async_to_sync(self.channel_layer.group_add)(
        self.room_group_name,
        self.channel_name
    )

    self.accept()
```

If a user disconnects, it is removed from the group with the group_ discard() method.

```
def disconnect(self, close_code):
    async_to_sync(self.channel_layer.group_discard)( self.
    room_group_name, self.channel_name)
```

Whenever a new message is received in a consumer, it will call the method group_send() method of the channel layer to which it belongs, which will send the data, automatically to all the active members of the group (refer to Listing 9-23).

Listing 9-23. Sending to group

```
def receive(self, text_data):
    text_data_json = json.loads(text_data)
    message = text_data_json['message']

    async_to_sync(self.channel_layer.group_send)(
        self.room_group_name,
```

357

```
    {
        'type':'chat_message',
        'message':message
    }
)
```

Here, the value of the type attribute is chat_message method. It is the method that internally calls the send() method to send data to each consumer.

Listing 9-24. Broadcast message

```
def chat_message(self, event):
    message = event['message']

    self.send(text_data=json.dumps({
        'type':'chat',
        'message':message
    }))
```

WebSocket Client Template

You have used a web page as the WebSocket client to interact with a stand-alone WebSocket server built with the websockets library. Its JavaScript code needs to modified to make it suitable for Django Channels and especially for Channel layers.

As described earlier, a simple HTML form is added to enter the messages and to display the chat log. In the JavaScript code (Listing 9-25), add a function that pops up a prompt box to let the user enter a name.

Listing 9-25. WebSocket client – updated

```
<script type="text/javascript">
        var user="";
        function myFunction() {
```

```
    user = prompt("Enter User name", "User1");
     document.getElementById("Log").innerHTML =
     "<h2>Hello " + user +"</h2>";
}
```

The onmessage event handler, as in Listing 9-26 is fired when an incoming message is notified. If it is from the group, the message text is appended to the chat log (a div element with messages as the id).

Listing 9-26. Chat log

```
chatSocket.onmessage = function(e){
    let data = JSON.parse(e.data)
    console.log('Data:', data)

    if(data.type === 'chat'){
        let messages = document.getElementById
        ('messages')

        messages.insertAdjacentHTML('beforeend', `<div>
                                <p>${data.message}</p>
                         </div>`)
    }
}
```

On the other hand, the message entered by a user is pushed into the group so that it can be broadcast to all the consumers. The Listing 9-27 has the relevant JavaScript code.

Listing 9-27. Sending in group

```
let form = document.getElementById('form')
form.addEventListener('submit', (e)=> {
    e.preventDefault()
    let message = e.target.message.value
```

```
chatSocket.send(JSON.stringify({
    'message':user+":"+message
}))
form.reset()
})
```

To test the WebSocket group chat, fire up the Daphne server as before, and open two browser windows as in Figure 9-5, pointing to the URL of the index page (http://localhost:8000/).

Try sending text from either window. The messages will appear in the chat log on both the browsers.

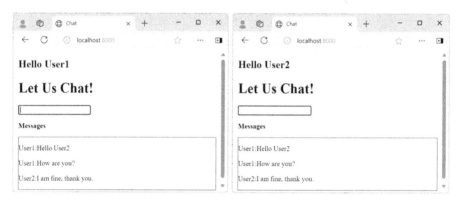

Figure 9-5. *Channels group chat*

Login/Logout

The channels.auth module includes login and logout functions, similar to the login and logout functions in the contrib.auth package in Django.

Within your consumer, use login() to log a user in:

```
login(scope, user, backend=None)
```

This requires that your scope has a session object; it can be done by wrapping the consumer in a `AuthMiddlewareStack`. The Listing 9-28 shows how this logic works.

Listing 9-28. Channels login (async)

```
from channels.auth import login

class ChatConsumer(AsyncWebsocketConsumer):
    ...
    async def receive(self, text_data):
        ...
        await login(self.scope, user)
        await database_sync_to_async(self.scope
        ["session"].save)()
```

Note that the session is populated but will not be saved automatically – you must call the `scope["session"].save()` method.

When calling from a synchronous consumer, you will need to use the `async_to_sync` wrapper, similar to Listing 9-29.

Listing 9-29. Channels login (sync)

```
from asgiref.sync import async_to_sync
from channels.auth import login

class SyncChatConsumer(WebsocketConsumer):
    ...
    def receive(self, text_data):
        ...
        async_to_sync(login)(self.scope, user)
        self.scope["session"].save()
```

You can log out a user with

```
async logout(self.scope)
```

or

```
async_to_sync(logout)(self.scope)
```

Summary

This chapter serves as a good introduction to Django Channels, with which you can add real-time capabilities to your Django application. You learned how to implement the WebSocket protocol to broadcast messages in a group. The Channels app provides additional features such as authentication, using Redis Channel Layer, and integrating IoT protocols like MQTT. However, discussion of these features is not within the scope of this book. Hence, you can experiment with them by referring to the official documentation and other resources.

The next chapter is a walkthrough for building a React frontend for your Django REST API app.

CHAPTER 10

ReactJS with Django

In the preceding chapters, you learned how to serve different protocols, i.e., REST, GraphQL, and WebSocket, with Django apps and consume the responses in the Django templates. This chapter focuses on developing a client application using ReactJS, a popular JavaScript-based framework.

These are the important topics that will be covered in this chapter:

- ReactJS

- React app

- React Developer Tools

- What is Promise?

- useState hook

- useEffect hook

- Axios

- DRF backend

- Axios frontend

- Apollo

- Graphene-Django backend

- Apollo frontend

- React for WebSocket

© Malhar Lathkar 2025
M. Lathkar, *Modern Django Web Development*,
https://doi.org/10.1007/979-8-8688-1472-3_10

ReactJS

As you have learned in the very first chapter, Django follows the MVT architecture, with the Template component taking care of the presentation layer of a web application. A template is a web page interspersed with DTL (Django Template Language) constructs to render dynamic content in response to the user's interaction.

However, the use of templates as a frontend of the applications has certain limitations. First of all, templates are rendered on the server and sent to the browser as static HTML. Hence, any changes in the UI require a full-page reload, which results in a considerably lower performance. The use of templates is suitable for simpler applications with minimal interactivity.

On the other hand, applications based on JavaScript-based frameworks provide client-side rendering; the DOM is updated dynamically without refreshing the page. React is one of the most popular JavaScript libraries for frontend development because it provides numerous advantages that make building user interfaces (UIs) efficient, scalable, and developer-friendly.

One of its advantages is the separation of concerns, with Django managing the backend logic while React is responsible for the UI. On one hand, Django's powerful ORM is ideal for handling large amounts of data and traffic. On the other, React with its virtual DOM feature leads to a smooth user experience.

React library was first used by Facebook in 2011. Since then, it is being maintained by Meta as a free and open source frontend JavaScript library, with version 18.3 being the latest.

While a detailed discussion of the React API is out of the scope of this book, a brief overview of its important features is taken here to give the interaction between React and Django a proper perspective.

Virtual DOM: While displaying a web page, the browser interprets the HTML code and builds the Document Object Model (DOM) as a tree of HTML components and renders it. In order to minimize the reloading action, ReactJS uses a virtual DOM, which is a lightweight, in-memory representation of the actual Document Object Model (DOM). When the state of any component is updated, React creates a new Virtual DOM tree and compares it with the real DOM to identify and apply only the differences, thus giving an improved performance in the case of dynamic updates to the UI.

Components: Component is a basic building block of the React code. One or more reusable components are added in hierarchical manner to construct a single root component, which is then added to the root element of the DOM. Components interact with each other through **props** (properties), much like the arguments or parameters in a programming language such as Python. You can declare a component as a function component or a class component.

Hooks: A hook is a JavaScript function that facilitates access to the features such as state and other lifecycle properties. The hook feature was introduced in React 16.8; therefore, you don't necessarily use the class components. Different types of hooks are available.

State hooks let a component "remember" information, for example, useState.

Context hooks let a component receive information from others, for example, useContext.

Effect hooks let a component connect to and synchronize with external systems, for example, useEffect.

React App

A React application code basically consists of HTML, JavaScript, and CSS. The two libraries needed – React and ReactDOM – can even be included in the code via CDN. However, the recommended approach is to use React build tools with the npm utility that is shipped with Node.js. The `create-react-app` build tool is based on webpack and has been quite popularly used. Nowadays, a new build tool – `Vite` – is the preferred build tool for the latest versions of React, owing to its speed and efficiency.

To use Vite, you'll need to ensure that you have Node.js and npm installed on your system (if not already, install the latest versions from the Node.js official website: `https://nodejs.org/en`).

To create a new React app, use the following command:

```
npm create vite@latest my-app
```

You may be prompted to choose a framework (choose React) and a variant (choose JavaScript). This command initializes a new Vite project with a React template. It will install the react and react-dom libraries.

Change to the project folder:

```
cd my-app
```

To install the necessary dependencies for your React project, run the following command:

```
npm install
```

It will install the react and react-dom libraries. This can be verified from the dependencies section in the `package.json` file inside the my-app folder.

```
"dependencies": {
  "react": "^18.3.1",
  "react-dom": "^18.3.1"
}
```

Now, start the Vite development server with the following command:

npm run dev

```
> my-app@0.0.0 dev
> vite
  VITE v6.0.7 ready in 430 ms
  → Local:   http://localhost:5173/
  → Network: use --host to expose
  → press h + enter to show help
```

By default, the server listens at http://localhost:5173. You can set alternative port number in the vite.config.js file. Visit the URL and you should get the default home page in the browser (as in Figure 10-1), if the installation steps are correctly executed.

Figure 10-1. *Home page of React app*

The project's root folder includes, along with the required node modules, *index.html*. This file (Listing 10-1) is the entry point of your application, where your React application is mounted. It is present in the root directory.

Listing 10-1. index.html

```
<body>
  <div id="root"></div>
  <script type="module" src="/src/main.jsx"></script>
</body>
```

The project folder has the following important files inside its src folder:

> **App.jsx**: The root component of your application
> is defined here, having a default UI designed. The
> App component displays the logos of React and Vite,
> each linked to the respective home pages. You will
> modify this code to add more components as per
> the needs of your project.
>
> **main.jsx**: This file (Listing 10-2) imports the App
> component and attaches it to the root element in
> the *index.html* file.

Listing 10-2. main.jsx

```
import { StrictMode } from 'react'
import { createRoot } from 'react-dom/client'
import './index.css'
import App from './App.jsx'

createRoot(document.getElementById('root')).render(
  <StrictMode>
    <App />
  </StrictMode>,
)
```

The createRoot() function lets you create a root to display React components inside a browser DOM node. The use of StrictMode is optional; it helps you find common bugs in your components.

Go ahead and edit the *App.jsx* file in your preferred IDE (such as VS Code) and modify the App component (as in Listing 10-3) to render the message React Frontend for Django API.

Listing 10-3. App.jsx

```
import './App.css'

function App() {
  return (

      <h1>Django + React</h1>

      <div className="App">
        React Frontend for Django API
      </div>

  );
}

export default App
```

You must have noted that the files containing a React code have the .jsx extension instead of .js, as a normal JavaScript file has. The JSX stands for JavaScript XML. The .jsx file holds the React component design and its logic and state. It allows you to write HTML-like and declarative code within JavaScript. However, a React project may also have the normal .js files. The convention says that jsx files contain the component-related code and the JS files the non-UI code.

Note that the src folder also includes *App.css*, to define the styles to be applied to different HTML elements.

React Developer Tools

Most popular browsers (Chrome, Edge, etc.) have built-in Developer tools with which you can debug HTML, CSS, and JavaScript code in your web page. To inspect and debug the React code, you need to add the React-specific development tools as the extensions available in the respective stores. If the current page uses React, the Components and Profile panels are visible. Figure 10-2 shows the React Developer Tools at the bottom of the browser window.

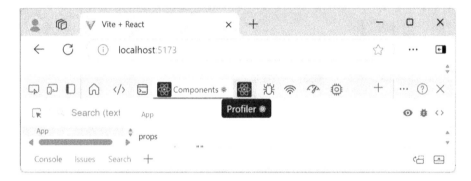

Figure 10-2. *React Developer Tools*

Whether you're a beginner or an experienced developer, a comprehensive set of features in the React Developer Tools help you to inspect the component hierarchy and optimize your applications. While it is not possible here to explore these tools in detail, one is well advised to look for other resources to master the React Developer Tools.

What Is Promise?

In JavaScript (and React), promises are a fundamental tool for handling asynchronous operations. A Promise is a special JavaScript object that returns a value after an asynchronous operation is successfully completed, or fails to complete successfully.

In life, you either fulfill a promise or you fail to keep it. The promise object in JavaScript has three possible states. It is in pending state when an executor function starts. It is said to be resolved when the operation succeeds, and rejected when it fails. Any which way, the object reaches a settled state. The Figure 10-3 illustrates how Promise works.

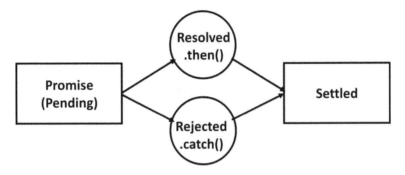

Figure 10-3. *How Promise works*

To create a Promise object, you need two parameters: resolve and reject.

```
const myPromise = new Promise((resolve, reject) => {
    // condition
});
```

If the condition is met, the Promise will be resolved; otherwise, it will be rejected. JavaScript uses then() for resolved Promises and catch() for rejected Promises.

```
myPromise.then((message) => {
    console.log(message);
}).catch((message) => {
    console.log(message);
});
```

In React, promises are often used to send and retrieve data from a server. They are combined with hooks like useEffect and useState to manage and render async data.

useState Hook

While you can declare regular JavaScript variables inside a React component, values of such local variables are not retained on every render of the component. React has the provision of the state variable.

The state variable stores the value of a React component, which can change as a result of user interaction. Change in the state variable triggers the component to be re-rendered so that React components can return active data updates and provide an ideal user experience.

Use the useState hook to add a state variable to the component. Import it from the react module.

```
import { useState } from 'react'
```

It returns an array with two elements: the current state value and a function to update that state value.

```
const [count, setCount] = useState(0)
```

The current value of count is 0, and the setCount() function causes it to be changed. Let us call this function on the onClick event of a button, as in the Listing 10-4. Every button click increments the count, and the App component is re-rendered showing the incremental count.

Listing 10-4. useState hook

```
function App() {
  const [count, setCount] = useState(0)

  return (

      <h1>Hello World</h1>
      <div className="card">
        <button onClick={() => setCount((count) => count + 1)}>
```

```
        count is {count}
      </button>

    </div>

  )
}
```

```
export default App
```

useEffect Hook

The useEffect hook causes a function to be invoked every time a component is rendered. Note that a component renders every time its associated state changes.

The useEffect hook needs two arguments: a callback function to be invoked and a dependency array.

```
useEffect(EffectCallback, deps)
```

The callback function is mandatory. If the deps array is provided, the function will be called only when the value in the array changes.

In this example, in Listing 10-5, the useEffect hook displays a message in the console every time the count state changes.

Listing 10-5. useEffect hook

```
import { useState, useEffect } from 'react'
import './App.css'

function App() {
  const [count, setCount] = useState(0)
```

```
  useEffect(() => {
    console.log('count changed:', count)
  }
  , [count])

  return (

      <h1>Hello World</h1>
      <div className="card">
        <button onClick={() => setCount((count) => count + 1)}>
          count is {count}
        </button>

      </div>

  )
}

export default App
```

However, if the deps array is empty (pass [] as the second argument to useEffect), the button click will increment the count, but the useEffect function will not be called. This can be verified by the console log that doesn't show the subsequent change in the count.

Axios

The primary objective of this chapter is to build a React app that acts as a client for the Django APIs. Basically, you need a tool to issue HTTP requests from within the React code. The two popular libraries used for this purpose are **Fetch** and **Axios**. Fetch is a native JavaScript library (hence, it doesn't need any installation) for handling operations such as GET/POST, whereas Axios is a third-party library (it needs to be installed with npm). Axios is found to be more convenient because of its simpler API, although Fetch also presents some significant advantages. We shall, however, implement Axios library in this chapter.

Axios is a Promise-based HTTP client for the browser and Node.js. (By the way, Fetch also supports Promise API.) It uses the native Node. js http module on the server-side, while on the client (browser), it uses XMLHttpRequests. This small yet simple-to-use library has a very extensible interface.

Install Axios in your React project by running the following command:

```
npm install axios
```

Your *package.json* should show the updated dependencies section as

```
"dependencies": {
  "axios": "^1.7.9",
  "react": "^18.3.1",
  "react-dom": "^18.3.1"
}
```

To send HTTP requests using Axios, you first need an instance of axios class (Listing 10-6), returned by the create() method.

Listing 10-6. Axios object

```
import axios from 'axios';

const API = axios.create({
    baseURL: 'https://example.com/api/'
});
```

Certain additional parameters such as timeout, headers, etc., may also be passed. The axios object has all the required methods to place GET, POST, PUT, and DELETE calls.

```
axios.get(url[, config])
axios.post(url[, data[, config]])
axios.put(url[, data[, config]])
axios.delete(url[, config])
```

As you can see, the post() and put() methods need to have a data parameter for creating a new resource and updating an existing one. The config parameter is optional.

The axios module also defines these convenience functions corresponding to the instance methods.

```
axios.get(url[, config])
axios.post(url[, data[, config]])
axios.put(url[, data[, config]])
axios.delete(url[, config])
```

Let us experiment a little with one of the many free API services available on the Internet for testing purpose. One such service is https:// restful-api.dev/; many publicly accessible endpoints of a REST API are listed. One of them is https://api.restful-api.dev/objects/7, which returns the details of a single object with the specified id.

```
{
  "id": "7",
  "name": "Apple MacBook Pro 16",
  "data": {
    "year": 2019,
    "price": 1849.99,
    "CPU model": "Intel Core i9",
    "Hard disk size": "1 TB"
  }
}
```

Let us use this endpoint as an argument to the axios.get() function. Create a new jsx file in your React project (Listing 10-7).

Listing 10-7. GET request with Axios

```
import React, { useEffect } from 'react'
import axios from 'axios'

function Api() {
    useEffect (() => {
        axios.get("https://api.restful-api.dev/objects/7")
        .then((Response) => {
            console.log(Response)
        })
    }, [])

  return (
    <div>
      GET API with Axios
    </div>
  )
}

export default Api
```

You also need to modify the *App.jsx* file and render the Api component in the App component, which is rendered as the root.

While this component simply renders a div element with a text (GET API with Axios), the response returned by the GET endpoint is displayed on the console. Open the Developer tools of your browser (shown in Figure 10-4) after running the project; click on the Console tab to check the data.

Figure 10-4. *Developer console*

The response object typically contains the following attributes:

> **data**: The actual data returned by the API

> **status**: The HTTP status code

> **headers**: The response headers

> **config**: The Axios request configuration

The Component tag in your browser's Developer tools shows (Figure 10-5) the Api component inside the App component and the useEffect() hook.

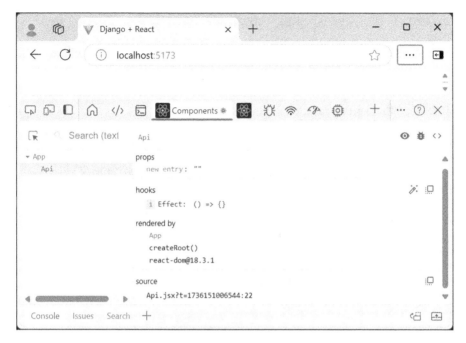

Figure 10-5. *Developer component tab*

The response retrieved from the API can also be rendered in a React component. Let's use another free API to display a list of users from the endpoint https://reqres.in/api/users?page=2.

This time, you will use useState along with the useEffect hook. The axios object returns a JSON response of the users, with the user object having attributes such as first_name, last_name, email, etc. The setData() function of the useEffect hook stores it in the userData array, which is in turn rendered in the component with the help of the map() function. Note that the map function in JavaScript is similar to the for loop in Python. The code snippet in Listing 10-8 obtains the response using the Axios library.

Listing 10-8. Get response with Axios

```
import React, { useEffect, useState } from 'react'
import axios from 'axios'

function Api() {
  const [userData, setData] = useState([]);
    useEffect  (() => {
        axios.get("https://reqres.in/api/users?page=2")
        .then((Response) => {
            console.log(Response)
            setData(Response.data)
        })
    }, [])

  return (
    <div>
      <h2>GET API with Axios</h2>
    {userData.data?.map((item, index) => {
      return (
        <div key={index}  style={{border: "1px solid", margin:
        "10px", padding: "10px"}}>
          <p><b>Name:</b> {item.last_name}, {item.first_name}
          <b>Email:</b> {item.email}</p>
        </div>
      )
    })}
    </div>
  )
}

export default Api
```

Fire the Vite server and visit the URL http://localhost:5173 to display the list of users returned by the REQRES API. The Figure 10-6 shows the output in the browser window.

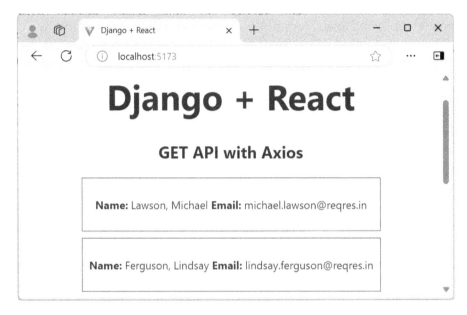

Figure 10-6. *Axios GET response*

Your React app is almost ready to be used as the frontend. You only have to replace the REQRES endpoint with that of a backend API built with Django REST Framework.

DRF Backend

In one of the earlier chapters, you learned how to build a Django API with serializers and generic views in Django REST Framework. The only difference here is that instead of the Django templates, the frontend would be a React app. This requires a significant modification in the project's settings.

Cross-Origin Resource Sharing (CORS)

By default, the Django server runs at http://localhost:8000, while the default URL of your React app is http://localhost:5173. To allow the Django server to respond to any requests outside its domain, you need to use the cross-origin resource sharing feature. If not, the server throws the An unauthorized status (403) error.

Servers usually have a same-origin policy. The CORS mechanism enables it to be bypassed. For that to happen, you need to tell the server which domains to allow access to its resources.

In the Django ecosystem, the django-cors-headers package allows in-browser requests to your Django application from other origins.

Naturally, you need to install it in the current Python environment with PIP:

```
pip install django-cors-headers
```

To enable CORS support in the Django project, add `'corsheaders'` in INSTALLED_APPS along with `'rest_framework'` and `'corsheaders.middleware.CorsMiddleware'` in the MIDDLEWARE list of its settings.py file.

The CORS_ALLOWED_ORIGINS parameter is a sort of a white list of domains allowed to send requests to the Django server. Add the URL of the Vite server in this list.

```
CORS_ALLOWED_ORIGINS = [
    "http://localhost:5173",
]
```

That's it. Your Django project is now capable of acting as a backend to the React app. The rest of the steps are similar to those done by you in the previous chapter (Chapter 7). Here is a quick run-through of the steps:

- **Model**: We shall use the Ticket model (Listing 10-9) that was used earlier in the book.

Listing 10-9. Ticket model

```
class Ticket(models.Model):
    flight_number = models.CharField(max_length=10)
    passenger_name = models.CharField(max_length=100)
    departure_time = models.DateTimeField()
    seat_number = models.CharField(max_length=5)
```

- **Serializer**: Write a ModelSerializer class based on the above model. Refer to the Listing 10-10.

Listing 10-10. TicketSerializer

```
class TicketSerializer(serializers.ModelSerializer):
    class Meta:
        model = Ticket
        fields = "__all__"
```

- **Views**: Define the generic views in views.py (Listing 10-11) – TicketListCreateView for handling GET and POST requests and TicketRetrieveUpdateDeleteView for handling GET, PUT, and DELETE requests.

Listing 10-11. Views

```
class TicketListCreateView(generics.ListCreateAPIView):
    queryset = Ticket.objects.all()
    serializer_class = TicketSerializer
class TicketRetrieveUpdateDeleteView(generics.
RetrieveUpdateDestroyAPIView):
```

```
queryset = Ticket.objects.all()
serializer_class = TicketSerializer
```

A view function acting as an API root is always useful.

```
@api_view(['GET'])
def api_root(request, format=None):
    return Response({
        'tickets': reverse('ticket-list',
        request=request, format=format),
        'ticket-detail': reverse('ticket-detail',
        args=[1], request=request, format=format),
    })
```

- Map these views to suitable URL routes in the urls.py file, as in Listing 10-12.

Listing 10-12. URL routes

```
urlpatterns = [
    path('', views.api_root, name='api-root'),
    path('tickets/', views.TicketListCreateView.as_
    view(), name='ticket-list'),
    path('tickets/<int:pk>/', views.TicketRetrieve
    UpdateDeleteView.as_view(), name='ticket-
    detail'),
]
```

Lastly, update the URLCONF of the project. Run the development server and test the functionality with DRF's browsable API. The expected output is shown in Figure 10-7.

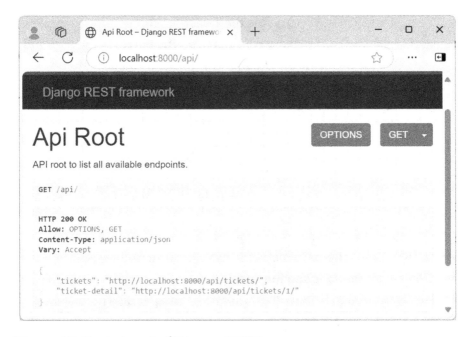

Figure 10-7. *Api root of Django REST app*

Axios Frontend

Create a new React project with the Vite build tool. Add the Api.jsx file in the src folder (Listing 10-13) to declare an object of axios class. This time use the URL of your Django API as the baseURL (follow the steps explained earlier).

Listing 10-13. Api.jsx

```
import axios from 'axios';

const API = axios.create({
    baseURL: 'http://127.0.0.1:8000/api/',
});

export default API;
```

Next, create a new file to define the TicketList component. It employs the useEffect and useState hooks to fetch all the tickets in the backend database and render the list in the App component. You will also be creating another component to display a form for the user to fill and use the data to send a POST request.

At this juncture, your root component should provide two things: one, a navigation bar to let the user select actions such as view the list, book a new ticket, and update or delete a ticket, and two, a routing mechanism (similar to URLCONF in Django) to map the URLS to the respective components.

First about the routing. The 'react-router-dom' is a declarative routing library that helps in matching the URL to components, thus providing navigation around the app.

First, you need to install this library with npm package manager.

```
npm install react-router-dom
```

BrowserRouter is an important component in this library. It uses the browser's built-in HTML5 history API to manage navigation between different pages or components in your React application and ensures the app's URL is updated in the browser as the user navigates. The typical usage of BrowserRouter is shown in Listing 10-14.

Listing 10-14. Routing in React

```
import { BrowserRouter as Router } from 'react-router-dom';

const App = () => (
  <Router>
    {/* Routes and components go here */}
  </Router>
);
export default App;
```

Multiple Route components are included inside the <Routes> … </Routes> construct. Each Route component is used to define a mapping between a specific URL path and the component.

Assuming that the TicketList component is mapped with the /**list** endpoint and the AddTicket component to the /**add** endpoint, the routing mechanism of your root App component would be as shown in Listing 10-15.

Listing 10-15. Routing in App.jsx

```
import { BrowserRouter as Router, Route, Routes, Link } from
'react-router-dom';
import TicketList from './TicketList';
import AddTicket from './AddTicket';
import Home from './Home';
<Router>
            <div>
              <Routes>
                <Route path="/" element={<Home />} />
                <Route path="/list" element=
                {<TicketList />} />
                <Route path="/add" element=
                {<AddTicket />} />
              </Routes>
            </div>
            </Router>
```

Additionally, providing a neat navigation bar will give an enhanced user experience. In React, the <Link> component is used to define hyperlinks (Listing 10-16). For example, <Link to="/">Home</Link> navigates to the root route (/).

Include the navigation code inside the Router component.

Listing 10-16. Navigation in App.jsx

```
<nav className="navbar">
    <ul className="navbar-list">
        <li className="navbar-item">
            <Link to="/">Home</Link>
        </li>
        <li className="navbar-item">
            <Link to="/list">List</Link>
        </li>
        <li className="navbar-item">
            <Link to="/add">New</Link>
        </li>
        <li className="navbar-item">
            <Link to="/update">Update</Link>
        </li>
        <li className="navbar-item">
            <Link to="/delete">Delete</Link>
        </li>
    </ul>
</nav>
```

TicketList Component

Let us now turn to the TicketList component. It employs the useState hook to fetch the list of tickets in a userData state variable. When the TicketList component is first rendered, the Api.get() method retrieves the data. The state change causes the list to be rendered. As before the map() function is used to iterate through the list. The code for ticketList.jsx component is as per the Listing 10-17.

Listing 10-17. ticketList.jsx

```
function TicketList() {
  const [userData, setData] = useState([]);

  useEffect(() => {
    API.get("tickets/")
      .then((response) => {
        console.log(response.data); // Check the structure of
                                    the data
        setData(response.data);
      })
      .catch((error) => {
        console.error("Error fetching data:", error);
      });
  }, []);

  return (
    <div>
      <h2>Ticket List</h2>
      {userData.map((item, index) => (
        <div key={index} style={{border: "1px solid", margin:
        "10px", padding: "10px"}}>
          <p><b>Name:</b> {item.passenger_name} <b>Flight
          No:</b> {item.flight_number}
          <b>Seat No:</b> {item.seat_number}</p>
        </div>
      ))}
    </div>
  );
}
```

When visited, the TicketList component renders the list (Figure 10-8).

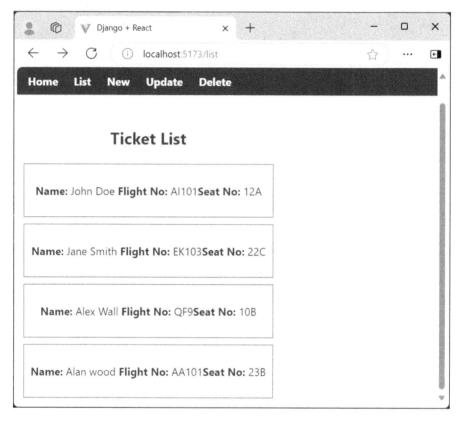

Figure 10-8. *TicketList component of React frontend*

AddTicket Component

This component is expected to render an HTML form for the user to fill the passenger data. We shall use the built-in browser <form> component that creates interactive controls for submitting information. For example:

```
<form action={search}>
    <input name="query" />
    <button type="submit">Search</button>
</form>
```

The <input> component lets you render different kinds of form inputs. You basically input component of text type to receive values for the model attributes such as name, flight number, etc. One such input element is shown in Listing 10-18.

Listing 10-18. Input element in React

```
<form onSubmit={handleSubmit}>
    <div>
        <label>Flight Number:</label>
        <input
            type="text"
            name="flight_number"
            value={ticket.flight_number}
            onChange={handleChange}
            required
        />
    </div>
```

The form submission is handled by the handleSubmit() function. Internally it raises the POST request to the tickets/ URL with the form data to be used for creating a new Ticket resource. The useState hook records the state of all the input elements. If the server responds with a success message, the form is again reset. Listing 10-19 shows the abbreviated code for the AddTicket component.

Listing 10-19. AddTicket component

```
const AddTicket = () => {
    const [ticket, setTicket] = useState({
        flight_number: '',
        passenger_name: '',
```

```
            departure_time: '',
            seat_number: '',
    });

    const [successMessage, setSuccessMessage] = useState('');
    const [errorMessage, setErrorMessage] = useState('');

    // Handle form input change
    const handleChange = (e) => {
        const { name, value } = e.target;
        setTicket({ ...ticket, [name]: value });
    };

    // Handle form submission
    const handleSubmit = (e) => {
        e.preventDefault();
        setSuccessMessage('');
        setErrorMessage('');

        axios.post('tickets/', ticket)
            .then((response) => {
                setSuccessMessage('Ticket added
                successfully!');
                setTicket({ flight_number: '', passenger_name:
                '', departure_time: '', seat_number: '' }); //
                Clear form
                console.log(response.data);
            })
            .catch((error) => {
                setErrorMessage('Failed to add ticket. Please
                try again.');
                console.error(error);
            });
    };
```

```
    return (
        <div>
            <h2>Book New Ticket</h2>
            <form onSubmit={handleSubmit}>
                <div>
                    //input component for flight_number
                </div>
                <div>
                    //input component for passenger_name
                </div>
                <div>
                    //input component for departure_time
                </div>
                <div>
                    //input component for seat_number
                </div>
                <button type="submit">Submit</button>
            </form>
            {successMessage && <p style={{ color: 'green'
            }}>{successMessage}</p>}
            {errorMessage && <p style={{ color: 'red' }}>
            {errorMessage}</p>}
        </div>
    );
};

export default AddTicket;
```

The AddTicket component renders a booking form as shown in Figure 10-9.

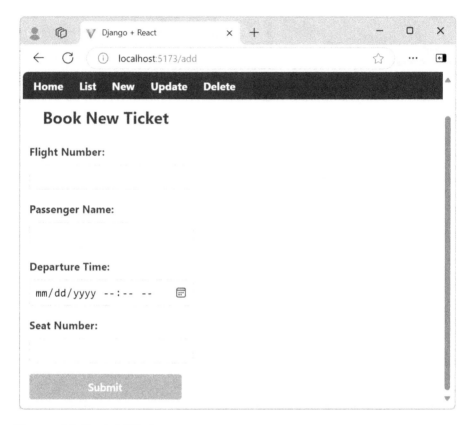

Figure 10-9. *AddTicket component*

Apollo

You already know how to build a Django app that serves a GraphQL API (Chapter 8). While you can consume the data served by the app (built with Strawberry-Django or Graphene-Django) with a Django view and template – for which you'll need to perform the HTTP operations using the requests library – a better approach would be to use a client-side application for this purpose. A frontend React app will provide an enhanced user experience while interacting with the GraphQL server.

Apollo is one of the popular and a comprehensive set of tools that helps in building scalable applications with GraphQL. Apollo has a server component (which we are not going to use here, as we already have a GraphQL server built with Django) and the Apollo Client library that is very easy to integrate in a React app.

Apollo Client is a JavaScript library that facilitates the state management of local and remote data with GraphQL. With its declarative data fetching mechanism, you can easily query and fetch the data without having to manually track the state manually.

To let your React app interact with Django's GraphQL server, you first need to install the Apollo Client library. With the command terminal logged in the React app directory, use the following command:

```
npm install @apollo/client graphql
```

The updated dependencies section of your *package.json* file should be like

```
"dependencies": {
  "@apollo/client": "^3.12.5",
  "graphql": "^16.10.0",
  "react": "^18.3.1",
  "react-dom": "^18.3.1"
},
```

Apollo Client is a comprehensive library with quite a few classes and methods defined in it. Out of which, a brief overview of some is worth taking a look in order to understand how the GraphQL data is handled by your React app.

The ApolloClient class is the most important part of Apollo's client-side library and is responsible for providing the view-layer integration with React. An ApolloClient object handles fetching, caching, and managing data from your GraphQL API. The constructor needs two arguments: uri (the endpoint of your GraphQL API) and cache (specifying the caching strategy). Listing 10-20 shows the construction of ApolloClient object.

Listing 10-20. ApolloClient object

```
import { ApolloClient, InMemoryCache } from '@apollo/client';
const client = new ApolloClient({
  uri: "GraphQL API endpoint",
  cache: new InMemoryCache(),
});
```

The ApolloProvider is a React component that connects your Apollo Client instance to your React app. It is also defined in the @apollo/client package. The root App component of your React app returns the ApolloProvider object, which makes it possible for the child components to execute GraphQL queries and mutations (Listing 10-21).

Listing 10-21. ApolloProvider component

```
import { ApolloProvider } from "@apollo/client";
function App() {
  return (
    <ApolloProvider client={client}>
      <div className="App">
        <h1>React with Django GraphQL</h1>
        <BookList />
      </div>
    </ApolloProvider>
  );
}
```

Here, the BookList component executes a GraphQL query to fetch all the books in a database.

You have used a couple of React hooks (useState and useEffect) in the previous section. Apollo Client provides its own React hook called useQuery. The useQuery() function uses a GraphQL query string as an argument and returns an object having the properties loading, error, and data. The query string is returned by the gql() function. It is a template literal tag provided by Apollo Client, used to write GraphQL queries and mutations.

For example, when the allBooks query you used in the previous chapter (Chapter 8) is passed to the gql() function, it parses into its Apollo-compatible form. Refer the Listing 10-22 for the typical use of gql() function.

Listing 10-22. gql() function

```
const GET_DATA = gql`
  query {
  MyQuery {
    field1
    field2

    . . .

  }
}
`;
```

The useQuery function then uses the object returned by gql().

```
const { loading, error, data } = useQuery(MyQuery);
```

Here, loading indicates if the query is in progress; its value is either True or False. Errors, if any, are stored in the error property. The data property contains the result of the query. It is then used to render the fetched rows in the App component.

Graphene-Django Backend

In a previous chapter (Chapter 8), you learned how to build a Graphene-Django project that serves a GraphQL API. We shall use the same code base with a few React-related tweaks. Let us quickly go through the steps to set up the GraphQL API:

- As in the previous section, you need to include 'corsheaders' in the INSTALLED_APPS list and also 'corsheaders.middleware.CorsMiddleware' in the MIDDLEWARE list in the settings.py file. You also have to add the URL of the React Vite server (http://localhost:5173) in the CORS_ALLOWED_ORIGINS list. You also need to tell Django to use Graphene Schema object from the app's schema.py file.

- We shall be using the Book model as done earlier (reproduced here in Listing 10-23).

Listing 10-23. Book model

```
class Book(models.Model):
    id = models.IntegerField(primary_key=True)
    title = models.CharField(max_length=50)
    author = models.CharField(max_length=50)
    price = models.IntegerField()
    publisher = models.CharField(max_length=50)

    class Meta:
        db_table = "books"
```

- Define a BookType class (Listing 10-24) that inherits DjangoObjectType.

Listing 10-24. BookType

```
class BookType(DjangoObjectType):
    class Meta:
        model = Book
        fields = ("id", "title", "author", "publisher",
        "price")
```

- Define a Query class with all_books and book properties and the corresponding resolver methods (as in Listing 10-25).

Listing 10-25. Graphene query

```
class Query(graphene.ObjectType):
    all_books = graphene.List(BookType)
    book = graphene.Field(BookType, id=graphene.Int())

    def resolve_all_books(self, info):
        return Book.objects.all()

    def resolve_book(self, info, id):
        try:
            return Book.objects.get(pk=id)
        except Book.DoesNotExist:
            return None
```

A Schema class constructor uses this Query to return the Schema object.

- As done earlier, define the generic views (TicketListCreateView and TicketRetrieveUpdateDeleteView), and register the GraphQLView with the "graphql/" endpoint. Listing 10-26 shows the updated urlpatterns list.

Listing 10-26. URL route for GraphiQL

```
from django.contrib import admin
from django.urls import path, include

from graphene_django.views import GraphQLView
from django.views.decorators.csrf import csrf_exempt
urlpatterns = [
    path('admin/', admin.site.urls),
    path('api/', include('api.urls')),
    path("graphql/", csrf_exempt(GraphQLView.as_
    view(graphiql=True))),
]
```

The URL http://localhost:8000/graphql/ should present the GraphiQL interface so that you can execute the allBooks query. Your GraphQL backend is now ready to be used as a backend to the React app.

Apollo Frontend

To start with, create a new React app with the Vite build tool. It renders the App component as the root of the DOM. Create a new JSX file (*BookList. jsx*) in the project's src folder. You need to declare an object of AppClient class in the *App.jsx* file (refer Listing 10-27), with the endpoint of Django's GraphQL API as its uri parameter.

Listing 10-27. Root component for Apollo app

```
import { ApolloClient, InMemoryCache, ApolloProvider } from
"@apollo/client";

import BookList from "./BookList";
```

```
const client = new ApolloClient({
  uri: "http://localhost:8000/graphql/",
  cache: new InMemoryCache(),
});

function App() {
  return (
    <ApolloProvider client={client}>
      <div className="App">
        <h1>React with Django GraphQL</h1>
      </div>
    </ApolloProvider>
  );
}

export default App
```

BookList Component

This React component is expected to fetch the result of a GraphQL query to be run over the Book model. The GraphQL query is first fed to the gql() function.

Listing 10-28. GET_BOOKS query

```
import { gql } from "@apollo/client";
const GET_BOOKS = gql`
  query {
  allBooks {
    id
    title
    author
```

```
    publisher
    price
  }
}
`;
```

The GET_BOOKS object (as in Listing 10-28) is used as an argument to the useQuery hook and fetches the JSON representation of the list of books (Listing 10-29).

Listing 10-29. BookList component

```
import { useQuery} from "@apollo/client";
function BookList() {
    const { loading, error, data } = useQuery(GET_BOOKS);

  console.log("Query Response:", { loading, error, data });

  if (loading) return <p>Loading...</p>;
  if (error) return <p>Error: {error.message}</p>;
    if (loading) return <p>Loading...</p>;
    if (error) return <p>Error: {error.message}</p>;

    return (
        <ul>
          {data.allBooks.map((book) => (
            <li key={book.id}>
              {book.title} by {book.author}
            </li>
          ))}
        </ul>
    );
  }

export default BookList;
```

The data returned by Apollo Client has the data attribute. Along with the other HTTP-related attributes, it returns the query result in allBooks property, which in turn is identified by the model attributes such as title, author, etc. Use the map() function to render the book details as a part of the BookList component.

Finally, update your *App.jsx* file (refer to the Listing 10-30) to include the BookList component inside the root App Component.

Listing 10-30. App.jsx for Apollo app

```
function App() {
  return (
    <ApolloProvider client={client}>
      <div className="App">
        <h1>React with Django GraphQL</h1>
        <BookList />
      </div>
    </ApolloProvider>
  );
}

export default App
```

That's it. Run the React app (ensure that the Django server is running and the GraphQL queries are executed correctly in the GraphiQL interface). You should get a list of all the books and their authors rendered in your browser.

As an exercise, you can add another component to perform mutation. You can also refer to the previous section to add routing in the App component.

React for WebSocket

In the previous chapter (Chapter 9), we had used JavaScript code inside an HTML script to establish connection with the WebSocket endpoint provided by a Django Channels application. Now, we shall build a simple React app that works as the client for the Channels application.

Start by creating a new React app with the help of the Vite build tool. You need to define a component that lets the user open a WebSocket connection on the server and send a message. The server broadcasts messages to all the connected clients.

Open a new code window in your IDE as *ChatApp.jsx*. In the WebSocket client code, you have to record the states of username and whether a username is set, the message to be sent, and a log of messages from all the clients (Listing 10-31). This is done with the useState() hook.

Listing 10-31. ChatApp states

```
const [name, setName] = useState('');
const [isNameSet, setIsNameSet] = useState(false);
const [message, setMessage] = useState('');
const [messages, setMessages] = useState([]);
const [chatSocket, setChatSocket] = useState(null);
```

When the ChatApp component is first rendered, the useEffect() hook will be invoked, and it will request a connection with the WebSocket server, which is live on the Django application that is running in the background.

```
const socket = new WebSocket('ws://127.0.0.1:8000/ws/socket-
server/');
```

Once the connection request is accepted, your React app will ask the user to enter a username, as per the Listing 10-32.

Listing 10-32. Chat app login screen

```
<form onSubmit={handleNameSubmit}>
  <h1>Welcome to the Chat</h1>

  <input
    type="text"
    placeholder="Enter your name"
    value={name}
    onChange={(e) => setName(e.target.value)}
    required
  />

<nbsp> </nbsp>
  <button type="submit">Join</button>
</form>
```

The browser should display an input text box for the username to be entered. Figure 10-10 represents the login screen of your chat app.

Figure 10-10. *Login screen of Chat app*

The user input will be stored in the state variable name and also isNameSet set to True. This is performed by the handleNameSubmit() function.

```
const handleNameSubmit = (e) => {
  e.preventDefault();
  setIsNameSet(true);
};
```

If the user has entered a username, you should get an interface (Listing 10-33) to enter and send a message. This is stored in a state variable message.

Listing 10-33. Chat interface

```
<h1>Welcome, {name}!</h1>
<form onSubmit={handleMessageSubmit}>
  <input
    type="text"
    placeholder="Type your message"
    value={message}
    onChange={(e) => setMessage(e.target.value)}
    required
  />
  <nbsp> </nbsp>
  <button type="submit">Send</button>
</form>
```

The browser shows the chat interface as in Figure 10-11.

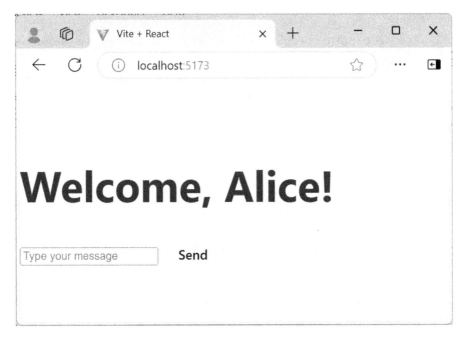

Figure 10-11. *Chat interface*

With the help of the handleMessagesubmit() function (the code given in 10-34), the text entered in the input element is sent with the chatSocket.send() method.

Listing 10-34. Handler to send message

```
const handleMessageSubmit = (e) => {
  e.preventDefault();
  if (chatSocket && chatSocket.readyState ===
  WebSocket.OPEN) {
    chatSocket.send(JSON.stringify({ message: `${name}:
    ${message}` }));
    setMessage('');
```

```
  } else {
    console.error('WebSocket is not open. Cannot send
    message.');
  }
};
```

In response, the server will broadcast the received messages to all the clients (Listing 10-35). The client component adds it to the list.

Listing 10-35. Handler to receive messages

```
socket.onmessage = (event) => {
  const data = JSON.parse(event.data);
  if (data.type === 'chat') {
    setMessages((prevMessages) => [...prevMessages, data.
    message]);
  }
};
```

The ChatApp component then renders all the message in the list by running the map() loop.

```
<div id="messages">
  {messages.map((msg, index) => (
    <div key={index}>
      <p>{msg}</p>
    </div>
  ))}
</div>
```

Now, all you have to do is to embed the ChatApp component inside the App component that is loaded as the root component (refer Listing 10-36) of the DOM.

Listing 10-36. Root component of Chat app

```
import React from 'react';
import ChatApp from './ChatApp';

const App = () => {
  return (
    <div>
      <ChatApp />
    </div>
  );
};

export default App;
```

The chat log will appear in the messages div element.

The screenshot of the browser output is shown in Figure 10-12.

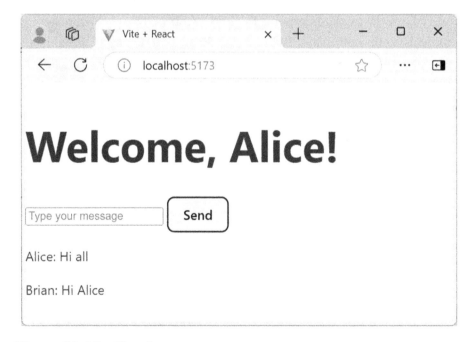

Figure 10-12. *Chat log*

As far as the backend is concerned, you don't need to make any changes to the Channels application used in the previous chapter (Chapter 9), except for adding the CORS settings. You can refer to the previous section of this chapter for the steps in CORS configuration.

Summary

This was the last chapter of this book. Our journey has reached the last stop, where you have learned how to provide React frontend solutions for the Django REST, GraphQL, and Channels apps. Along the way, the JavaScript libraries Axios and Apollo Client were introduced.

Starting with the basics of HTTP and `asyncio`, this book navigated you through the core concepts of Django (such as model, view, and templates) as well as the advanced concepts such as messages framework, authentication, and using `SQLAlchemy`. The second half of the book covered how Django implements the REST, GraphQL, and WebSocket protocols, culminating in this chapter on React with Django. With this, hopefully this book has given an experience of full-stack web application development with the Django ecosystem as its backend and React as its frontend.

Index

© Malhar Lathkar 2025
M. Lathkar, *Modern Django Web Development*,
https://doi.org/10.1007/979-8-8688-1472-3

HTML form, 270, 271
HTML templates, 267
ListView, 122–125
request handlers, 269
special-purpose class, 114
syntax pattern, 268
TemplateView, 114–116
UpdateView, 118, 119
urlpatterns, 268, 270
get() method, 67, 71
getbook() function, 105, 110
getbook() view function, 175
get_context_data() method, 123
get_cookie() method, 189
GET method, 4
get_object() method, 120
Google Remote Procedure Call
        (gRPC), 232
gql() function, 397, 401
Graphene, 308, 309
    execute() function, 325, 326
    features, 322
    mutations, 328
    mutation string, 329
    object type, 323
    query, 324, 327
    resolver method, 324, 325, 327
    scalar types, 323
    schema-first approach, 322
Graphene-Django, 289
    abstractions, 330
    schema, 334
    configuration, 331
    DjangoObjectType class, 331

installation, 330
mutation, 333
ORM models, 308
queries, 332
root schema, 331
URLCONF, 332
Graphene-Django project, 398–400
GraphiQL interface, 312, 313,
        315, 319
GraphQL
    API technology, 299
    architecture, 301, 302
    Graphene, 322–330
    Graphene-Django, 330–334
    mutation, 314
    and Python, 308, 309
    vs. REST, 300, 301
    schema, 308
    SDL (*see* Schema definition
        language (SDL))
    Strawberry, 309–316
    Strawberry-Django, 316–322
GraphQLView, 317, 332
group_add() method, 357
group_discard() method, 357
Groups, 356, 357
group_send() method, 357

H

handleMessagesubmit()
        function, 407
handleNameSubmit()
        function, 406

N

R

S

U

GPSR Compliance
The European Union's (EU) General Product Safety Regulation (GPSR) is a set
of rules that requires consumer products to be safe and our obligations to
ensure this.

If you have any concerns about our products, you can contact us on

ProductSafety@springernature.com

In case Publisher is established outside the EU, the EU authorized
representative is:

Springer Nature Customer Service Center GmbH
Europaplatz 3
69115 Heidelberg, Germany